COMMUNISM

A POLITICAL READER

COMMUNISM

A POLITICAL READER

Edited By

R. C. GETTEL

and

W. A. DUNNING

Cosmo Publications

2004 **New Delhi**

A DAUGHTER OF THE REVOLUTION

John Reed

Chapter-1

That night there was one of those Paris rains, which never seem to wet one as other rains do. We sat on the terrasse of the Rotonde, at the corner table—it was a warm night, though November-Fred, Marcelle and I, sipping a Dubonnet. The cafes all closed at eight sharp because of the war, and we used to stay until then almost every night before we went to dinner.

Next to us was a young French officer with his head done up in a bandage, and his arm comfortably around Jeanne's green-caped shoulder. Beatrice and Alice were farther down along under the glare of the yellow lights. Behind us we could peek through a slit in the window-curtain and survey the smoke-tilled room inside, an uproarious band of men sandwiched between girls, beating on the table and singing, the two old Frenchmen at their tranquil chess-game, an absorbed student writing a letter home, his *amie's* head on his shoulder, five utter strangers and the waiter listening breathlessly to the tales of a muddy-legged soldier back from the front...

The yellow lights flooded us, and splashed the shining black pavement with gold; human beings with umbrellas Bowed by in a steady stream; a ragged old wreck of a man poked furtively for cigarette-butts under our feet; out in the roadway the shuffling feet of men marching fell unheeded upon our accustomed ears, and dripping slanted bayonets passed athwart a beam of light from across the Boulevard Montparnasse.

This year all the girls at the Rotonde dressed alike. They had little round hats, hair cut short, low-throated waists and long capes down to their feet, the ends tossed over their shoulders Spanish-fashion. Marcelle was the image of the others. Besides, her lips were painted scarlet, her cheeks dead white, and she talked obscenities when she wasn't on her dignity, and sentimentalities when she was. She had regaled us both with the history of her very rich and highly respectable family, of the manner of her tragic seduction by a Duke, of her innate virtue—and had remarked proudly that she was no common ordinary street-walker...

At this particular instant she was interlarding a running fire of highly-flavored comment upon what passed before her eyes with appeals for money in a harshened little voice; and I thought to myself that we had got to the bottom of Marcelle. Her comments upon things and persons were pungent, vigorous, original—but they palled after while; a strain of recklessness and unashamed love of life held only a little longer. Marcelle was already soiled with too much handling...

We heard a violent altercation, and a tall girl with a bright orange sweater came out from the cafe, followed by a waiter gesticulating and exclaiming:

"But the eight anisettes which you ordered, *nom de Dieu!"*

"I have told you I would pay," she shrilled over her shoulder. "I am going to the Dome for some money," and she ran across the shiny street. The waiter stood looking after her, moodily jingling the change in his pockets.

"No use waiting," shouted Marcelle, "There is another door to the Dome on the Rue Delambre!" But the waiter paid no attention; he had paid the *caisse* for the drinks. And, as a matter of fact, the girl never reappeared.

"That is an old trick," said Marcelle to us. "It is easy when you have no money to get a drink from the waiters, for they dare not ask for your money until afterward. It is a good thing to know now in time of war, when the men are so few and so poor."...

"But the waiter!"objected Fred. "He must make his living!"

Marcelle shrugged. "And we ours," she said.

"There used to be a *belle type* around the Quarter," she continued after a minute, "who called herself Marie. She had beautiful hair—*épatante,*—and she loved travelling...Once she found herself on a Mediterranean boat bound for Egypt without a *sou,*—nothing except the clothes on her back. A monsieur passed her as she leaned against the rail, and said,'You have marvellous hair, mademoiselle.

"'I will sell it to you for a hundred francs,' she Bashed back. And she cut off all her beautiful hair and went to Cairo, where she met an English lord..."

The waiter heaved a prodigious sigh, shook his head sadly, and went indoors. We were silent, and thought of dinner. The rain fell.

I don't know how it happened, but Fred began to whistle absent-mindedly the *Carmagnole.* I wouldn't have noticed it except that I heard a voice chime in, and looked around to see the wounded French officer, whose arm had fallen idly from the shoulder of Jeanne, staring blankly across the pavement, and humming the *Carmagnole.* What visions was he seeing, this sensitive-faced youth in the uniform of his country's army, singing the song of revolt! Even as I looked, he caught himself up short, looked self-conscious and startled, glanced swiftly at us, and rose quickly to his feet, dragging Jeanne with him.

At the same instant Marcelle clutched Fred roughly by the arm.

"It's défendu—you'll have us all pinched," she cried, with something so much stronger than fear in her eyes that I was interested. "And, besides, don't sing those dirty songs. They are revolutionary—they are sung by *voyous*—poor people—ragged men—"

"Then you are not a revolutionist yourself?" I asked.

"I? *B'en* no, I swear to you!" she shook her head passionately. "The *méhants,* the villains, who want to overturn everything—!" Marcelle shivered.

"Look here, Marcelle! Are you happy in this world the way it is? What does the System do for you, except to turn you out on the street to sell yourself?" Fred was launched now on a boiling flood of propaganda. "When the red day comes, I know which side of the Barricades I shall be on—!"

Marcelle began to laugh. It was a bitter laugh. It was the first time I had ever seen her un-self-conscious.

"*Ta gueule,* my friend," she interrupted rudely. "I know that talk ! I have heard it since I was so high…I *know!"* She stopped and laughed to herself, and wrenched out—"MY grandfather was shot against a wall at Père Lachaise for carrying a red Bag in the Commune in 1870." She started, looked at us shame-facedly, and grinned. "There, you see I come of a worthless family…"

"Your grandfather!" shouted Fred.

"Pass for my grandfather," said Marcelle indifferently. "Let the crazy, dirty-handed old fool rest in his grave. I have never spoken of him before, and I shall burn no candles for his soul…"

Fred seized her hand. He was exalted. "God bless your grandfather!"

With the quick wit of her profession, she divined that, for some mysterious reason, she had pleased. For answer she began to sing in a low voice the last lines of the *Internationale.*

"C'est la lutte finale—" She coquetted with Fred.

"Tell us more about your grandfather," I asked.

"There is no more to tell," said Marcelle, half-ashamed, half-pleased, wholly ironical. "He was a wild man from God knows where. He had no father and mother. He was a stone-mason, and people say a fine workman. But he wasted his time in reading books, and he was always on strike. He was a savage, and always roaring 'Down with the Government and the rich!' People called him 'Le Farrou.' I remember my father telling how the soldiers came to take him from his house to be shot. My father was a lad of fourteen, and he hid my grandfather under a mattress of the bed. But the soldiers poked their bayonets in there and one went through his shoulder—so they saw the blood. Then my grandfather made a speech to the soldiers—he was always making speeches—and asked them not to murder the Commune…But they only laughed at him—" And Marcelle laughed, for it was amusing.

"But my father—" she went on; "Heavens ! He was even worse. I can remember the big strike at the Creusot works.—wait a minute,—it was the year of the Great Exposition. My father helped to make that strike. My brother was then just a baby,—eight years he had, and he was already working as poor children do. And in the parade of all the strikers, suddenly my father heard a little voice shouting to him across the ranks,—it was my little brother, marching with a red flag, like one of the comrades!

"'Hello, old boy!' he called to my father. *'Ca ira!'*

"They shot many workmen in that strike." Marcelle shook her head viciously. "Ugh ! The scum !"

Fred and I stirred, and found that we had been chilled from resting in one position. We beat on the window and ordered cognac.

"And now you have heard enough of my miserable family," said Marcelle, with an attempt at lightness.

"Go on," said Fred hoarsely, fixing her with gleaming eyes.

"But you're going to take me to dinner, *n'est-ce pas?"* insinuated Marcelle. I nodded. *"Pardié!"* she went on, with a grin. "It was not like this that my father dined—hè! After my grandfather died, my old man could get no work. He was starving, and went from house to house begging food. But they shut the door in his face, the women of my grandfather's comrades, saying 'Give him nothing, the *salaud;* he is the son of Le Farrou, who was shot.' And my father sneaked around the cafe tables, like a dog, picking up crusts to keep his soul and body together. It has taught me much," said Marcelle, shaking her short hair. "To keep always in good relations with those who feed you. It is why I do not steal from the waiter like that girl did; and I tell everybody that my family was respectable. They might make me suffer for the sins of my father, as he did for his father's."

Light broke upon me, and once more the puzzling baseness of humanity justified itself. Here was the key to Marcelle, her weakness, her vileness. It was not vice, then, that had twisted her, but the intolerable degradation of the human spirit by the masters of the earth, the terrible punishment of those who thirst for liberty.

"I can remember," she said, "how, after the Creusot strike was ended, the bosses got rid of their troublesome workmen. It was winter, and for weeks we had had only wood that my mother gathered in the fields, to keep us warm-and a little bread and coffee that the Union gave us. I wasn't but four years old. My father decided to go to Paris, and we started—walking. He carried me on his shoulder, and with the other a little bundle of clothes. My mother carried another—but she had already tuberculoSis, and had to rest every hour. My brother came behind...We went along the white, straight road, with the light snow lying on it, between the high naked poplars. Two days and a night...We huddled down in a deserted roadmender's hut, my mother coughing, coughing. Then out again before the sun rose, tramping along through the snow, my father and my brother shouting revolutionary cries, and singing.

'Dansons la Carmagnole
'Vive le son—Vive le son—
'Dansona la Carmagnole
'Vive le son du canon!'"

Marcelle had raised her voice unconsciously as she sang the forbidden song; her cheeks flushed, her eyes snapped, she stamped her foot. Suddenly she broke off and looked fearfully around. No one had noticed, however.

"My brother had a high, little voice like a girl, and my father used to break off laughing as he looked down at his son stamping sturdily along beside him, and roaring out songs of hate like an old striker.

"'*Allons! Petit cheminot,*—you little tramp you! I'll bet the police will know you some day!' And he would slap him on the back. It made my mother turn pale, and sometimes at night she would slip out of bed and go to the corner where my brother slept, and wake him up to tell him, weeping, that he must always grow up to be a good man. Once my father woke up and caught her...But that was later, at Paris...

"And they would sing—

'Debout freres de misere!
(Up ! Brothers of misery !)
'Ne voulons plus de frontieres
(We want no more frontiers)
'Pour egorger la bourgeoisie
(To loot the bourgeoisie)
'Et supprimer la tyrranie
(And suppress tyranny)
'Il faut avoir du coeur
(We must have heart)
'Et de l'energie!'
(And energy!)

"And then my father would look ahead with flashing eyes, marching as if he were an army. Every time his eyes sashed like that, my mother would tremble,—for it meant some reckless and terrible fight with the police, or a bloody strike, and she feared for him...And I know how she must have felt, for she was law-abiding, like me — and my father, he was no good." Marcelle shuddered, and gulped her cognac at one swallow.

"I really did not begin myself to know things until we came to Paris," she went on, "because then I began to grow up. My first memory, almost, is when my father led the big strike at Thirion's, the coal-yard down there on the avenue de Maine, and came home with his arm broken where the police had struck him. After that it was work, strike,—work, strike,—with little to eat at our house and my mother growing weaker until she died. My father married again, a religious woman, who finally took to going continually to church and praying for his immortal soul...

"Because she knew how fiercely he hated God. He used to come home at night every week after the meeting of the Union, his eyes shining like stars, roaring blasphemies through the streets. He was a terrible man. He was always the leader. I remember when he went out to assist at a demonstration on Montmartre. It was before the Sacre Coeur, the big white church you see up there on the top of the mountain, looking over all Paris. You know the statue of the Chevalier de la Barre just below it? It is of a young man in ancient times who refused to salute a religious procession; a priest broke his arm with the cross they carried, and he was burned to death by the Inquisition. He stands there in chains, his broken arm hanging by his side, his head lifted so,—proudly. *Eh b'en,* the workingmen were demonstrating against the Church, or something, I don't know what. They had speeches. My father stood upon the steps of the basilica and suddenly the *curé* of the church appeared. My father cried, in a voice of thunder, *'A bas* the priests! That pig burned him to death I he pointed to the statue. 'To the Lanterne with him! Hang him! Then they all began to shout and surge toward the steps,—and the police charged the crowd with revolvers…Well, my father came home that night all covered with blood, and hardly able to drag himself along the street.

"My step-mother met him at the door, very angry, and said,'Well, where have you been, you good-for-nothing?'

"'At a manifestation, *quoi!'* he growled.

"'It serves you right,' she said. 'I hope you're cured now.'

"'Cured?' he shouted, roaring through the bloody toothlessness of his mouth. 'Until the next time. *Ca ira!'*

"And true enough, it was at the guillotining of Leboeuf that the cuirassiers charged the Socialists, and they carried my father home with a sabre cut in his head."

Marcelle leaned over with a cigarette in her mouth to light it from Fred's.

"They called him *Casse-tete* Poisot—the Headbreaker, and he was a hard man…How he hated the Government! ... Once I came home from school and told him that they had taught us to sing the Marseillaise.

"'If I ever catch you singing that damned traitors' song around here,' he cried at me, doubling up his fist,'I'll crack your face open.'"

To my eyes came the picture of this coarse, narrow, sturdy old warrior, scarred with the marks of a hundred vain, ignoble fights with police, reeling home through squalid streets after Union meeting, his eyes blazing with visions of a regenerated humanity.

"And your brother?" asked Fred.

"Oh, he was even worse than my father," said Marcelle, laughing. "You could talk to my father about some things, but there were things that you could not talk to my brother about at all. Even when he was a little boy he did dreadful things. He would say,'After school come to meet me at such and such a church,—I want to pray.' I would meet him on the steps and we would go in together and kneel down. And when I was praying, he would suddenly jump up and run shouting around the church, kicking over the chairs and smashing the candles burning in the chapels...And whenever he saw a cure' in the street, he marched along right behind him crying, *'A bas les calolres! A bas les calories!'* Twenty times he was arrested, and even put in the Reformatory. But he always escaped. When he had but fifteen years he ran away from the house and did not come back for a year. One day he walked into the kitchen where we were all having breakfast.

"'Good morning,' he said, as if he had never gone away. 'Cold morning, isn't it?'

"My step-mother screamed.

"'I have been to see the world,' he went on. 'I came back because I didn't have any money and was hungry.' My father never scolded him, but just let him stay. In the daytime he hung around the cafes on the corner, and did not come home at night until after midnight. Then one morning he disappeared again, without a word to anyone. In three months he was back again, starving. My step-mother told my father that he ought to make the boy work, that it was hard enough with a lazy, fighting man to provide for. But my father only laughed.

"'Leave him alone,' he said. 'He knows what he's doing. There's good fighting blood in him.'

"My brother went off and came back like that until he was almost eighteen. In the last period, before he settled down in Paris, he would most always work until he had collected enough money to go away. Then he finally got a steady job in a factory here, and married...

"He had a fine voice for singing, and could hold people dumb with the way he sang revolutionary songs. At night, after his work was finished, he used to tie a big red handkerchief around his neck and go to some music hall or cabaret. He would enter, and while some singer was giving a song from the stage, he would suddenly lift up his voice and burst out into the *Ca ira* or the *Internationale.* The singer on the stage would be forced to stop, and all the audience would turn and watch my brother, up there in the top benches of the theatre.

"When he had finished, he would cry 'How do you like that?' and then they would cheer and applaud him. Then he would shout 'Everybody say with me "Down with the Capitalists! *A bas* the police! To the Lanterne with the *flics!*"' Then there would be some cheers and some whistles. 'Did I hear somebody whistle me!' he'd cry. 'I'll meet anybody at the door outside who dared to whistle me!' And afterward he would fight ten or fifteen men in a furious mob in the street outside, until the police came...

"He, too, was always leading strikes, but had a laughing, gallant way that made all the comrades love him..'. He might perhaps some day have been a deputy, if my father had not taught him lawlessness when he was young—"

"Where is he now?" asked Fred.

"Down there in the trenches somewhere." She waved her arm vaguely Eastward. "He had to go with the others when the war broke out, though he hated the Army so. When he did his military service, it was awful. He would never obey. For almost a year he was in prison. Once he decided to be promoted, and within a month they made him corporal, he was so intelligent...But the very first day he refused to command the soldiers of his squad...'Why should I give orders to these comrades?' he shouted. 'One orders me to command them to dig a trench. *Yoyons,* are they slaves?' So they degraded him to the ranks. Then he organized a revolt, and advised them to shoot their officers...The men themselves were so insulted, they threw him over a wall.—So terribly he hated war! When the Three Year Military Law was up in the Chamber, it was he who led the mob to the Palais Bourbon...And now he must go to kill the *Boches,* like the others. Perhaps he himself is dead.—I do not know, I have heard nothing." And then irrelevantly, "He has a little son five years old."

Three generations of fierce, free blood, struggling indefatigably for a dim dream of liberty. And now a fourth in the cradle! Did they know why they struggled? No matter. It was a thing deeper than reason, an instinct of the human spirit which neither force nor persuasion could ever uproot.

"And you, Marcelle?" I asked.

"I?" She laughed. "Shall I tell you that I was not seduced by a Duke?" She gave a bitter little chuckle. "Then you will not respect me—for I notice that you friends of passage want your vice seasoned with romance. But it is true. It has not been romantic. In that hideousness and earnestness of our life, I always craved joy and happiness. I always wanted to laugh, be gay, even when I was a baby. I used to imagine drinking champagne, and going to the theatre, and I wanted jewels, fine dresses, automobiles. Very early my father noticed that my tastes led that way; he said,'I see that you want to throw everything over and sell yourself to the rich. Let me tell you now, that the first fault you commit, I'll put you out the door and call you my daughter no more.'

"It became intolerable at home. My father could not forgive women who had lovers without being married. He kept saying that I was on the way to sin—and when I grew older, I wasn't permitted to leave the house without my step-mother. As soon as I was old enough, he hurried to find me a husband, to save me. One day he came home and said that he had found one—a pale young man who limped, the son of a restaurant-keeper on the same street. I knew him; he was not bad, but I couldn't bear to think of marrying. I wanted so much to be free." We started, Fred and I. "Free !" Wasn't that what the old man had fought for so bitterly?

"So that night," she said, "I got out of bed and put on my Sunday dress, and my everday dress over that, and ran away. All night I walked around the streets, and all the next day. That evening, trembling, I went to the factory where my brother worked and waited for him to come out. I did not know whether or not he would give me up to my father. But soon he came along, shouting and singing with some comrades. He spied me.

"'Well, old girl, what brings you here?' he cried, taking my arm. 'Trouble?' I told him I had run away. He stood off and looked at me. 'You haven't eaten,' he said. 'Come home with me and meet my wife. You'll like her. We'll all have dinner together!' So I did. His wife was wonderful. She met me with open arms, and they showed me the baby, just a month old...And so fat! All was warm and happy there in that house. I remember that she cooked the dinner herself, and never have I eaten such a dinner! They did not ask me anything until I had eaten, and then my brother lighted a cigarette and gave me one. I was afraid to smoke, for my step-mother had said it was to bring hell on a woman...But the wife smiled at me and took one herself.

"'Now,' said my brother.'What are your plans?'" 'I have none,' I answered. 'I must be free. I want gaiety, and lovely clothes. I want to go to the theatre. I want to drink champagne.'

"His wife shook her head sadly.

"'I have never heard of any work for a that will give her those things,' she said.

"'Do you think I want work?' I burst out. 'Do you think I want to slave out my life in a factory for ten francs a week, or strut around in other women's gowns at some *couturiere's* on the Rue de la Paix? Do you think I will take orders from anyone? No, I want to be free!'

"My brother looked at me gravely for a long time. Then he said,'We are of the same blood. It would do no good to argue with you, or to force you. Each human being must work out his own life. You shall go and do whatever you want. But I want you to know that whenever you are hungry, or discouraged, or deserted, that my house is always open to you—that you will always be welcome here, for as long as you want.'..."

Marcelle wiped her eyes roughly with the back of her hand.

"I stayed there that night, and the next day I went around the city and talked with girls in the cafes—like I am now. They advised me to work, if I wanted a steady lover; so I went into a big department score for a month. Then I had a lover, an Argentine, who gave me beautiful clothes and took me to the theatre. Never have I been so happy!

"One night when we were going to the theatre —as we passed by my brother's house, I thought I would stop in and let him know how wonderful I found life. I had on a blue charmeuse gown—I remember it now, it was lovely! Slippers with very high heels and brilliants on the buckles, white gloves, a big hat with a black ostrich feather, and a veil. Luckily the veil was down; for as I entered the door of my brother's tenement, my father stood there on the steps ! He looked at me, I stopped. My heartstood still. But I could see he did not recognize me.

"'Va t'en" he shouted. 'What is your kind doing here, in a workingman's house? What do you mean by coming here to insult us with your silks and your feathers, sweated out of poor men in mills and their consumptive wives, their dying children? Go away, you whore!'

"I was terrified that he might recognize me!

"It was only once more that I saw him. My lover left me, and I had other lovers...My brother and his wife went out to live near my father, in St. Denis. I used sometimes to go out and spend the night with them, to play with the baby, who grew so fast. Those were really happy times. And I used to leave again at dawn, to avoid meeting my father. One morning I left brother's house, and as I came onto the street, I saw my father, going to work at dawn with his lunch pail! He had not seen my face. There was nothing to do but walk down the street ahead of him. It was about five o'clock—few people were about. He came along behind me, and soon I noticed that he was walking faster. Then he said in a low voice, 'Mademoiselle, wait for me. We are going the same direction, *hein?* I hurried. 'You are pretty, mademoiselle. And I am not old. Can't ne go together some place?' I was in a panic. I was so full of horror and of fear that he might see my face. I did not dare to turn up a side street, for he would have seen my profile. So I walked straight ahead—straight ahead for hours, for miles...I do not know when he stopped...I do not know if now he might be dead...My brother said he never spoke of me..."

She ceased, and the noises of the street became again apparent to our ears, that had been so long deaf to them, with double their former loudness. Fred was excited.

"Marvelous, by God!" he cried, thumping the table. "The same blood, the same spirit ! And see how the revolution becomes sweeter, broader, from generation to generation! See how the brother understood freedom in a way which the old father was blind to!"

Marcelle shot him an astonished look. "What do you mean?" she asked.

"Your father—fighting all his life for liberty—yet turned you out because you wanted *your liberty.*"

"Oh, but you don't understand," said Marcelle. "I did wrong. I am bad. If I had a daughter who was like me, I should do the same thing, if she had a frivolous character."

"Can't you *see?*" cried Fred. "Your father wanted liberty for men, but not for women!"

"Naturally," she shrugged. "Men and women are different. My father was right. Women must be *respectable!*"

"The women need another generation," sighed Fred, sadly.

I took Marcelle's hand.

"Do you regret it?" I asked her.

"Regret my life?" she Bashed back, tossing her head proudly, *"Dame,* no ! I'm *free!* ."

THE FIGHT FOR SOCIALISM: THE PRINCIPLES AND PROGRAM OF THE SOCIALIST WORKERS PARTY

Max Shachtman's

Chapter-2

A Workers' Government and Socialism

SOCIALISM, based upon the planned organization of production for use by means of the common ownership and democratic control of the means of production, is the abolition of all classes and class differences.

"As an ideal, it would be a good thing to have socialism; but it is only an ideal which cannot be realized in practice." This is said by many people who have a poor understanding not only of socialism but of capitalism as well. Let us see. Is socialism merely a noble ideal, or is it more than that—a practical possibility and urgent necessity?

The First Steps of a Workers' Government

Without production, society cannot live. The first step that a genuine Workers' Government would take would be directed toward assuring continuous production so as to satisfy the needs of the people.

How could that be assured? There would be all sorts of difficulties in the way. Most of them would come from the big capitalists. If they saw that this government was really serious in applying its principle of serving the interests of society and not merely of serving the profit-lust of capitalism, they would set up all the obstacles they could. Their aim would be to throw monkey-wrenches into all the machinery of industry and administration, to weaken the government, to undermine its authority, to discredit it, and to overthrow it as soon as possible. When the capitalists feel that their property and profits are in any way endangered, there are no lengths to which they will not go to preserve them. The interests and welfare of the people are their very last concern.

What would they do? They would refuse to carry out the orders of the government, or carry them out in such a way as to nullify their purpose. They would sabotage production in a thousand different ways, or shut down their plants on one pretext or another. They would conceal their real stocks and assets. By their control of the banking system, they would deny the government the funds required to carry out a progressive program. They would even create an artificial financial panic, as they have done on other occasions. They would use their great economic power to finance bands of thugs and reactionaries assigned to the job of creating turmoil, of impeding the smooth operation of the government, and eventually of overthrowing it by force or the threat of force. By their monopoly of the press and radio, they would keep up a running fire of misrepresentation, lies and slander against the government with the aim of undermining it, sabotaging its efforts, and confusing and misleading the people. They would soon show the Workers' Government what it means for them to have a monopoly of social power!

These are not mere predictions. They have already occurred in many countries. The capitalist class acted in exactly that way not only in Russia, when a revolutionary Workers' Government took political power, but also in England, Austria, Spain, Germany, France and other countries, where there were only conservative and timid Labor Governments or half-Labor Governments. The only country in which this campaign was properly dealt with was in Russia, in the revolution of 1917. A genuine Workers' Government in any other country would have to deal with the capitalist class in fundamentally the same way—if only in simple self-defense.

A Workers' Government would, first of all, nationalize the key, basic industries, the means of transportation, and the banking system. These are the main strongholds of monopoly capitalism and the foundations of modern production. By nationalizing and centralizing them in the hands of the state, the Workers' Government accomplishes two objectives with one stroke. It is now in a position to organize production and distribution in a planful and systematic way, and it deprives the reactionary monopolists of the economic power to interfere with production and the functioning of the government.

In undertaking the nationalization of industry and finance, several questions of first-rate importance immediately face the Workers' Government. Let us consider them one by one.

First: *Shall the property of the big capitalists be confiscated without compensation?*

The very word "confiscation," especially when the words "without compensation" are added to it, raises shrieks of horror from the ranks of the capitalists. Outrageous! Inconceivable! Yet the whole system of capitalism is based on confiscation. The original accumulation of capital, as will be recalled, was accomplished for the most part by an elaborate system of confiscating (expropriating) the wealth and resources of small producers, independent peasants and farmers, and entire colonial peoples. Day-in and day-out capitalism exists only because it confiscates the surpius-value produced by the worker over and above the wages he receives for his labor. Capitalism has developed confiscation to a forcibly-maintained, scientific process of exploitation. If we understand the fact that the value of all the products of society has been produced by labor, it would be perfectly proper for labor to confiscate without further ado.

Nevertheless, confiscation of capitalist property without any compensation to its former owners is not an absolutely necessary step for the Workers' Government to take. If the capitalists reconcile themselves quietly to the new government and the social progress it undertakes to achieve, it might very well prove to be a wise step to compensate them for the property that has been nationalized. Or, compensation might be offered them in order to show that the new government is not interested merely in vengeance. Its primary concern is the organization of economic life for the benefit of the whole of society. There is room in this organization even for former capitalists who wish to cooperate and are ready to place at the disposal of society whatever technical and managerial skill they may possess. Under these conditions, compensation would be a cheap way of assuring a smooth and speedy reorganization of economic and social life.

Naturally, even if compensation were decided on, it would certainly not be based on calculations arbitrarily made by the former capitalists, but on estimates made by the government. The capitalist would not be permitted to present the government with any claim he himself saw fit to make and to demand, "This is what my property is worth. Pay me off in full." In addition, whatever compensation he received would be for his personal wealth, but could not be used to acquire ownership of the means of production all over again so that the exploitation of labor might be resumed. Finally, all incomes would be subject to a progressive tax with a democratically-fixed schedule.

All experience indicates, however, that the capitalist class will not quietly submit to a Workers' Government. Wherever it seemed on the verge of coming into existence, the capitalists always organized all the armed forces at their disposal to crush it. Wherever it did take power, the capitalists fought tooth and nail to overturn it by the same armed force. In all likelihood, that is how they will act in every country where their immense power to rule society is threatened. It goes without saying that where the capitalist class or any part of it tries to overturn the Workers' Government, tries to impose the will of the minority upon the majority by force and violence, tries to throw the country into a bloody civil war, it would be treated like any traitor. These capitalists would be declared outlaws, they would be deprived of all civil rights and their properties confiscated outright by the state.

In other words, the choice is really theirs. If they recognize that the day of their despotic domination over society has ended, and that they had best cooperate as useful citizens, then chaos and bloodshed will be averted, and smooth and speedy progress assured for all. If they do not reconcile themselves, and seek to turn progress into reaction by sword and bomb, they can hardly complain about the inevitable consequences.

Second: *Shall all private property be nationalized immediately?*

Certainly not! In the first place, we are concerned not with private property but with capitalist private property, that is, privately-owned means of production and exchange, that is, with capital, or wealth used for the creation of more wealth by exploiting the labor of others. We do not have in mind such things as clothing, the family home, radio or automobile, furniture, your own fishing boat or hobby equipment, and other items of purely personal property. If anything, the aim of the Workers' Government is to make such "property" available in larger quantities to millions who have never enjoyed them. The basic problem of society is related to such property as is represented by the means of production and exchange. It is these that must be nationalized, and forthwith.

Does this mean the Workers' Government will immediately take over every corner grocery, every shoe store and tailor shop, every little farm? Certainly not! In the first place, it would be foolish for the Workers' Government to alienate the members of the middle classes and drive them into the arms of monopoly-capitalist reaction. In the second place, the evils of capitalist society do not grow out of the little farm or grocery store, but out of the big industrial monopolies that are linked with the big banking institutions. In the third place, the Workers' Government can act with complete confidence in the superiority of the way it will organize and manage economic life. It can afford to let the evidence of this superiority convince the small farmer that it is far more economical and far less back-breaking to work collectively with other agriculturists on highly-mechanized, scientifically-exploited, efficiently-managed, socially-owned-and-operated big farms. It is wrong and quite unnecessary to try *forcing* the farmer to rive up his farm for a collective farm. Essentially the same attitude may well be adopted toward the small merchant and producer. The Workers' Government has no need or interest in forcing these small property-owners, producers and merchants into the machinery of state-industry, state-farming. It can fully rely on the persuasive power of example.

Third: *Shall economic life be centrally organized and planned?*

Most decidedly! If not, what sense would there be to the nationalization of the means of production? The government would have the responsibility for solving the economic problems of the country. It could not possibly discharge this weighty responsibility unless it had the power to do so. It cannot have this power unless it has the economic machinery in its hands and is in a position to gear all its wheels so that they operate smoothly.

There are people who argue against a Workers' Government nationalizing the means of production and exchange. They say that it is not so much that they oppose the formation of a Workers' Government, but that they are against it having "too much economic power." As a "compromise," they propose that some industries be nationalized and others remain private property.

But this does not make sense. If private property is superior to nationalized or socialized property, then the nationalization of property should be opposed altogether, which is as good as saying that a Workers' Government has no reason for existence. If both are equally good or equally bad, there is supply no point in bothering to replace one with the other. If nationalized property is superior to capitalist property, then, even if only part of industry were nationalized, its superiority would be demonstrated so quickly that private property could not properly be maintained. The worst aspect of this argument is this: If only part of the means of production were nationalized and centralized in the hands of the Workers' Government, it would not find it possible to *organize and plan production on a national scale*. It is not possible to *plan* the production and distribution of goods if part of the machinery is under one control and direction and the other part under different control. The whole purpose of the nationalization of property would be defeated in advance.

The purpose of planning, long-term planning, is to assure the harmonious expansion of industry and the systematic raising of the standard of living. The raw materials, machinery and labor power of the nation would be brought together into an integrated whole. The waste of capitalist competition and the stagnation of monopoly capitalism would be overcome. Production would not be organized on the basis of the blind push and pull of the capitalist market, but in accordance with the needs of the people. Production for profit would give way to production for use.

Fourth: *Shall economic life be democratically managed and controlled?*

Absolutely! It is the maintenance of capitalist domination of society that demands, more and more, the abandonment of democracy. A Workers' Government would have to extend democracy continually, not merely because it is a desirable ideal, but because it is indispensable to the planning of production for use.

Capitalism produces bombs for the destruction of homes just as readily as it constructs homes, if not more readily. It produces barbed wire to tear the flesh of men just as readily as it produces clothing to cover them. It produces luxurious palaces while millions live in shacks. Its motive of production was, is, and always will be profit. It is not the needs of the people that dictate its production.

If, however, production were carried on for use, to satisfy the needs of the people, the question immediately arises: Who is to determine what is useful and what would satisfy these needs? Will that be decided exclusively by a small board of government planners? No matter how high-minded and wise they might be, they could not plan production for the needs of the people. Production for use, *by its very nature,* demands constant consultation of the people, constant control and direction by the people. The democratically-adopted decision of the people would have to guide the course of production and distribution. Democratic control of the means of production and distribution would have to be exercised by the people to see to it that their decision is being carried out.

Otherwise, the government and its planning would undergo a complete perversion of its purpose. At best, we would have a benevolent regimentation of the people "for their own good." A government which declares itself to be "for" the workers, but is not a government *of* and *by* the workers, is a Workers' Government only in name. Instead of being regulated by the blind market, as under capitalism, production would be regulated by the autocratic, uncontrolled will of a bureaucracy. Economic distortions, social conflict, exploitation and oppression would inevitably result. Production for use, aimed at satisfying the needs of society and of freeing all the people from class rule, would be impossible. Democratic control, the continual extension of democracy, is therefore an indispensable necessity under a Workers' Government. The idea of a Workers' Government is thus inseparably connected with the idea of nationalization of the means of production and exchange, the centralized organization and planning of production and distribution, and the continual extension of democracy and democratic control of industry, there must be planing of production. To plan production, the economic machinery of the country must be socially owned and centrally operated. To nationalize the means of production and exchange, a Workers' Government must be established with power to act. For it to be a Workers' Government, it must be democratically run and controlled by the workers. None of these is possible without having all.

Now, what must be emphasized at this point is this:

The Workers' Government has taken the first important steps toward the achievement of Socialism!

Socialism is not a utopian ideal, a blueprint for society that exists in the minds of some people. It is a social necessity; it is a practical necessity. It is the direction that the masses of the people must take in order to save society from disintegration, in order to satisfy their social needs. To be a socialist, merely means to be conscious of this necessity, to make others conscious of it, and to work in an organized manner for the realization of the goal.

How Capitalism Prepares Socialism

How is the goal of a socialist society to be realized? Is it really possible to realize it? In order to answer these questions, we must retrace our steps a little, and deal with two highly important matters. One is the way in which capitalism prepares the economic groundwork for socialism. The other is the way in which capitalism provides the social force capable of destroying capitalism and building up the new society. The great superiority of capitalism over the societies that came before it, lies in the fact that it has enormously developed the forces of production. Under slavery and feudalism, life, economic life in particular, barely moved along. For centuries, people used the same primitive tools. For centuries, people worked as individuals or, at most, in twos or threes or fours, on the farm and in tiny shops.

Capitalism lifted society out of this stagnation and sent it off at a furious gallop. Machines replaced hand labor; big industries replaced small ones. Labor productivity was raised to astounding heights. With modern machinery and production methods, one man produces what it took hundreds and thousands of men to produce a century or more ago. In addition, commodities are produced that our forefathers never even dreamed of seeing.

One of the results of this development is that *production is already carried on socially*. Labor has been socialized. The basis of production is no longer one man on a farm or a couple of men in a little shop. In some industries, tens of thousands of people work together under a single direction, under one roof, so to speak. Capital has become concentrated and centralized. The most important industries are owned and operated as monopolies.

In itself, this is highly desirable. One huge enterprise, which organizes a great multitude of little operations under single direction, is far more productive, far more economical and efficient, than a thousand little enterprises each of which does one or two little operations independently of all the others, or each of which tries to compete with all the others. The only important thing that has not been socialized is the *ownership* and the *appropriation* of the products of industry. They remain private. And therein lies the root of capitalist exploitation and oppression, of the anarchy of production, of crises and imperialist wars.

Social production, in large-scale mechanized industry, represents, however, *the seeds of the socialist society growing right in the soil of capitalist society itself.* Socialism could not possibly be built up on the basis of the tens of thousands of isolated, independent, competing little enterprises that existed generations ago. But it can be built on the basis of modern production which is already carried on socially. And it must be built because *private ownership*, which is the basis of *private appropriation*, now *stands in the way* of the further development of the productive forces. The reason why it is now possible is that the only remaining step to be taken is the removal of this last obstacle to human progress—private ownership.

Once this is done, the seeds of socialism, sown by capitalism itself, will bloom and flourish.

Capitalism also produces the force capable of reorganizing society on a rational basis. That force is the modern working class, brought into existence and developed by capitalism itself. Capitalist production organizes the workers as a class. The very way in which it is carried on assembles the workers for cooperative labor, so that they are accustomed to work together in a planful way by tens of thousands in the larger enterprises.

By monopolizing the means of production and depriving the formerly independent worker of his tools, capitalism wipes out the basis for the workers' interest in maintaining private property. The workers are now *propertyless workers*, who no longer own the tools and machines with which they produce. At the same time, however, they have become the principal productive force. Of all the people in society, the workers suffer most intensely from the rule of capitalism. Their interests are diametrically opposed to those of the capitalists. Of all the conflicts in society, the struggle between working class and capitalist class is the sharpest and most irreconcilable.

The workers cannot rid themselves of their sufferings without abolishing the domination that the machine has over them. They can do this only if they gain control of the machine itself. In doing so, they must destroy capitalism and proceed with the complete reorganization of society.

No other class is capable of doing this historic task. The middle classes are, it is true, ground under by monopoly capitalism. But they are incapable of leading the fight against it. They are isolated and dispersed. Their economic position in society does not make it possible for them to unite as an organized force. As tiny isolated producers or merchants, they are at the mercy of big industry and finance. They may oppose the monopolists, but they cannot fight, much less lead the fight, against the capitalist system of private property—they are little property-owners themselves.

To the extent that they have a program of their own, it is to "break the trusts." These mighty concentrations of capital, however, should not (and cannot) be broken up into ineffective and inefficient little units. They should be taken over by society itself. Even if they could, by some magic, be divided into the small productive units that once existed, the law of capitalist development would operate incessantly to merge them all over again. The program of the middle class is utterly utopian, unrealizable. It is reactionary, for it tries to turn back the wheels of social development.

Furthermore, the middle classes are doomed to social and political instability. Because they find themselves forced to oppose the industrial and financial monopolists, they seek an alliance with the workers. This is, so to speak, the progressive side of the middle classes of town and country. But because they seek to preserve their hopeless position as property-owners, and because they must intensify the exploitation of the few workers they employ in order to compete with large-scale industry, they oppose the working class and lean upon the big capitalists for support. This is the conservative or reactionary side of the middle class.

It does not follow that the middle classes are exactly "in the middle" between the two main classes or that their interests are as much opposed to the one as to the other. Capitalism destroys them not only as small property-owners, but as human beings. It makes them the helpless slaves of the banks, the railroads, the mills, the packing houses. Or it deprives them altogether of their half-independent position and throws them into the ranks of the working class or of the "surplus population." It oppresses and degrades them, depriving them of both material and intellectual independence. This is true of all the middle classes, from the farmer at one end to the teacher and writer at the other.

Under the rule of the working class the small property interests of the middle classes cannot of course be assured forever. The working class can pledge itself—because it is to its interests to do so—not to deprive them of their little holdings by force, or arbitrary law. But more important than that, the working class can release the middle classes from the oppression and humiliation they endure at the hands of monopoly capitalism. The working class can release them from the murderous grubbing for existence which characterizes the life of the middle classes—sun-up to sun-down toil on farm or in store; the constant feverish race to meet the to meet the notes of creditors and mortgagors; the virtual enslavement of wife and children on farm and in store in the attempt to keep head above water; the suffering, insecurity, misery and—in war-time—the death which the middle classes share with all the other little people in society. The working class can offer them the prospects of useful citizenship, freedom and equality as producers in a socialist society. The best interests of the middle classes therefore lie in joining the working class in its fight.

But the very nature of the situation dictates that it is the working class that must lead in this necessary alliance. It is the decisive class in production, and the only one that can reorganize it. It is the most numerous and the most socially-representative class. It is the best organized class, certainly better organized than the middle classes are or can be. But above all, for the reasons set forth in the comparison above, it is the only *consistently progressive class*.

That is why, throughout these pages, we have spoken of a *Workers'* Government and not, for example, of a "People's Government." At the same time, we have spoken of the Workers' Government basing itself upon and being supported by the masses of the people, and not by the working class alone. The reason for this should now be clear. The fight against capitalist anarchy and devastation can be *led* only by the working class, but it must draw into the fight all the people, middle classes of town and country included, who suffer under the domination of monopoly capital and find in it their common enemy. The words, *Workers'* Government, express the fact that the *leadership* in the reorganization of society can be taken only by the working class. But in the very course of reorganizing society, such a government must liberate not only the workers, but all the people. The workers take the leadership of the nation only in order to emancipate all humanity from exploitation, class distinctions, class privileges, class conflict, to establish social equality for all.

The working class is thus the bearer of socialism. Can it realize it? How would it work?

Between Capitalism and Socialism

The abolition of private ownership would remove the last barrier to the development of production. Production would be organized, planfully carried on and expanded, and aimed at satisfying the needs of society. But this does not mean that all classes and class distinctions could be wiped out overnight.

There would still be classes and social differences, and heaps of material and mental rubbish inherited from generations of capitalist society. A considerable period would elapse between the overturn of the political power of the capitalist class and the establishment of the socialist society. Man did not step directly from the ox-cart into the modern automobile. There was a transition between the two. So will there be a transitional period between capitalism and socialism.

It is precisely in this transitional period that the Workers' Government—a workers' state—will be required. At this point, we recall that the state has always been an instrument of force and repression in the hands of the ruling class. Is that also the case with the workers' state? To reply with a simple "Yes" or "No" would be misleading. It is better to deal with this question in more detail, so that we can see in what sense the workers' state will resemble the state we have known in the past, and in what sense it would differ from it.

First, the workers' state *would* be an instrument of force. It would have to be. It would have to have at its disposal armed men and prisons. Against whom? Against what? Well, it would not make any sense to set up a Workers' Government and then leave it so thoroughly disarmed from the first day of its existence that any group of capitalists could come along with its armed bands at home, or with armies provided by a foreign country still ruled by capitalism, to overthrow the new government by violence. The Workers' Government would have to have the organized strength—arms—with which to deal with such reactionary forces, and prisons in which to confine them and any other violent anti-social elements.

All modern experience shows that it is foolhardy to expect the whole capitalist class and all the reactionaries to give up their tremendous power and wealth without a bitter fight, even after the Workers' Government has taken control. If they resist so violently the demands of the workers for an extra few cents per hour in wages, how much more violently will they resist the efforts of the workers to take from them all their power to dominate society?

Second, the workers' state would tolerate inequality. This, also, it would have to do. The greatest heights of production yet reached by capitalism are still low by the standards of socialism. Capitalism lays the economic groundwork for socialism, and provides the class that can bring socialism about, but neither the groundwork nor the class inherited from capitalism is what it will and must be in a truly socialist society.

For example, there are skilled workers and unskilled workers. There are those who work mainly with their hands and those who work mainly with their brain. There are day laborers and highly skilled technicians, industrial organizers and managers. In so far as all of them contribute to the process of production, their labor can be reduced to so many and so many units of simple labor. But the number of units, so to speak, is different in the different categories of skill and occupation.

Could the Workers' Government say, on the first day of its formation, that everyone will receive exactly the same income, exactly the same share of the total national production? It seems obvious that it could not and would not make such a rule. The working class is not utopian, and neither are the socialists. Different categories would have to be established in the first period of the social reorganization. No one would any longer receive special privileges and rights merely because of his ownership of capital. But the skilled worker or technician or industrial organizer, who is able to contribute more to production than the unskilled worker, would receive a correspondingly higher income. Whether he received it in the form of money or some other certificate entitling him to a given share of goods produced, is of secondary importance. The important point is that the more skilled man would have a larger income than the less skilled. In other words, there would still be a form of inequality. The state would tolerate it and take it into account in organizing the production and distribution of products, *while working to eliminate this inequality too.*

These characteristics of the Workers' Government show its similarities with the preceding state. But it is in its fundamental differences with it that the workers' state shows, as the founders of scientific socialism have put it, that it is no longer a state in the classic sense of the word. A whole world of difference separates the two.

First, the force at the disposal of the workers' state would not reside in bodies of armed men separated from the people, as under capitalism or feudalism or slavery. The arms would be in the hands of the workers themselves. The government which could summon these arms into action would be in the hands of the workers themselves.

Second, the state power would no longer be the instrument of an exploiting minority for the domination of the exploited majority. For the first time in history, the state would be in the hands of the majority to be used whenever necessary against the reactionary or anti-social minority.

Third, the state power would no longer be governed by a special or professional bureaucracy. It would be ruled and controlled by the people. It would have no permanent officials, and all elected officers would be subject to immediate recall by their electors. By virtue of its system of democratic representation, which will be dealt with in detail further on, every worker will participate directly in the affairs of government, from the humblest to the most prominent.

That is not all. The workers' state, which is compelled to tolerate inequality in the initial period of its existence, nevertheless aims consciously at the abolition of inequality.

Capitalism has already accomplished a great deal in eliminating the need for high skills by simplifying the operations in production. The workers' state would go much further, but in a radically different sense. With the constantly increasing national wealth at its disposal, education, specially higher education, would cease to be restricted to the few. The spread of education to all would gradually eliminate the difference between skilled and unskilled labor, between mental and physical labor. One or two generations of normal evolution, and everyone would not only be required to divide his contribution to society between physical and mental work, but would be able to do so.

In addition, all the unnatural differences between town and country would be eliminated. Agriculture, under capitalism, has remained the most backward section of economic life. The Workers' Government would work to make a long-over-due revolution in agriculture. Step by step, the small farmer would be shown in practice the enormous advantages both to himself and to society of large-scale cooperative exploitation of the soil. As has already been said, the government would take no steps to force the small farmer into such cooperative labor. It would not need to. The advantages would speak for themselves, and lead the agricultural population to share in them voluntarily. The most advanced scientific knowledge would be placed at the disposal of agriculture, and it would soon show that the methods that were "good enough for grandfather" are not nearly as good as the newest methods. Instead of the exhausting duplication of work on small tracts of land, the most modern machinery—efficient, time-saving, labor-saving—would be applied to agriculture on a large scale. The horse-drawn plow is as outmoded as the hand-loom. Agriculture would become industrialized; the distinction between agricultural labor and industrial labor would vanish. Rural isolation would vanish as well. As for rural prejudices, originating in hostility to the wealth of the industrial centers and to the fact that industry and finance lived at the expense of agriculture, they would disappear with the disappearance of rural poverty and misery.

Hand in hand with this development would go another of equal importance. Once the profit barrier is removed, and the huge wastes and destructions of capitalism eliminated, productivity and production would reach undreamed-of peaks.

Man would no longer be the slave of the machine. The machine would be the fertile slave of man. Every increase in productivity would bring with it two things: an increase in the things required for the need, comfort and even luxury of all; and an increase in everyone's leisure time, to devote to the free cultural and intellectual development of humankind. Man will not live primarily to work; he will work primarily to live.

A most practical perspective! Even today, with all the restrictions that capitalism places upon production, there are capitalist experts who declare that industry, properly organized, can produce the necessities of life for all in a working day of four hours or less. Organized on a socialist basis, even this figure could be cut down.

As the necessities and comforts of life become increasingly abundant, and the differences between physical and mental labor, between town and country are eliminated—the need for tolerating even the last vestiges of inequality will disappear as a matter of course. This may seem incredible to a mind thoroughly poisoned with capitalist prejudices. But why should it be incredible?

Thirsty men will fight tooth and nail for a drink at a desert oasis. But if they are up to their hips in water they may have a thousand differences among themselves, but they will not even dream of fighting for a drink. A dozen men in a prison cell with only one tiny window may trample over each other in the fight to get to that tiny source of fresh air. But outside, who ever thinks of fighting for air to breathe, or for more air than the next man? Announce a shortage of bread, and immediately a long line will form, with everyone racing to get there first, and a policeman on hand to "keep order." But if everyone knew that there is an ample supply of bread today, and there will be just as large a supply tomorrow and the next day, there would be no line, no race, no conflict; nobody would try to hoard an extra loaf in order to make sure of eating the next day; and there would be no need of a policeman to back up his orders by force. If society could assure everyone of as ample and constant a supply of bread as there is of air, why would anyone need or want a greater right to buy bread than his neighbor? Bread is used here only as the simplest illustration. But the same applies to all other foods, to clothing, to shelter, to books, to means of transportation.

A planfully organized society, efficiently utilizing our present productive equipment and the better equipment to come, could easily assure abundance to all. In return, society could confidently expect every citizen to contribute his best voluntarily.

In the initial period of development, a capitalist morality is still prevalent. Many of the people, even many workers, are still poisoned with the old spirit of greed, selfishness, cheating and other evils of a class society where only the few enjoy abundance and opportunity. One of the reasons for a workers' *state* is to enforce sternly the principle, "He who does not work shall not eat."

But in the midst of abundance for all and of the high cultural development that will accompany it, there is no reason to believe that special force will be needed to maintain this principle. Labor to the best of one's ability will be as natural an act as breathing, eating, clothing and sheltering oneself. Under those circumstances, let any strange creature try to be so capitalistically "old-fashioned" as to draw on the public stores without contributing his labors The scorn of all around him would quickly make him a social outcast such as policemen and prisons could never make him under capitalism. He would not be long in coming to his senses and performing his social duty.

What happens to the workers' state? There is abundance for all. There is ample opportunity for the intellectual development of all. All perform their social duty as a matter of course. What need is there for compulsion, for a machinery of force? To prevent burglary? What will there be to steal in the midst of abundance? To prevent rape or murder? Such cases will be exceedingly rare, we may be sure, and in any case they will require medical attention or confinement for the guilty one, and not prison confinement. To regulate traffic? But for that and similar tasks there will be needed, not policemen, as we know them now, but ordinary citizens assigned to perform that social duty in about the same way that traffic dispatchers work on the railway.

The important thing is that there will be no need of a public coercive force to maintain the power of one class over another, to protect the property of one from the assaults of the other, to assure the continuation of oppression and exploitation. The workers' state itself will die out for lack of any social need or function. The transition from the class society of socialism will be completed. There will be the simple administration of things, but no longer the rule of man over man.

In this most important of all respects, the Workers' State will be fundamentally different from the state we have known in all past history. Paradoxical though it may seem at first glance, it becomes clear upon reflection that the workers' state imperatively needed precisely in order to carry society through the transition to socialism in which the state itself dies away.

Such a bold historical prospect, even though scientific and practical, may seem preposterous to a mind that capitalism has taken good care to keep in a dull and conservative condition. Abundance for all? Freedom for all? A society without a state? Impossible! Never had it in all history!

If they could have reasoned and talked, the common ancestors of man and ape could easily have spoken the same way. "We tree-animals will always have to fight among ourselves and with other animals for food. Our fathers and forefathers had to do it before us, and so will our offspring after us. The idea of growing our own food is very attractive, but it is utopian and impractical. As for tails, those we shall always have with us. Our fathers and forefathers found tails indispensable for swinging from branch to branch, and for a third support when trying to stand on two legs. Our offspring will never be able to do without tails. That animal there, who just dropped to the ground and is trying to move on two legs alone, is sure to break his fool neck in no time at all. The idea of moving around without tails is very attractive, because in many ways they are a nuisance, but it will never work in practice. The idea of walking upright on two legs might be an interesting experiment for crackpots, but we know from experience that we need tails for balance and we shall always have them with us".

Man, as is known, has proved that these hypothetical tree-animals were somewhat conservative and wrong.

Man will also prove that class divisions, poverty and oppression are not unavoidable and the state not indispensable. In the socialist society he will show that abundance, freedom and equality are not only possible but the natural condition for the new history of the human race.

INDUSTRIAL UNIONISM AND CONSTRUCTIVE SOCIALISM

James Connolly

Chapter-3

There is not a Socialist in the world today who can indicate with any degree of clearness how we can bring about the co-operative commonwealth except along the lines suggested by industrial organization of the workers.

Political institutions are not adapted to the administration of industry. Only industrial organizations are adapted to the administration of a co-operative commonwealth that we are working for. Only the industrial form of organization offers us even a theoretical constructive Socialist programme. There is no constructive Socialism except in the industrial field.

The above extracts from the speech of Delegate Stirton, editor of the Wage Slave, of Hancock, Michigan, so well embody my ideas upon this matter that I have thought well to take them as a text for an article in explanation of the structural form of Socialist society. In a previous chapter I have analysed the weakness of the craft or trade union form of organization alike as a weapon of defence against the capitalist class in everyday conflict on the economic field, and as a generator of class consciousness on the political field, and pointed out the greater effectiveness for both purposes of an industrial form of organization.

Organizing Constructively

In the present article I desire to show how they who are engaged in building up industrial organizations for the practical purpose of today are at the same time preparing the framework of the society of the future. It is the realization of that feet that indeed marks the emergence of Socialism as a revolutionary force from the critical to the positive stage. Time was when Socialists, if asked how society would be organized under Socialism, replied invariably, and airily, that such things would be left to the future to decide. The fact was that they had not considered the matter, but the development of the Trust and Organized Capital in general, making imperative the Industrial Organizations of Labour on similar lines, has provided us with an answer at once more complete to ourselves and more satisfying to our questioners.

Now to analyse briefly the logical consequences of the position embodied in the above quotation.

> "Political institutions are not adapted to the administration of industry."

Here is a statement that no Socialist with a clear knowledge of the essentials of his doctrine can dispute. The political institutions of today are simply the coercive forces of capitalist society they have grown up out of, and are based upon, territorial divisions of power in the hands of the ruling class in past ages, and were carried over into capitalist society to suit the needs of the capitalist class when that class overthrew the dominion of its predecessors.

The Old Order and the New

The delegation of the function of government into the hands of representatives elected from certain districts, States or territories, represents no real natural division suited to the requirements of modern society, but is a survival from a time when territorial influences were more potent in the world than industrial influences, and for that reason is totally unsuited to the needs of the new social order, which must be based upon industry.

The Socialist thinker, when he paints the structural form of the new social order, does not imagine an industrial system directed or ruled by a body of men or women elected from an indiscriminate mass of residents within given districts, said residents working at a heterogeneous collection of trades and industries. To give the ruling, controlling, and directing of industry into the hands of such a body would be too utterly foolish.

What the Socialist does realize is that under a social democratic form of society the administration of affairs will be in the hands of representatives of the various industries of the nation; that the workers in the shops and factories will organize themselves into unions, each union comprising all the workers at a given industry; that said union will democratically control the workshop life of its own industry, electing all foremen etc., and regulating the routine of labour in that industry in subordination to the needs of society in general, to the needs of its allied trades, and to the departments of industry to which it belongs; that representatives elected from these various departments of industry will meet and form the industrial administration or national government of the country.

Begin in the Workshop

In short, social democracy, as its name implies, is the application to industry, or to the social life of the nation, of the fundamental principles of democracy. Such application will necessarily have to begin in the workshop, and proceed logically and consecutively upward through all the grades of industrial organization until it reaches the culminating point of national executive power and direction. In other words, social democracy must proceed from the bottom upward, whereas capitalist political society is organized from above downward.

Social democracy will be administered by a committee of experts elected from the industries and professions of the land; capitalist society is governed by representatives elected from districts, and is based upon territorial division.

The local and national governing, or rather administrative, bodies of Socialists will approach every question with impartial minds, armed with the fullest expert knowledge born of experience; the governing bodies of capitalist society have to call in an expensive professional expert to instruct them on every technical question, and know that the impartiality of said expert varies with, and depends upon, the size of his fee.

No 'Servile State'

It will be seen that this conception of Socialism destroys at one blow all the fears of a bureaucratic State, ruling and ordering the lives of every individual from above, and thus gives assurance that the social order of the future will be an extension of the freedom of the individual, and not the suppression of it. In short, it blends the fullest democratic control with the most absolute expert supervision, something unthinkable of any society built upon the political State.

To focus the idea properly in your mind you have but to realize how industry today transcends all limitations of territory and leaps across rivers, mountains and continents; then you can understand how impossible it would be to apply to such far-reaching intricate enterprises the principle of democratic control by the workers through the medium of political territorial divisions.

Under Socialism, States, territories, or provinces will exist only as geographical expressions, and have no existence as sources of governmental power, though they may be seats of administrative bodies.

Now, having grasped the idea that the administrative force of the Socialist republic of the future will function through unions industrially organized, that the principle of democratic control will operate through the workers correctly organized in such industrial unions, and that the political territorial State of capitalist society will have no place or function under Socialism, you will at once grasp the full truth embodied in the words of this member of the Socialist Party whom I have just quoted, that "only the industrial form of organization offers us even a theoretical constructive Socialist programme."

The Political State and its Uses

To some minds constructive Socialism is embodied in the work of our representatives on the various public bodies to which they have been elected. The various measures against the evils of capitalist property brought forward by, or as a result of, the agitation of Socialist representatives on legislative bodies are figured as being of the nature of constructive Socialism.

As we have shown, the political State of capitalism has no place under Socialism; therefore, measures which aim to place industries in the hands of, or under the control of, such a political State are in no sense steps towards that ideal; they are but useful measures to restrict the greed of capitalism and to familiarize the workers with the conception of common ownership. This latter is, indeed, their chief function.

But the enrolment of the workers in unions patterned closely after the structure of modem industries, and following the organic lines of industrial development, is par excellence the swiftest, safest, and most peaceful form of constructive work the Socialist can engage in. It prepares within the framework of capitalist society the working forms of the Socialist republic, and thus, while increasing the resisting power of the worker against present encroachments of the capitalist class, it familiarizes him with the idea that the union he is helping to build up is destined to supplant that class in the control of the industry in which he is employed.

The Union Can Build Freedom

The power of this idea to transform the dry detail work of trade union organization into the constructive work of revolutionary Socialism, and thus make of the unimaginative trade unionist a potent factor in the launching of a new system of society, cannot be overestimated. It invests the sordid details of the daily incidents of the class struggle with a new and beautiful meaning, and presents them in their true light as skirmishes between the two opposing armies of light and darkness.

In the light of this principle of industrial unionism every fresh shop or factory organized under its banner is a fort wrenched from the control of the capitalist class and manned with the soldiers of the revolution to be held by them for the workers.

On the day that the political and economic forces of Labour finally break with capitalist society and proclaim the Workers' Republic, these shops and factories so manned by industrial unionists will be taken charge of by the workers there employed, and force and effectiveness be thus given to that proclamation. Then and thus the new society will spring into existence, ready equipped to perform all the useful functions of its predecessor.

Industrialism and the Trade Unions

In the second part of my book Socialism Made Easy, I have endeavoured to establish two principles in the minds of my readers as being vitally necessary to the upbuilding of a strong revolutionary Socialist movement. Those two principles are: First, that the working class as a class cannot become permeated with a belief in the unity of their class interests unless they have first been trained to a realization of the need of industrial unity; second, that the revolutionary act—the act of taking over the means of production and establishing a social order based upon the principles of the working class (labour)—cannot be achieved by a disorganized, defeated and humiliated working class, but must be the work of that class after it has attained to a commanding position on the field of economic struggle. It has been a pleasure to me to note the progress of Socialist thought towards acceptance of these principles, and to believe that the publication of that little work helped to a not inconsiderable degree in shaping that Socialist thought and in accelerating its progress. In the following article I wish to present one side of the discussion which inevitably arises in our Socialist party branches upon the mooting of this question. But as a preliminary to this presentation I would like to decry, and ask my comrades to decry and dissociate themselves from, the somewhat acrid and intolerant manner in which this discussion is often carried on. Believing that the Socialist Party is part and parcel of the labour movement of the United States, and that in the growth of that movement to true revolutionary clearness and consciousness it, the Socialist Party, is bound to attract to itself and become mentor and teacher of elements most unclear and lacking in class consciousness, we should recognize that it is as much our duty to be patient and tolerant with the erring brother or sister within our ranks as with the rank heathen—outside the fold. No good purpose can be served by wildly declaiming against "intellectuals", nor yet by intriguing against and misrepresenting "impossibilists". The comrades who think that the Socialist Party is run by "compromisers" should not jump out of the organization and leave the revolutionists in a still more helpless minority; and the comrades who pride themselves upon being practical Socialist politicians should not too readily accuse those who differ with them of being potential disrupters. Viewing the situation from the standpoint of an industrialist I am convinced that both the industrialist and those estimable comrades who pander to the old style trade unions to such a marked degree as to leave themselves open to the suspicion of coquetting with the idea of a "labour" party, both, I say, have the one belief, both have arrived at the one conclusion from such different angles that they appear as opposing instead of aiding, auxiliary forces. That belief which both share in common is that the triumph of Socialism is impossible without the aid of labour organized upon the economic field. It is their common possession of this one great principle of action which impels me to say that there is a greater identity of purpose and faith between those two opposing (?) wings of the Socialist Party than either can have with any of the intervening schools of thought. Both realize that the Socialist Party must rest upon the economic struggle and the forces of labour engaged therein, and that the Socialism which is not an outgrowth and expression of that economic struggle is not worth a moment's serious consideration.

There, then, we have found something upon which we agree, a ground common to both, the first desideratum of any serious discussion. The point upon which we disagree is: Can the present form of American trade unions provide the Socialist movement with the economic force upon which to rest, or can the American Federation of Labour develop towards industrialism sufficiently for our needs? It is the same problem stated in different ways. I propose to state here my reasons for taking the negative side in that discussion.

Let it be remembered that we are not, as some good comrades imagine, debating whether it is possible for a member of the American Federation of Labour to become an industrialist, or for all its members, but we are to debate whether the organization of the American Federation of Labour is such as to permit of a modification of its structural formation to keep pace with the progress of industrialist ideas amongst its members. Whether the conversion of the membership of the American Federation of Labour to industrialism would mean the disruption of the Federation and the throwing of it aside as the up-to-date capitalist throws aside a machine, be it ever so costly, when a more perfectly functioning machine has been devised.

At this point it is necessary for the complete understanding of our subject that we step aside for a moment to consider the genesis and organization of the American Federation of Labour and the trade unions patterned after it, and this involves a glance at the history of the labour movement in America. Perhaps of all the subjects properly pertaining to Socialist activity this subject has been the most neglected, the least analysed. And yet it is the most vital. Studies of Marx and popularizing (sic) of Marx, studies of science and popularizing of science, studies of religion and application of same with Socialist interpretations, all these we have without limit. But of attempts to apply the methods of Marx and of science to an analysis of the laws of growth and incidents of development of the organizations of labour upon the economic field the literature of the movement is almost, if not quite, absolutely barren. Our Socialist writers seem in some strange and, to me, incomprehensible manner to have detached themselves from the everyday struggles of the toilers and to imagine they are doing their whole duty as interpreters of Socialist thought when they bless the economic organization with one corner of their mouth and insist upon the absolute hopelessness of it with the other. They imagine, of course, that this is the astutest diplomacy, but the net result of it has been that the organized working class has never looked upon the Socialist Party as a part of the labour movement, and the enrolled Socialist Party member has never found in American Socialist literature anything that helped him in strengthening his economic organization or leading it to victory.

Perhaps some day there will arise in America a Socialist writer who in his writing will live up to the spirit of the Communist Manifesto that the Socialists are not apart from the labour movement, are not a sect, but are simply that part of the working class which pushes on all others, which most clearly understands the line of march. Awaiting the advent of that writer permit me to remind our readers that the Knights of Labour preceded the American Federation of Labour, that the structural formation of the Knights was that of a mass organization, that they aimed to organize all toilers into one union and made no distinction of craft, nor of industry, and that they cherished revolutionary aims. When the American Federation of Labour was organized it was organized as a dual organization, and although at first it professed a desire to organize none but those then unorganized, it soon developed opposition to the Knights and proceeded to organize wherever it could find members, and particularly to seek after the enrolment of those who were already in the Knights of Labour. In this it was assisted by the good will of the master class, who naturally preferred its profession of conservatism and identity of interest between capital and labour to the revolutionary aims and methods of the Knights. But even this assistance on the part of the master class would not have assured its victory were it not for the fact that its method of organization, into separate crafts, recognized a certain need of the industrial development of the time which the Knights of Labour had failed up to that moment to appraise at its proper significance.

The Knights of Labour, as I have pointed out, organized all workers into one union, an excellent idea for teaching the toilers their ultimate class interests, but with the defect that it made no provision for the treating of special immediate craft interests by men and women with the requisite technical knowledge. The scheme was the scheme of an idealist, too large-hearted and noble-minded himself to appreciate the hold small interests can have upon men and women. It gave rise to jealousies. The printer grumbled at the jurisdiction of a body comprising tailors and shoemakers over his shop struggles, and the tailors and shoemakers fretted at the attempts of carpenters and bricklayers to understand the technicalities of their disputes with the bosses.

To save the Knights of Labour and to save the American working class a pilgrimage in the desert of reaction, it but required the advent of some practical student of industry to propose that, instead of massing all workers together irrespective of occupation, they should, keeping the organization intact and remaining bound in obedience to one supreme head, for administrative purposes only, group all workers together according to their industries, and subdivide their industries again according to crafts. That the allied crafts should select the ruling body for the industry to which they belonged, and that the allied industries again should elect the ruling body for the whole organization. This could have been done without the slightest jar to the framework of the organization; it would have recognized all technical differences and specialization of function in actual industry; it would have kept the organization of labour in line with the actual progress of industrial development; and would still have kept intact the idea of the unity of the working class by its common bond of brotherhood, a universal membership card, and universal obligation to recognize that an injury to one was an injury to all.

Tentative steps in such a direction were already being taken when the American Federation of Labour came upon the scene. The promoters of this organization, seizing upon this one plank in the Knights of Labour organization, specialized its work along that line, and, instead of hastening to save the unity of the working class on the lines above indicated, they made the growing realization of the need of representation of craft differences the entering wedge for disrupting and destroying the earlier organization of that class.

Each craft was organized as a distinct body having no obligation to strike or fight beside any other craft, and making its own contracts with the bosses heedless of what was happening between these bosses and their fellowlabourers of another craft in the same industry, building, shop or room. The craft was organized on a national basis, to be governed by the vote of its members throughout the nation, and with a membership card good only in that craft and of no use to a member who desired to leave one craft in order to follow another. The fiction of national unity was and is still paid homage to, as vice always pays homage to virtue, by annual congresses in which many resolutions are gravely debated, to be forgotten as soon as congress adjourns. But the unifying (?) qualities of this form of organization are best revealed by the fact that the main function of the congress seems to be to provide the cynical master class with the, to them, pleasing spectacle of allied organizations fiercely fighting over questions of jurisdiction.

This policy of the American Federation of Labour coupled with the unfortunate bomb incident of Chicago, for which the Knights of Labour received much of the blame, completed the ruin of the latter organization and destroyed the growing unity of the working class for the time being. The industrial union, as typified today in the Industrial Workers of the World, could have, as I have shown, developed out of the Knights of Labour as logically and perfectly as the adult develops from the child. No new organization would have been necessary, and hence we may conclude that the Industrial Workers of the World is the legitimate heir of the native American labour movement, the inheritor of its principles, and the ripened fruit of its experiences. On the other hand the American Federation of Labour may truly be regarded as a usurper on the throne of labour, a usurper who occupies the throne by virtue of having strangled its predecessor, and now, like all usurpers, raises the cry of "treason" against the rightful heir when it seeks to win its own again. It is obvious that the sway of the American Federation of Labour in the American labour movement is but a brief interregnum between the passing of the old revolutionary organization and the ascension into power of the new.

But, I fancy I hear some one say, granting that all that is true, may we not condemn the methods by which the American Federation of Labour destroyed, or helped to destroy, the Knights of Labour, and still believe that out of the American Federation of Labour we may now build up an industrial organization such as we need, such as the Industrial Workers of the World aims to be?

This we can only answer by clearly focusing in our mind the American Federation of Labour system of organization in actual practice. A carpenter is at work in a city. He has a dispute with the bosses, or all his fellow-carpenters have. They will hold meetings to discuss the question of a strike, and finding the problem too big for them they will pass it on to the headquarters, and the headquarters pass it on to the general membership. The general membership, from San Francisco to Rhode Island, and from Podunk to Kalamazoo, will have a vote and say upon the question of the terms upon which the Chicago carpenters work, and if said carpenters are called out they will expect all these widely scattered carpenters to support them by financial and moral help. But while they are soliciting and receiving the support of their fellow-carpenters they are precluded from calling out in sympathy with them the painters who follow them in their work, the plumbers whose pipes they cover up, the steamfitters who work at their elbows, or the plasterer who precedes them. Yet the co-operation of these workers with them in their strikes is a thousand-fold more important than the voting of strike funds which would keep them out on strike—until the building season is over and the winter sets in. In many cities today there is a Building Trades' Council which is looked upon by many as a beginning of industrialism within the American Federation of Labour. It is not only the beginning but it is as far as industrialism can go within that body, and its sole function is to secure united action in remedying petty grievances and enforcing the observance of contracts, but it does not take part in the really important work of determining hours or wages. It cannot for the simple reason that each of the thirty-three unions in the building industry are international organizations with international officers, and necessitating international referendums before any strikes, looking to the fixing of hours or wages, are permissible. Hence, although all the building trade branches in a given district may be satisfied that the time is ripe for obtaining better conditions, they cannot act before they obtain the consent of the membership throughout the entire country, and before that is obtained the moment for action is passed. The bond that is supposed to unite the carpenter in New York with the carpenter in Kokomo, Indiana, is converted into a wall of isolation which prevents him uniting, except in the most perfunctory fashion, with the men of other crafts who work beside him. The industrial union and the craft union are mutually exclusive terms. Suppose all the building trades branches of Chicago resolved to unite industrially to form an industrial union. Every branch which became an integral part of said union, pledged to obey its call to action, would by so doing forfeit its charter in the craft union and in the American Federation of Labour, and outside Chicago its members would be considered as scabs. The Brewers Union has been fighting for years to obtain the right to organize all brewery employees. It is hindered from doing so, not only by the rules of the American Federation of Labour, but by the form of organization of that body. Breweries, for instance, employ plumbers. Now if a plumber, so employed, would join the Brewers Union and obey its call to strike he would be expelled from his craft union, and if he ever lost his job in the brewery would be considered as a scab if he went to work where union plumbers were employed. A craft union cannot recognize the right of another association to call its members out on a strike. A machinist works today in a machine shop; a few months from now he may be employed in a clothing factory attending to the repairs of sewing machines. If the clothing industry resolves itself into an industrial union and he joins them, as he needs must if he believes in industrialism, he loses his membership in the International Association of Machinists. And if ever he loses his factory job and seeks to return to the machine shop he must either do so as a non-union man or pay a heavy fine if he is permitted to re-enter the International Association of Machinists. A stationary engineer works today at the construction of a new building, three months from now he is in a shipyard, six months from now he is at the mouth of a coal mine. Three different industries, requiring three different industrial unions.

The craft card is good today in all of them, but if any of them chose to form industrial unions, and called upon him to join, he could only do so on penalty of losing his craft card and his right to strike benefits from his old organization. And if he did join, his card of membership in the one he joined would be of no value when he drifted to any of the others. How can the American Federation of Labour avoid this dilemma? Industrialism requires that all the workers in a given industry be subject to the call of the governing body, or of the vote of the workers in that industry. But if these workers are organized in the American Federation of Labour they must be subject only to the call of their national or international craft body; and if at any time they obey the call of the industry in preference to the craft they are ordered peremptorily back to scab upon their brothers.

If in addition to this organic difficulty, and it is the most insuperable, we take into consideration the system of making contracts or trade agreements on a craft basis pursued by old style unions we will see that our unfortunate brothers in the American Federation of Labour are tied hand and foot, handcuffed and hobbled, to prevent their advance into industrialism. During the regent shirt-waist makers' strike in New York when the question was mooted of a similar strike in Philadelphia our comrade Rose Pastor Stokes, according to our Socialist press, was continually urging upon the shirt-waist makers of Philadelphia the wisdom of striking before Christmas, and during the busy season. No more sensible advice could have been given. It was of the very essence of industrialist philosophy. Industrialism is more than a method of organization—it is a science of fighting. It says to the worker: fight only at the time you select, never when the boss wants a fight. Fight at the height of the busy season, and in the slack season when the workers are in thousands upon the sidewalk absolutely refuse to be drawn into battle. Even if the boss insults and vilifies your union and refuses to recognize it, take it lying down in the slack season but mark it up in your little note book. And when work is again rushing and master capitalist is pressed for orders squeeze him, and squeeze him till the most sensitive portion of his anatomy, his pocket-book, yells with pain. That is the industrialist idea of the present phase of the class war as organized labour should conduct it. But, whatever may have been the case with the shirt-waist makers, that policy so ably enunciated by comrade Rose Pastor Stokes is utterly opposed to the whole philosophy and practice of the American Federation of Labour. Contracts almost always expire when there is little demand for labour. For instance the United Mine Workers' contract with the bosses expires in the early summer when they have before them a long hot season with a minimum demand for coal. Hence the expiration of the contract generally finds the coal operators spoiling for a fight, and the union secretly dreading it. Most building trade contracts with the bosses expire in the winter. For example, the Brotherhood of Carpenters in New York, their contract expires in January. A nice time for a fight, in the middle of a northern winter, when all work in their vicinity is suspended owing to the rigours of the climate!

The foregoing will, I hope, give the reader some food for consideration upon the problem under review. That problem is intimately allied with the future of the Socialist Party in America. Our party must become the political expression of the fight in the workshop, and draw its inspiration therefrom. Everything which tends to strengthen and discipline the hosts of labour tends irresistibly to swell the ranks of the revolutionary movement, and everything which tends to divide and disorganize the hosts of labour tends also to strengthen the forces of capitalism. The most dispersive and isolating force at work in the labour movement today is craft unionism, the most cohesive and unifying force, industrial unionism. In view of that fact all objections which my comrades make to industrial unionism on the grounds of the supposedly, or truly, anti-political bias of many members of the Industrial Workers of the World is quite beside the mark. That question at the present stage of the game is purely doctrinaire. The use or non-use of political action will not be settled by the doctrinaires who may make it their hobby today, but will be settled by the workers who use the Industrial Workers of the World in their workshop struggles. And if at any time the conditions of a struggle in shop, factory, railroad or mine necessitate the employment of political action those workers so organized will use it, all theories and theorists to the contrary notwithstanding. In their march to freedom the workers will use every weapon they find necessary.

As the economic struggle is the preparatory school and training ground for Socialists it is our duty to help guide along right lines the effort of the workers to choose the correct kind of organization to fight their battles in that conflict. According as they choose aright or wrongly, so will the development of class consciousness in their minds be hastened or retarded by their everyday experience in class struggles.

From *Socialism Made Easy, 1908*

MARXISM AND BOLSHEVISM: DEMOCRACY AND DICTATORSHIP

Karl Kautsky

Chapter-4

The Beginnings of Marxism

On March 14, 1933, we marked the fiftieth anniversary of the death of Karl Marx. Simultaneously with this anniversary we might also have commemorated the fiftieth anniversary of the birth of Marxism, if it were practicable to assign an exact date to the founding of a school of thinkers and fighters.

In 1881 Eduard Bernstein took over the editorship of the "Sozialdemokrat" in Zurich in order to fashion it into a Marxist fighting organ. Together we had struggled our way through to Marxism.

In 1883 there appeared in Stuttgart the first issue of the "Neue Zeit," founded by me, the first scientific organ of Marxism, excepting those, of course, published by Marx himself.

Both the "Sozialdemokrat" and the "Neue Zeit" were German periodicals. But the growth of Marxist thought was not limited to the German-speaking circles of international Socialism. The shift from Bakuninism and revolutionary Popularism to Marxism in Russia began at the same time. Plekhanov, Axelrod and Vera Zasulitch were then the first to attain to the Marxist conception. At about the same time, in France, Jules Guesde, an erstwhile Bakuninist, became the leader of Marxist thought, along with Paul Lafargue, who even before Guesde had found his way to Marxism from Proudhonism. At the Congress of St. Etienne (September 1882) Lafargue and Guesde broke away from the other Socialists, and at the Congress of Roanne (September 27) formed a party of their own, "Le Parti Ouvrier."

In England Marxism, too, dates from the early eighties. There the first to take up the Marxist ideas and present them before the public were H. M. Hyndman and E. Belfort Bax. This was done through the Democratic Federation, founded in 1881, which under the influence of the Marxists, among them Marx's youngest daughter Eleanor, assumed in 1883 the name of "The Social-Democratic Federation."

Thus the year in which Marx succumbed to great physical sufferings saw everywhere the victorious advance of the ideas which he had sown. It was a tragic fate that he who throughout his life had to combat not only his bourgeois opponents, but also misunderstanding in the ranks of his own comrades and friends, closed his weary eyes precisely at the time when his first sympathetic disciples and continuators appeared on the scene.

Since then these, too, have left us one by one. Only last year we accompanied, personally or in spirit, our unforgettable comrade and friend, Eduard Bernstein, to his place of eternal rest. At the time of his death he had completed sixty years of indefatigable, devoted activity in the Social-Democratic Party and a half-century of labor as a Marxist thinker and fighter.

The others mentioned above had departed long before him. I alone remain as the last of the Mohicans of the family—alas, so small in number—of "original" Marxists, if one may designate by the name those Marxists who were privileged to receive instruction and enlightenment from the lips of the teacher himself.

In our efforts to expound and apply the Marxist ideas we I often encounter the reproach that we are fanatics of a dogma, incapable of anything but swearing by the words of their teacher.

The reproach is invalidated by the fact that the Marxists are not a uniform school, but are divided into different groups and varieties with individual and national distinctions. Not only are there German Marxists with a separate Austrian Marxism, but there is also a French Marxism, a British Marxism and a Russian Marxism, in its turn divided into a Menshevik and a Bolshevik Marxism.

Every form of doctrinaire fanaticism, every attempt to turn Marxism into an unalterable dogma is contrary to Marxist thought, which recognizes no absolute truth but only relative truth. This is not scepticism, which denies the very possibility of absolute perception of the world, but only a recognition of the limitations of our perception. All the truths which we recognize are not truths in themselves, independent of time and place, but truths only as far as we are concerned, valid only for us, for our time, for the space in which we live. Every such truth must govern our actions until more advanced perception has exposed and removed the bit of error residing in the previously accepted truth.

There was nothing that Marx feared so much as the degeneration of his school into a rigid sect. The same fear was entertained by Engels, whose scientific work is indissolubly linked with that of his friend Marx, so that we always keep in mind both Marx and Engels whenever we speak of the Marxist theory.

The worst reproach that Engels could make against the first English Marxists was that they were applying Marxism in a sectarian spirit. What would he have said, had he lived to see it, about a school of Marxists who after succeeding in capturing the state power proceeded to make a state religion of Marxism, a religion whose articles of faith and their interpretation are watched over by the government, a religion, the criticism of which, nay, the slightest deviation from which, is sternly punished by the State; a Marxism ruling by the methods of the Spanish Inquisition, propagated with fire and sword, practicing a theatrical ritual, as illustrated by the embalmed body of Lenin: a Marxism reduced to the status not only of a state religion but of a medieval or oriental faith? Such a Marxism may indeed be called a doctrinaire fanaticism.

To Marx there was no ultimate knowledge, only an infinite process of learning. Therefore, his own theory is not to be conceived as a collection of tenets which we must accept on faith. Marxism itself is nothing but a definite process of learning, founded upon a definite method, a process introduced by Marx and Engels which we, Marxists must continue and which is to be called Marxist so long as the method of inquiry and reasoning which our teachers discovered has not been either superceded or improved upon by another method. This method itself, which Marx and Engels called the materialist conception of history, is not unalterable. It is being constantly improved, like a machine, through continued gain in experience accumulated in its application. The principles underlying a given method of intellectual activity often do not change as rapidly as do the results of that activity. The views of people under the influence of constantly changing experiences tend to change more easily than do *the methods and forms of thought by which they are attained.* Both, however, are regarded as in constant process of development. Even the materialist conception of history did not like Minerva spring fully armed from the head of its procreator; as a matter of fact it had two such procreators. These two were constantly developing it through their lives and to the Marxists bequeathed the task of continuing the process.

To know and understand the line of this development is of the highest importance to every Marxist as well as to any one who wishes to make a critical study of Marx, prompted by a sincere desire for knowledge, and not by the motives of the trickster lawyer who seeks to obtain a conviction of his opponent's client at any cost.

Remarkable as it may seem, there are a number of Marxists who see the highest point of the development of Marxism at its very inception, from which point it is supposed to be constantly declining.

It is clear that as a philosopher and economist as well as a Socialist and revolutionary Marx was able to advance beyond the ideas of his time only after he had assimilated them in their highest forms. The new I Marxist method had been attained already in 1844, but it still bore the traces of its Hegelian, Feuerbachian, Ricardian origin as well as those of utopian Socialism and Jacobin-Blanquist conceptions. To some of our present-day Socialists these traces seem to be the most important and beautiful thing about Marxism.

Yet not every one of these traces is of equal attractiveness to each of these Socialists.

We may distinguish two large groups among these pre-Raphaelite Marxists. One of them seeks to establish Socialism in a backward community immediately. To these people it is the Jacobin-Blanquist elements that are especially attractive as expressions of the Marxist spirit. The other group, on the contrary, is favorably impressed with the fact that Marx at the beginning had no economic views of his own, that he accepted the economics of Ricardo just as he found it and that once in a while he still justified his Socialist bias on ethical grounds.

The existence of a strong social ethos is no doubt the prerequisite for any kind of Socialism. But that is something quite self-evident about which Marx later did not think it even necessary to speak. But with ethos alone, without a deeper economic and historical perception, one can not get very far.

Without this perception one may, by starting from the same moral considerations, arrive at Christian charity or at liberal philanthropy. And even where it does lead to the idea of Socialism, we still do not know what kind of Socialism it is to be, whether that of Owen, or of St. Simon, of Proudhon or of Marx. No one is more ambiguous, more unreliable than the purely ethical Socialist, even when he remains true to his ethical ideal. Yet this kind of Socialism possesses one great advantage. By affecting a proud contempt for the "low" and "vulgar" economic theories of Marxist Socialism one is spared the need of studying the difficult theory of Marxist economics. This study is, indeed, a hard task, but it is also a mental exploit without equal. Great gain in social knowledge beckons to the one who masters it. Today, as it was true fifty years ago, Marx's "Capital" is studied much too little. I regard its study as one of the most urgent tasks of Socialist education. It is more important than the study of the beginnings of Marxism. Of course, this too is of great significance to any one who wishes to understand the development of Marxist thought. But it does not facilitate but rather makes more difficult the understanding of Marxism when it is undertaken for its own sake and not in conjunction with the study of Marx's later works.

These later works constitute his more perfect achievements. Marx and Engels always regarded them as such. This is proved by the fact that most of their writings belonging to the early period

Marx and Engels left lying in their desks in manuscript form, without ever making any attempt to publish them.

Naturally, the lion's claw was evident even in those beginnings. They already surpassed the most mature works of the other Socialists of that time. But these beginnings, in part, were quite imperfect as compared with the later works which Marx and Engels brought to light with so much broader practical experience, so much more extensive knowledge and so much greater precision of method.

The last four decades of his life during which Marx developed his ideas constituted an epoch of the greatest advance in all natural sciences as well as in the humanities. Thus for example, up to the forties of the last century, there had been practically no systematic study of economic history and of prehistoric epochs. How tremendous has been their subsequent development! And no less tremendous has been the development of the forms and the extension of capitalist production. Marxism has stood the test as a doctrine of development in that it proved able not only to adapt itself to all the changes, but also to assume a more perfect form as the changes occurred.

The evolution not only of its philosophy of history and its theory of capitalist production but also of the political principles of the proletarian class struggle was furthered thereby. This came about principally through the progress of democracy. We shall now examine this more closely.

Marx and Revolution

Quite early in his career Marx realized, and in this he proved superior to the other Socialists of his day, that the liberation of the working class could be achieved only by the working class itself, that no paternalistic friend from the bourgeoisie, nor a select proletarian vanguard could accomplish this task for the masses. But like other Socialists he had to admit that the masses were not yet ripe for the struggle. How was this ripeness to be achieved? Through well meaning tutors from above? Grown-up people will not submit to the guardianship of tutors. Where this attempt is made either by

Christians or by atheists it usually degenerates into a loathsome, priestly presumptuousness on the part of the tutor and a hypocritical submission of the tutored.

Grown-ups can be taught by life alone. Marx expected the education of the proletariat to come from life, that is to say, he expected it to come from capitalist development and its effect upon the proletariat. Marx pointed this out already in the "Communist Manifesto." Industry draws the workers together in large numbers and thereby increases their class consciousness. At the same time conflicts with the employers grow, trade unions develop. The extension of the conflicts to all industry transforms the occasional local clashes into a class struggle. This class struggle becomes political, finding expression in political changes. But the proletariat was not strong enough to overcome the forces tending toward the pauperization of the masses, which was the predominant feature of capitalism everywhere. The "Communist Manifesto" had yet to prove the absolute impoverishment of the industrial proletariat. "The modern worker, instead of improving his condition with the progress of industry, sinks deeper and deeper under the circumstances affecting his own class. The worker becomes a pauper and pauperism develops even faster than population and wealth."

Under such conditions, whence could come that moral and intellectual advancement which alone could make possible the self-liberation of the proletariat?

Marx expected it to come as a result of revolution, the advent of which he correctly foresaw. He had studied the French Revolution. It bore at the beginning a purely bourgeois character but grew more and more radical, and finally led to the rule, only for a short time, to be sure, of the working classes. The revolution developed enormously not only the political courage but also the political understanding of the masses of the people, until then inert and ignorant. Opposed as Marx already was at the time of the "Communist Manifesto" to the policy of plots and coups des mains preached by the Blanquists, he was still strongly influenced by their Jacobin traditions. In the first months of 1850, in his articles on "The Class

Struggles in France," published in 1895 by Engels in pamphlet form, he regarded the Blanquists as properly the workers' party of France. They, above all others, held his sympathies.

In 1847 Marx assumed that the forthcoming revolution would run the same course as did the Great Revolution but with a proletariat "much further advanced" by the growth of large industries. The revolution was to last long enough to lift the proletariat quickly to the necessary mental level. Hence "the German bourgeois revolution could serve only as a direct prelude to a proletarian revolution."

This expectation was not realized. The force of the German revolution of 1848 spent itself within a few months and the proletariat as an independent factor played no part in it. What happened then was the same thing that was to happen to Marx often enough later, and still more often to us Marxists. He correctly foresaw the direction in which events were moving but he misjudged the rate at which they were moving.

Yet none learned so readily from experience as did Marx, even when the experience ran counter to his innermost wishes. It was precisely his materialist method that facilitated this learning from experience, for it stressed the study of the surrounding world and not that of personal wishes and emotions.

Already in September 1850 he came out against the view that "we must strive to gain power immediately" and declared that the workers might have to go through "15, 20, 30 years of civil strife and foreign wars in order to change not only conditions but to change yourselves, to qualify yourselves for rulership."

This sounded quite different from the expectation that the coming bourgeois revolution would be the "direct prelude to a proletarian revolution." Yet even this new, more prudent hope proved too sanguine. Since it was first uttered, not only 15, 20, 30 years but 80 years have passed. To be sure, these have not been years of stagnation. The strides made by the proletariat toward the achievement of political independence and skill during the intervening period has been enormous.

Though Marx in 1850 rose superior to the majority of his Communist comrades who at that time were still dreaming of the immediate seizure of political power by the proletariat, he had not yet fully rid himself of his old Jacobin-Blanquist traditions. In armed struggle, in "civil strife and foreign wars" he still saw the means of lifting the proletariat to a higher level. He had not yet realized that every bloody struggle, including a popular war, inspiring and uplifting as it may appear at the beginning, in the long run demoralizes its participants and, far from increasing, actually reduces their capacity for constructive effort in the field of production as well as in political life.

During the decade following 1850, Marx had opportunity to study the laws underlying commodity production in England, namely its capitalist form, and expounded them more clearly than had been done by any student before him. But he also perceived the opportunity for effective action by the English working class under the democratic political institutions prevailing in England. He saw that under such freedom it was possible for the proletariat to overcome the tendency under capitalism to absolute impoverishment of the workers. In his inaugural address (1864) as well as in "Capital" (1867) he welcomed the salutary results of the ten hour work day, as an improvement over the longer hours then prevailing in English factories and plants. Of course, this did not blind him to the fact that the possessing classes in England were able amazing gain in wealth and power, while at the same time the absolute pauperization of those proletarian groups which were not protected either by state laws or by strong trade unions advanced still further, and that among those protected by the law the improvement in conditions lagged behind the increase in the wealth of capital, so that their position became relatively if not absolutely worse.

Nevertheless, the proof was furnished that under conditions of adequate freedom the workers could by their own efforts lift themselves to a high enough level to be able finally to achieve political power not through "civil strife and foreign wars" but through the class struggle waged by their political and economic mass organizations. The condition prerequisite for such a struggle is an adequate measure of political freedom. Where this is lacking, where it has yet to be won, "civil strife and foreign wars" may be necessary to achieve democracy as essential to the rise of the working class. Where democracy exists, it is not necessary for the working class to resort to armed force as a means of attaining power.

Here is what Marx said in 1872 at a public meeting in Amsterdam following the Congress of the International at The Hague (as reported by the Leipziger "Volkstat" of October 2, 1872):

> "The worker must some day achieve political power, in order to found the new organization of labor; he must overthrow the old political machine upon which the old institutions are based, if, like the old Christians, who neglected and despised such matters, he does not wish to renounce 'the kingdom of this world.'
>
> "But we do not maintain that the means of attaining this objective are everywhere the same.
>
> "We know that we must take into consideration the institutions, the habits and the customs of different regions, and we do not deny that there are countries like America, England and—if I knew your institutions better I would perhaps add Holland—where the workers can attain their objective by peaceful means. But such is not the case in all other countries."— By "other countries" Marx evidently meant, first of all, the great centralized police and military states of continental Europe as they existed at that time.

On April 12, 1871, in a letter to Kugelman at the time of the Paris Commune, Marx pointed out that the next attempt of revolution in France would be "no longer as heretofore to effect a change of hands of the bureaucratic military apparatus, but to demolish it, and that is the prerequisite for every true popular revolution on the continent." It was not granted to Marx to witness a third phase of the labor movement, besides the two indicated by him, which was already shaping itself about the time of his death. The "civil strife and foreign wars" of 1789-1871 were not sufficient to destroy the bureaucratic-military apparatus of the continental powers, but their effects were yet strong enough to wrest from these powers a certain measure of freedom for the toiling masses, which enabled them to acquire not only great political skill but also to build strong trade unions and proletarian parties. Unfortunately, this new phase was characterized by great obstacles at the beginning. In France the revolution of September 4, 1870, was followed by the bloody suppression of the Commune in May, 1871, and thereafter by a period of dark reaction and oppression of the proletariat which lasted almost until Marx's death. In Austria after 1866 came an era of liberalism which, however, did not last long. Nor did the liberal era that set in Germany after 1866 prove of long duration. It ended with the anti-Socialist law of Bismark.

Marx thus had little opportunity to observe the effects of democracy on the development of the proletariat in the military-bureaucratic countries of continental Europe.

Engels survived his great friend. He lived to witness the abolition of the exception laws in Austria, the rescinding of the Anti-Socialist law in Germany, the beginning of the rapid growth of the labor movement all over Europe. He was thus in a position to sum up the results of this particular phase of development for Marxism. He did this in his famous introduction to Marx's "Class Struggles in France".

A peculiar situation developed in the military-bureaucratic countries at that time. From 1890 the labor movement grew by leaps and bounds, marching from victory to victory. Side by side with this continued the domination of the military, the police and the centralized government administration, with the monarch as its head. But now with this domination was associated a rapidly growing class of capitalists headed by great monopolists representing banks and heavy industry. These capitalists allied themselves more and more readily with the large landowners against whom previously they had fought. The magnates in the cities and country together dominated the government.

The conflict between the two camps—the proletarians and the profit makers—became ever sharper. It was bound to culminate in a violent clash. But Social-Democracy had no reason to hasten a violent collision. Under the conditions prevailing it was growing in power from year to year. The number of proletarians grew faster than that of any other part of the population. And the influence of Social-Democracy on the proletariat was increasing in the same measure. The number of proletarians and Social-Democrats in the army also increased. And this army was less and less to be relied upon by the government in case of internal war.

It was vitally important for Social-Democracy not to disturb this state of affairs by a premature, violent collision with the government. It had to strive to postpone this collision as long as possible. Our opponents thought quite differently. The unscrupulous element among them endeavored to hasten the clash by provoking the masses into premature action.

Thus the revolutionary tactics of the Socialists as pursued hitherto were reversed. Engels pointed out: "We the 'revolutionaries' the 'overthrowers' thrive better by the use of legitimate methods than by using illegitimate ones and revolution."

Marx had never believed in the possibility of bringing about a revolution at will. Therein he differed already in his early works from the Blanquists. But as long as there was no political freedom for the proletariat, he was impelled to wish ardently for the speediest possible coming of the revolution, first as a democratic-bourgeois revolution, which would bring the necessary political freedom. During the fifties and sixties he eagerly looked for signs of the coming revolution arising either from war or civil conflicts.

But now the situation was quite different. Engels, too, saw the coming of the revolution, but he hoped it might be postponed. And he feared new wars. They might bring on the revolution but they threatened to ruin the proletariat, the only revolutionary class that still existed. They might destroy the revolution and impair the ability of the proletariat to utilize it, for what was expected from the revolution was that it would bring not merely political freedom, but power itself.

This was true of the situation in all military states of continental Europe, with one important exception: Russia. That country had not yet come out of the stage of absolutism. Its people were denied every vestige of freedom. The country needed first of all a democratic revolution, and it needed it immediately. The sooner the revolution came the better. Nothing could be gained by further delay. In Russia, too, however, it was impossible to kindle the revolution by artificial means. But its coming, its immediate coming, was ardently desired not only by all Socialists of whatever faction throughout the world, but also by wide circles outside the proletariat.

Marx in 1872 divided the countries of Europe into two groups. In one—essentially Anglo-Saxon—it seemed possible that the proletariat would attain power without violence. In the other group Marx included most of the countries of the continent where the gaining of power without a revolution appeared impossible.

After the rescinding of the anti-Socialist law in Germany there came into view a third sub-division. As heretofore it still appeared impossible for the proletariat in the military countries of the continent to come into power without a revolution. But in most of these countries it was now highly desirable to postpone the decisive clash with the state as long as possible. In Russia, on the other hand, it was most imperative that the uprising of the people against the absolutist regime should take place as soon as possible.

We find, therefore, in the Second International, whose period covered this new phase of development, three well-defined currents. They are geographically distinct and spring from the different types of government prevailing. Each of them represents an adaptation to conditions, and from a Marxist point of view is fully justified. Each of them could and did exist alongside the others, but not without friction.

The human mind craves absolute solutions. It is against its nature to contend with relativities. And so, in each of the three above-mentioned divisions, there were many Socialists who regarded the particular stand on the question of revolution which was suited to their own countries as something that had an absolute validity, independent of space and time. This was enhanced by the brisk international intercourse which made it possible for ideas to circulate even faster than commodities. Born of the three views representing the different sub-divisions, all of which were reconcilable with Marxism, came three factions which opposed one another not only within the International but in some of the separate countries as well.

To this was added the influence of the new conditions on Marxism itself. Its literature and, to a still larger extent, the conception of Marxism prevalent among the workers of the different countries, still bore the traces of the traditions of the revolutionary movement which culminated in the insurrections of 1848, even traces of the century-old traditions of the Great French Revolution. For that reason there was an inconsistency between the ideology and phraseology of the movement as it existed at the end of the nineteenth century on the one hand, and its practice on the other. Marx's "Capital" was now a generation old. It said nothing about the new economic phenomena such as the preponderance of the heavy industries over the textile industries, or the trusts, for example. The crises themselves had assumed a different form. Instead of ten-year cycles of crises there were now periods of crises as well as of prosperity of such long duration that some regarded the crisis of the eighties, for example, or the prosperity that followed, as the enduring state of capitalism.

At any rate all this provided the occasion for new critical studies and discussions which became mingled with those arising out of the geographical differences of the International.

The new current which arose as a consequence of these studies and discussions was called "Revisionism" and was referred to also as the "Crisis of Marxism." Our opponents were jubilant. Marxism was breathing its last, it was being given up by its own advocates. In reality Marxism emerged from the struggles of the time unscathed, even strengthened. The theoretical criticism directed against it soon exhausted itself, without causing any reverberations. It merely strengthened the striving of the younger Marxists toward further theoretical development of the doctrine of their teacher.

However, what did not come to an end as quickly as did was imminent and therefore to be reckoned with, or whether the discussion about the economic theory of Marxism were the tactical differences as to whether or not the revolution it was possible to avoid it. It was these tactical differences and not the theoretical ones that now and then, as in France, appreciably hurt the unity of the Socialist movement at the turn of the century. Eventually, however, these difficulties too were overcome.

From year to year the Socialist parties grew in size, in unity, in intellectual power. The party of the proletariat, Social-Democracy, became the equal of the other parties; nay, proved superior to them. This is proved by some of its deserters who, thanks to the schooling they received from us, subsequently became prominent politicians in the bourgeois camp, as, for example, Millerand, Briand, Mussolini, MacDonald.

In the bourgeois parties one naturally finds more men with an academic training, but Social-Democracy has become the only party that still possesses high ideals and opens wider horizons to the intellect of its adherents. The bourgeois parties champion only temporary and limited group interests; hence the growing superiority of Social-Democracy, which constantly increases its capacity to exercise political power more purposefully than can the other parties. Our opponents had imagined that with the death of Marx, or at least with the death of Engels, the movement whose intellectual foundations were laid by the two, would collapse. But even with the sowers gone the seed continued to grow. Harvest time seemed approaching. Then came the inclement weather of the World War, with its inundations and hailstorms. Nevertheless it proved possible to bring new life out of the ruins.

Marxism Since the War

The last days of the World War brought great progress, above all the overthrow of the military monarchy in the three great powers of Eastern Europe—a revolution whose consummation had until then been the frightfully difficult but yet indispensable task of Social-Democracy. At the same time the World War immensely increased the army of the dispossessed, while the economic collapse during the war brought despondency and perplexity into the ranks of the possessing classes. It appeared as though the time had arrived for the political rule of the proletariat, for Socialism. Unfortunately, however, this proved only a fleeting illusion.

A great protracted war which strains the energies of a nation to the utmost always carries frightful damage in its trail; not only huge losses in property and human life, which are quite obvious, but also profound economic and psychologic disturbances whose effects are not immediately discernible.

Already before the World War economic thought among the possessing classes was being supplanted by militaristic thought. People dominated by economic thought find themselves compelled to study economic law, and upon the basis of the knowledge thus gained they seek to give it practical application. Militaristic thought on the other hand despises such knowledge. It considers brutal force all powerful. In autocratic monarchies and among their army officers and bureaucrats militaristic thought had always been predominant. This is also true of the feudal nobility. But in the field of capitalist production this thought was being increasingly superceded by the growing influence of capitalists who sought to build their actions and those of the state upon the foundation of economic knowledge.

During the generation preceding the war, however, there occurred a change of attitude in the capitalist class, arising from the new importance which heavy industry, the banks, trusts and colonial policies had assumed for it. The capitalists, too, became more inclined to make brutal force instead of economic knowledge their servant. They united for that purpose with the great landowners, the higher bureaucracy, the generals, the monarchy. Like the latter, the capitalist magnates sought to utilize their growing influence in the state to the end that they might plunder it and exploit the shortsighted conflicting interests of the smaller groups, and sometimes even of large individual concerns or family fortunes, to their own advantage.

The World War greatly increased and accelerated these tendencies. Every war means the disregard of the laws of production in the respective fields. A war of the extent and duration of the last one makes this disregard general throughout the world. And equally universal did the World War make the belief in the omnipotence of brutal force. This was demonstrated not only during the war but even more fatally at its termination and after.

The economic terms of the peace treaty, especially those dealing with reparations, were sheer madness which can be explained only by the fact that the militaristic way of thinking in the previously existing military monarchies as well as in the government circles of the great western democracies had crushed out all economic thought. Naturally, in the course of time it was proven that the force of economic law is still stronger than that of violence. The reparations had to be constantly reduced until they practically vanished altogether. But that happened too late, only after the economically impossible claims had brought with them new economic disturbances, to remove which brutal force for the most part was again resorted to, making the economic chaos still worse.

To unscrupulous people relying upon compulsion no other condition is more favorable than this for forcing themselves into the economic affairs of the nation and satisfying their uncontrollable greed at the expense of the community, for securing by most shameful methods exemptions, subventions and other favors for their personal advantage.

The result of that is the desperate condition of the world today. It is said that it denotes the final collapse of capitalism. This is not true if what is meant is that this collapse is the natural result of the development of capitalist production according to the laws inherent in that production. No, it proceeds from the disregard of these laws by men in authority who are as ignorant as they are unscrupulous, men who have set up the cult of brutal force in place of a striving for economic insight. Today it is the great capitalist magnates themselves who are bringing on the collapse of capitalism.

Unfortunately this suicidal policy of the leaders of capitalist economy has found its socialist counterpart. In Russia it was a Marxist sect that dedicated itself resolutely to the cult of brutal force, which the World War unleashed also in circles other than those of the ruling class. The Bolsheviki, too, agreed among themselves to establish the rule of brutal force instead of economic insight. They thereby succeeded in setting up throughout the immense Russian state in place of the overthrown Czarist autocracy, an autocracy of their own. They succeeded perfectly, if the purpose of a socialist party is to be regarded as making its own leaders the rulers of the State. They failed dismally if the purpose of a socialist party is to be the use of its power for the realization of the party's program. This program demands the freedom and welfare of the entire people. The Bolsheviki erased freedom from their program the minute they seized power. The welfare of the masses they could strive to attain, considering their disregard of economic law, only by bringing about the robbing of one portion of the population by another. First the interests of the proletarians and the peasants were to be satisfied by robbing the capitalists and the big landowners. This did not accomplish much. Then it was sought to improve the condition of the industrial manual workers at the expense of the peasants and the intellectuals. Soon Soviet economy declined to such an extent that the despoilment of the cities, too, became necessary in order to maintain the instruments of power of the ruling Communist party. Ultimately this party itself may make robbery one of its articles of official belief.

In the capitalist states it is the leaders of capitalist economy and their agents in the army and among the bureaucracy that are ruining capitalist economy. In Soviet Russia it is not capitalistically trained leaders but economic leaders who came from the ranks of Social-Democracy that are similarly ruining the economic administration of their state, which they call Socialist merely because instead of private ownership of the means of production they have established government ownership of these means. But they have at the same time transformed the State into the property of the ruling dictators and instead of democratically socializing production they have autocratically militarized it. As a result we have the same dreadful conditions existing in both cases: the same degradation and slavery, although for different reasons and in different form.

But let us assume that capitalism is about to break down. Will it not mean the same thing as the victory of Socialism? Unfortunately, not. When the capitalistically managed factories are stopped it will mean, first of all, only the stoppage of production; it will not mean the carrying on of production under Socialist forms.

We must, therefore, guard against interpreting the materialist conception of history in an automatically-mechanistic way, as if social development went on by itself, being impelled by necessity. Human beings make history, and the course of history is propelled by necessity only to the extent that human beings living under the same conditions and prompted by the same impulses will of necessity react in the same manner.

Marx expected the victory of Socialism to come not from the collapse of capitalism; this I pointed out as early as 1899 in my polemical discourse against Bernstein. Marx expected it to come as a result of the growing power and maturity of the proletariat, in consequence of circumstances already discussed. It is true that the paralysis of production greatly arouses the discontent of the masses against the existing economic conditions or, rather, against the mismanagement of economic affairs. But such discontent predisposes the proletariat to destruction and plunder, and not to Socialist construction. Like war, mass unemployment arouses the impulse to strike down and despoil the opponent, the passion for immediate success, whatever the consequences. The cult of violence, the contempt for all economic law is intensified by economic crisis no less than by war. The one as well as the other has a tendency to demoralize not alone the profit-making classes but the working classes as well. This demoralization is primarily responsible for the ascendency of Hitlerism in Germany.

Up to the World War the German Socialists were rapidly achieving a majority and approaching the final struggle with the monarchy. After the collapse of the monarchy it seemed as if we had attained our goal. But it soon became evident that under the material and psychological conditions resulting from the war a large portion of the proletariat became a rather insecure foundation for our power. The terrible aggravation of the crisis within the last few years drove millions of proletarians into the arms of the champions of short-sighted brutal force, into the arms of the Communists and National Socialists.

As long as this condition continues the proletariat can attain neither the power nor the ability to control the State and use it for Socialist purposes. We must have no illusions on this point. We must and will do our utmost only to assert ourselves but also to attract new followers to the idea of gaining political power for Socialist construction. But our work will be very difficult as long as the political and economic conditions described here continue to exist. The immediate moment is one of great trial for the Socialist movement in the defeated countries, which have suffered most from the perturbations of the war and of the present economic depression. Fascism alone has profited by these conditions, but it has gathered about itself only loose quicksand which the wind has swiftly heaped to a huge mountain only to scatter it tomorrow in all directions.

Democracy and Dictatorship

The recrudescence of militarist thought brought about by the war and its social and economic perturbations pushed to the fore the question of dictatorship and democracy. This was the central feature of the discussions at the last congress of the Austrian Social-Democracy in Vienna in 1932. The outstanding event of the proceedings was Otto Bauer's address. In the discussion that followed one speaker said:

> "Democracy may be a means (toward an end) but we must not forget that democracy can never be an end in itself. The goal must be Socialism, to which we may come by following the road

of democracy."

This point of view is widely held and therefore merits attention. If it were correct it might become very dangerous, seriously weakening our zeal in fighting for democracy. Fortunately this point of view is utterly false.

Democracy is not merely a pathway to the Socialist goal. It is an integral part of that goal, which is not only economic welfare but also freedom and equality for all. At any rate, this integral part can be achieved much earlier than can the economic aspect of Socialist construction, *i.e.* its social economy.

In sharp contradiction to the belief that democracy is only a way to Socialism is another viewpoint which is also quite popular in Socialist ranks, namely, that true democracy is possible only in a Socialist society and that what we have now as democracy is an illusion and has only a formal character.

I maintain quite to the contrary that not only is Socialism impossible without democracy but that there is no other way to Socialism except through democracy, which must be attained, in some degree at least, before Socialism can be attempted. He who thinks that there are various ways of achieving Socialism and that democracy is merely one of them, and the most ineffective at that, regards democracy exclusively from the viewpoint of the conquest of state power. No one contends that different methods of achieving this conquest are conceivable and possible. State power may be captured through an insurrection. It may fall into our hands by itself, as it were, as a result of the collapse of the government apparatus due, for example, to a military defeat. But that is only one side of the question. In this particular form it arises before us only when we begin the decisive struggle with the dominant classes and parties.

But long before that time and quite indispensable under all conditions, even in an imperfect form, democracy becomes of great importance as a means of educating the proletariat to that state of political and social maturity which shall enable it to keep the power after it has been won and use that power efficiently for its own and the common good.

The class struggle is the primary school of the working class. I mean the struggle itself and the resultant changes in organization and legislation.

The results of class conflicts will be all the greater the more democracy there is in the state, the greater the benefits derived from it by the working class, and the more numerous the gains in democratic rights which ordinarily the working class achieves by allying itself with other laboring elements, the lower middle class, the farmers and intellectuals. Sometimes the working class is aided in this even by capitalists.

The masses of the workers can not be organized in secret, conspiratory organizations. They can be organized only in rree and open associations. To explain their situation to them it is not enough to have circulars printed illegally. For this is needed a daily press of wide circulation and literature easily accessible to the masses. Freedom of association, the right to vote on the basis of universal, secret and direct balloting are the necessary means of educating and developing the proletariat and hastening its maturity. Every extension of freedom for the laboring classes in the state has not only a formal but a real value of the highest degree. It is of tremendous educational importance to the working class. Without the preliminary attainment of democracy the working class can not acquire those qualities which it needs for its own liberation and the building of a new and higher social order.

Democracy is indissolubly bound up with Socialism both a means to an end and as integral part of the final goal. The Socialist who underestimates democracy, however provisionally, cuts the very branch on which he sits and whence he aims to climb higher.

The ruling classes know very well what democracy means to the laboring classes and above all to the wage-earning proletariat. They oppose democracy as long as they can. Where its establishment has been compelled they readily avail themselves of every opportunity to limit it by arbitrary acts or abolish it altogether.

We must always reckon with this possibility. It has become stronger in our own time. Is there anything we can oppose to force? Only force, of course, and not indignant protests. But we must also realize that "force of arms" is not the only form of force that is at the disposal of the working class. Moreover, of all possible means of coercion that the working class may use, arms are not the most effective. On the contrary they are most ineffective where the opponent has a well disciplined and well organized army and police. In the last few decades the general strike has been considered by many our most effective weapon.

Where democracy is being destroyed by violence we have the moral right, despite our democratic principles, to fight violence with violence. But we are not bound to do so by immediately resorting to arms. The reactionaries who are backed by the power of organized armies always try, whenever they are seized by fear of democracy, to arouse the anger of the laboring masses by some acts of violence, in order to provoke them to come out openly against the armed forces of the State and thus create an opportunity for bloody suppression. We must not yield to such provocations.

Hence we do not in any way regard ourselves as driven to the necessity of answering the destruction of democracy by an armed insurrection. One might object that we should not openly expound this view because it might encourage the reaction. But we are not at all refusing to oppose force with force. We reserve to ourselves the right to do so at such time and in such form as will insure our success. We reserve to ourselves the fullest freedom of tactics.

The expectation that we shall be compelled to meet every act of violence by an immediate call to arms may encourage the lovers of violence, thirsting for Marxist blood, to attempt to destroy the constitution, if they should think the moment favorable to themselves and unfavorable to us. And this very same expectation, should it be shared by many of our comrades, may be responsible for the profound disappointment of the masses in the event that our leaders, realizing the unfavorable situation, will refuse to embark upon a policy of opposing force with violence, as in Austria.

There is yet another circumstance that must be taken into consideration while appealing to force. The only weapon that gives the laboring masses an advantage over their exploiters is their numerical superiority. When it comes to decisive social clashes we have a chance to win only where that numerical superiority is on our side. This is true not only in cases where the fight is conducted by methods of democracy but also in a larger measure in conflicts where violence is employed. We should not think that the use of force will exempt us from the difficult duty of attracting to our side the majority of the population. On the contrary, we shall perish if we are going to be opposed not only by the machine guns and cannons of the army and the police but also by the majority of the people. In that case even a general strike will not help us. In the general strikes which resulted in victory for the revolutionists the majority of the population was invariably with the latter. It was so in 1905 in Russia, and it was so in 1920 at the time of the Kapp putsch in Germany.

We must not forget that it is not only the working class that is interested in the existence of democracy. Where it is organized and maintains its unity and where there are other groups vigorously opposed to dictatorship we have every chance to overcome eventually the forces of dictatorship.

Our tactics in opposing violence must be adapted to conditions in each individual case. It would be a mistake to arouse expectations which in case of serious developments might force us to use wrong methods or bring keen disappointment to our followers among the various classes of the population.

Whatever be the methods which we choose in defending ourselves against force, our aim must be always the same: the restoration of democracy, and not the substitution of a new regime of force for the one demolished by us. We shall attract the broad masses more easily for the purpose of reestablishing democracy than for the purpose of replacing one form of dictatorship with another. Besides, dictatorship can never be our road to Socialism. Such a road can only be democracy. I think that on the question of democracy I concur on all points with Otto Bauer and the Vienna Congress. But in my discussion of democracy I finally touched upon the subject of dictatorship, and here unfortunately our ways must part, at least for the moment, as regards the question of Soviet Russia.

There is one thing at any rate in which I agree with Otto Bauer and that is in wishing that the Soviet dictatorship may succeed in its "Socialist construction" work. This wish of his I fully share, but I lack faith in its fulfillment.

We have all heard of the Utopians who in the first half of the last century tried to make Socialism an immediate reality through the establishment of Communist colonies. With a backward proletariat, it was inevitable that these efforts should assume the character of a ready-made community plan, brought from above and carried out under the guidance of a dictatorship. Every Socialist was bound to wish ardently for the success of those efforts. Every failure was a heavy blow to us, and weakened, at least temporarily, the force of Socialist propaganda. But since the time of Marx and Engels we have learned that these efforts were doomed to failure because of an undeveloped proletariat. Since this became clear to us we have never helped in the organization of Socialist colonies and always opposed the very idea of such colonies, however desirable their success might have been. We knew that this was impossible and that all such efforts could not help being unsuccessful. Must we now give our approval merely because the same attempt is being made not on a small but on a tremendous scale? In other words, approve it because its failure must carry with it not an insignificant debacle but a terrible calamity?

From the time when the Socialist movement was placed upon a Marxist foundation and until the World War this movement grew steadily and developed without any serious setbacks, for Marxism taught us that the success of every cause depended not only upon our will and our wish but also upon the circumstances under which it was being advanced. Thanks to Marxism we have never undertaken tasks unrealizable under given conditions. Therein lay the great significance of Russian Marxism founded by Plekhanov and

Axelrod and accepted, at that time, by Lenin. It grew out of the incessant struggle with the early Socialist-Revolutionists, who thought that it was possible to build immediately a Socialist economy in Russia on the basis of village communism. To this the Marxists opposed the view that Socialism could be realized only by a working class that had reached a higher level of development. Such a working class can arise only under a system of highly developed industrial capitalism and after a prolonged exercise by the masses of the people of democratic liberties making possible the formation of large class organizations and the development of the proletarian class-struggle.

Unfortunately, the Russian Social-Democrats split into two approximately equal factions. One consisted of Mensheviki, who were organizing the party by democratic methods, as was always insisted upon by Marx. Against them appeared the Bolsheviki led by Lenin, who strove to establish in the party the dictatorial power of the leaders.

Then came the World War; the collapse of the Russian armies, of the power of the land barons and capitalists. The Socialists found themselves riding the tide in Russia. But at the same time the Bolsheviki began a fierce struggle against the other Socialists—the Mensheviki and the Socialist-Revolutionists. The latter were supported by the majority of the population. The Bolsheviki under Lenin's leadership, however, succeeded in capturing control of the armed forces in Petrograd and later in Moscow and thus laid the foundation for a new dictatorship in place of the old Czarist dictatorship.

Having seized control, Lenin at once conceived himself powerful enough to undertake from above and by utopian methods the carrying out of a task which until then he himself as a disciplined Marxist had regarded as unrealizable, namely, the immediate establishment of the Socialist order of production with the aid of an immature proletariat. It should be noted that it was a question not of village communism, for the private economy of the individual peasant was preserved, but of state economy in industry and commerce.

This was the task undertaken by Lenin, in opposition to the Mensheviki and the Socialist-Revolutionists, who declared the undertaking utopian and unrealizable. They likewise denounced the dictatorship and the destruction of democracy.

The grandiose experiment undertaken by the Bolsheviki could not help influencing the Socialist parties of the Western countries. These parties, until then united, now split. A part of them enthusiastically joined the Bolsheviki and began to apply their methods in Western Europe and America. This led to the rise of the Communist parties. The majority remained faithful to the old principles of our party and rejected the Communist methods under all circumstances as non-Marxist. As between these two currents there soon appeared a third one. This rejects the Bolshevik methods for its own country but believes that these methods are justified in Russia.

Wherein do the Russian people differ from other peoples of our capitalist civilization? First of all, of course, in their economic and political backwardness. As a result of this backwardness any Socialist party in present-day Russia would be unavoidably driven to the methods of utopianism and dictatorship if it were placed in power by the force of extraordinary circumstances, without support of the majority of the population, and if its own illusions impelled it to undertake the immediate task of building Socialism. Therein lies the explanation of the Bolshevik methods in Russia. The experiments of the utopian Socialists in Western Europe one hundred years ago were likewise impelled by the insufficient development of the proletariat in their countries. The methods of both the old utopians and the Bolsheviki are not mere accidents, but derive their logic from existing conditions. But this explanation offers just as little proof now as it did in the time of the utopians that these methods can lead to the desired aim. To prove the wisdom of the Bolshevik methods one would have to prove first that the Russian proletariat possesses some peculiar inherent socialist powers which the proletarians of Western Europe lack. So far the existence of such powers has not been established. Therefore, there is not the slightest reason for thinking that in Russia the road to Socialism will be different from that elsewhere.

This in fact was the view held by Lenin himself as late as 1918. He believed that the revolution in Russia would be the signal for the social revolution in Western capitalist countries, and that only the establishment of the Socialist order in these countries could furnish the direction and the means for Socialist construction in Russia. Lenin undertook this construction in the hope of a world revolution which, according to his belief, was to break out immediately.

In this he was deceived. Instead of the world revolution came civil war in Russia. This war helped to some extent in the establishment of a militarized state economy. This, indeed, is the result of every war, even in capitalist countries, if the war is of long duration and demands great sacrifices. But this compulsory economy can by no means be regarded as a higher, Socialist economy. It is only a temporary measure necessitated by an extreme emergency.

When the civil war in Russia subsided and all the hopes for a world revolution vanished, doubts began to arise in the minds of the Bolshevist rulers as to whether "military communism" would last long. Lacking a basis in the initiative and discipline of the working class, this new regime could be maintained only with the aid of a bureaucratic apparatus, as unwieldy as it was inefficient, and by means of military discipline in the factories and brutal terrorism practiced by an all-powerful political police throughout the state. "Military communism" resulted in a constant fall of production and brought the country to an ever growing economic decline.

This was soon recognized by the majority of the Bolsheviki themselves. Lenin created a breach in this Communism by making some concessions to private economy (Nep, 1921), and that gave the country a short breathing spell. Lenin himself called it a respite. And, in fact, Russia under "military Communism" was gasping for breath.

We do not know whether Lenin would have continued the Nep. He died in 1924. After his death differences arose among the

Bolsheviki on the question of the Nep. And indeed the development of the Nep demanded the adoption of a definite policy. It was necessary either to extend the system, which promised an economic upturn but threatened the existence of the dictatorship, or to abolish the Nep and return to integral communism. It was the latter that was decided upon by Stalin, who had gained unlimited authority among Lenin's followers.

State industry, however, was in a precarious condition and facing imminent ruin. Its production apparatus had to be overhauled. And so once more the Bolsheviki recalled Marx's doctrine, upon which after all Bolshevism at the beginning was founded, namely, that modern Socialism could develop only on the basis of a highly advanced heavy industry. It was decided therefore to create this industry at express train speed with the aid of a Five-Year Plan. Within five years, beginning with 1928, it was planned to build an industrial organization that was to eclipse that of the United States.

The plan was immediately put into execution with all the zeal and energy available. During the "Piatiletka" there were accomplished indeed colossal things that aroused the admiration and amazement of the capitalist world and of many Socialists who previously had maintained a sceptical attitude toward the Bolshevist experiment. Now some of them take the view which they themselves had previously rejected. They say, "Well, it is true that the Bolshevik methods are not suitable for us, nevertheless they seem to lead to Socialist construction in Russia."

An indirect criticism of this view was once offered by Lenin himself in the days of Czarism, when he was ridiculing the Czarist government. In January 1905 he published in the newspaper "Vperiod" an article about the Russian reverses in the war with Japan, where he clearly proved that those reverses were the result of Russia's lack of freedom, which hindered the efforts of energetic and self-reliant people without whom it was impossible to win a war.

"Events have proved," wrote Lenin, "how right those foreigners were who laughed at the way tens and hundreds of millions of rubles were wasted on the purchase and construction of magnificent dreadnaughts, and who pointed out that all these expenditures were useless in the absence of people capable of handling modern military machinery and navigating modern vessels."

This applies to both machines intended for destruction and those built for production. Machines are useless if there are no competent people to tend them.

Indeed, what characterizes modern production is not only a highly developed technique but also highly qualified workers who know how to operate the latest machinery and who are to be found in sufficient numbers only in a democracy. These workers even to a larger extent than the machines are the prerequisites for a true Socialist society that guarantees welfare and freedom to all.

In Russia, however, under the Czar as well as under the Bolsheviki, all efforts have always been directed toward importing the modern technique of capitalist countries, but not the freedom which creates modern men.

In the sixties of the past century, under the influence of the defeats suffered in the Crimean war, a liberal movement sprang up among a section of the Russian nobility. This faction, after abolishing serfdom, wanted to emulate the English aristocracy in conducting a modern economy. The abolition of serfdom brought to some of the landowners large indemnities which they used in the purchase of agricultural machinery in England. But they could not import English workers along with the machinery, or if they could it was only in small numbers. The peasants, who by law had just been freed from serfdom but who in reality continued to be the slaves of the landowners and of absolutism, showed little capacity for handling modern machinery. The machines soon fell into disrepair and became junk.

The promoters of the "Piatiletka" disregarded these early experiences. They too believed that all that was necessary was to import from the industrial countries as many new machines as possible. They forgot that it was necessary also to create the political and social conditions that further the development of modern men. Still less did they think of the fact that such men cannot be developed as fast as new machines are created, and that for this purpose a Five-Year plan is not enough.

But to create new machines in the face of a lack of qualified workmen means not to increase the productive forces of the country but to waste its resources.

Furthermore, Stalin and his men during the "Piatiletka" were wasting national wealth in a manner quite different from the method employed in the sixties by the liberal landowners. These last spent for the purchase of machinery only such funds as would have been wasted anyway in gambling, in trips to Paris, etc. The condition of their peasants did not grow worse on account of it. Quite different is the case with Stalin. All the wealth of Russia which her exploiters had been able to garner before the World War by accumulating the surplus value that flowed into their pockets had been spent or destroyed first in the war, then in the civil war and finally in consequence of the establishment of a bureaucratic state economy by the Bolsheviki. The large sums of money needed for the creation of the new industrial apparatus could be raised only by extracting as much as possible of the newly-created surplus value from the laboring masses. But the productiveness of these masses is quite low. Under Czarism the wages and standard of living of the workers were pitifully low. They declined further during the World War and civil war. During the Nep period they rose somewhat. Now they have been greatly reduced again in order to obtain money for the purchase of numerous machines.

Foreign tourists in Russia stand in silent amazement before the gigantic enterprises created there, just as they stand before the pyramids, for example. Only seldom does the thought occur to them what enslavement, what lowering of human self-esteem was connected with the construction of those gigantic establishments.

The Russian landowners imported machinery without improving the condition of the peasants or adding to their freedom. This was the cause of the failure of their technical reform plan. The Bolsheviki, on the other hand, import machinery by rendering the condition of the workers immeasurably worse and curtailing their freedom. They extract the means for the creation of material productive forces by destroying the most essential productive force of all the laboring man. In the terrible conditions created by the "Piatiletka" people rapidly perish. Soviet films, of course, do not show this. But to convince oneself one only has to inquire of Western European and American workers who went to work in Russia, wishing to escape the capitalist hell and find happiness in the Soviet paradise. After a short stay these workers hurry back to their former hell where conditions now, of course, are bad enough but yet more bearable than is the condition of the workers or even of privileged persons on the other side of the Soviet border.

The results of the "Piatiletka" have turned out to be terrible largely because the Bolsheviki, not content with setting up a large number of gigantic industrial establishments, undertook to transform the individual peasant economy forthwith into a gigantic collective economy, doing precisely that which Lenin had prudently abstained from. For Lenin was able to win because he energetically supported the demands of the peasants who were bent on taking possession of the land of the landowners. It must be remarked, however, that this support was quite unnecessary to the peasants, inasmuch as the Socialist-Revolutionists and the Mensheviki sided with the peasants in this question and had promulgated the division of the land among the peasants before the Bolsheviki had seized power.

But Stalin needed money for a program of rapid industrialization on a gigantic scale. Those enterprises which already existed were working on a deficit, therefore the expedient of extracting more from the peasants seemed all the more necessary. This method of procedure encountercd many difficulties when applied to the individual, free peasant who had enough resistance power. Hence the idea of combining the individual peasant holdings into gigantic collectives, the so-called kolkhozy, ruled by the state. From such enterprises the State thought to collect a much larger share of their production than from individual peasants. But the peasants would not join the kolkhozy. Therefore they must be compelled to enter them by force. Thus the diligent and willing toil of free peasants is replaced with the compulsory labor of unwilling serfs. And the yield of such labor is always poor in quality and quantity. It can be managed only with the aid of the most primitive and simple tools of production. A man working under compulsion will quickly damage any kind of complicated tool. And yet the kolkhozy were supposed to be the last word of modernity and efficiency in agricultural economy. They are supplied with the best American implements. With the change to the new methods of production cattle were to a large extent slaughtered. The member of the kolkhoz is compelled to work with the new implements of production which are not suited to him, for they demand free, highly skilled workers. The old implements to which he has become accustomed are gone. It is easy to imagine the results accomplished by a man working against his will and interests. And in fact the productivity of Russian agriculture since the introduction of "Socialist construction" has been falling appreciably. At present there is real famine in that agricultural country. In the days of the Czar we were perfectly justified in denouncing famine in Russia as evidence of the rottenness of the political order. But the famine in Russia this year exceeds anything known before. It rages practically all over the Ukraine, in Northern Caucasus and the Lower Volga region—the most fertile sections of the country—the very ones in which the collectivization of agriculture has been most extensive. Must we therefore welcome famine as the inevitable attendant of Socialist construction?

Gigantic enterprises have been created in agriculture and industry. But they owe their existence to the use of methods which compel the broad masses of the people to starve, to live in rags and filth. This is not the road that will lead us to Socialism, but one that will lead farther away from it, for it increasingly deprives the workers of their capacity to work successfully. It also degrades them in a spiritual sense. For along with want grows dissatisfaction, and to combat this dissatisfaction all sorts of deceptions are employed, and oppression, enhancing the fear that holds the people in subjection, is increased. Resort to capital punishment increases.

According to the laws of social development established by Marx, a backward agricultural country cannot show the way to

Socialism to other countries. Its failure in this respect is foreordained. It is merely a question of when and how this failure will finally manifest itself. Until now the Bolsheviki have been skillful in disguising their failure under the mask of promises of a glorious future. The last such promise was the Five-Year plan. But the Bolshevist state economy has been in existence now more than fifteen years. For more than ten years the USSR has been enjoying complete peace. And yet, contrary to all promises, things under the Bolshevist state economy have been getting worse every year, (excepting the short period of the Nep), and the day is not far distant when even the most credulous will become convinced that the Bolshevist way leads not upward, toward Socialism, but downward, to open ruin or slow disintegration.

He, who, like myself, has come to this conviction cannot consider it his duty to help in the dissemination of false views regarding the Russian experiment. On the contrary, he must regard it as his duty to point out to the world that what is going on in Russia is not the bankruptcy of the Socialist methods of Marxism, but evidence of the failure of the methods of utopianism. It is also evidence of the bankruptcy of dictatorship, which we reject under all circumstances in times of peace as a means of political ascendancy and Socialist construction. Only in a democracy is Socialism possible.

Otto Bauer himself does not claim that the existing order in Russia constitutes Socialism. He merely speaks of the possibility of the success of Socialism under Soviet dictatorship, and he admits that for this it is necessary to "wrest from the dictatorship that freedom of thought without which no true Socialism can exist." Of course, capitalism has been destroyed in Russia, but that does not mean that Socialism has been achieved. It would be nonsensical if out of hatred for capitalism we were to welcome every non-capitalistic form of production, even though it might mean more want and enslavement for the workers than was the case under the domination of Capital.

I expect that soon the failure of the attempts to transform Russia into a Socialist community by methods of dictatorship will become apparent to all. The failure of the Communist experiment in Russia, however, does not mean the downfall of the Bolshevik regime. The two things are not necessarily linked together. Nay, they are mutually exclusive. The same backwardness that makes Socialism in Russia at the present time impossible favors the strengthening of despotism once it has taken root.

The Soviet dictatorship may continue long after the world has recognized the fact that Socialism is no longer the essential purpose of that dictatorship but is only a delusion by means of which it strives to prolong its life and which is uses to deceive itself and others. The Bolsheviki may continue in power for a more or less extended period of time but their power will become increasingly incapable of withstanding serious trials. One such trial may overthrow it over night. We should always be prepared for the unexpected in Russia.

Otto Bauer fears the unexpected that may lead to the crash of the dictatorship. He thinks that the "dictatorship of the Reds can be replaced only by a dictatorship of the Whites."

This view is widely held at the moment. But I cannot share it.

Bauer also admits that democracy in Russia is necessary. But he hopes that it may come as soon as the dictatorship has succeeded in creating a more or less prosperous regime. I, too, wish with all my heart that democracy may come in this peaceful way. But here, too, I must side with those who lack the faith, that this will happen. I think my friend Otto Bauer is putting the cart before the horse. He hopes that prosperity will lead to freedom. I, on the other hand am convinced that as long as then is no freedom no ascent toward prosperity is possible, but only a descent to increasing want.

Like every absolutism in history, Bolshevist absolutism will be compelled to grant freedom to the Russian masses only under the pressure of an irresistible movement of the people.

To avoid all misunderstanding, I want first of all to remark that I am not at all advocating the organization of open rebellion against the rulers residing in the Kremlin, and that I am still less in favor of any kind of foreign intervention. The latter if attempted would bring incalculable harm, and the organization of an insurrection against such a powerful government apparatus as the Bolshevist is bound to fail. If this apparatus is not wrecked as a result of dissension within the ruling group itself then there is no other way of shortening its tenure except through an elemental upsurge of the people whose pressure will prove irresistible.

So that the question before us is not whether we should encourage the Russian Socialists to organize an insurrection. The question is altogether different, namely, how are we to act when, without our help but solely under pressure of the desperate condition of the state and its economic life, there will break out a mass movement of such power as to threaten the domination of the Communist party? Will such an insurrection lead inevitably to the establishment of the dictatorship of the Whites, so that in order to fight it the Socialist International will have to mobilize all the forces at its command?

That, of course, will be of little help to the dictators in the Kremlin. Popular movements that pass into revolutions have such a sweep that the efforts of foreign parties and emigres living just across the border are insignificant by comparison. This, however, will not absolve us from the duty which we owe to the proletariat of the entire world to take a definite stand for or against the movement.

First of all, however, we must ask ourselves the question as to just what is meant by "White Dictatorship." "White Guards" is the name given to those who favor the return of the Czar and the landowners. They played a part in the Russian civil war of 1918-1920. Now there remain only small remnants of that element. They may seize upon this or that occasion to parade in Europe or in China, but on the Russian people, the Russian workers and peasants, they have no influence whatever. In this respect the revolution has brought about a radical change.

Just what form the workers' and peasants' movement may take in present-day Russia is hard to say. We are dealing with an utterly abnormal state organism. The Communist Party may split, units of the Red Army may refuse to obey their officers, hunger may lead to an explosion of despair, the bureaucratic apparatus may stop working, the dictatorship itself may become more moderate and make some concessions, breaches may appear in the dike of terror and cause the whole structure eventually to be swept away. Many other things may happen. But what ground have we for thinking that in that case the representatives of Czarism, large industry and capital will gain such mastery as to be able to put the laboring masses under the harness of a new dictatorship? Against whom will the peasants and workers rise up if Bolshevism should collapse? Against the state economy? The workers will prefer private enterprise only in cases where they are assured better living and working conditions than they can get from the government-owned economy. But even the peasants will not oppose state industry if it can supply them with commodities of good quality and at low prices. True, the majority of peasants will abandon the kolkhozy as soon as government coercion is removed, but this they will do only if they receive the necessary means of production. At first the kolkhozy will simply stop delivering their supplies to the government for next to nothing. Perhaps many of them, under a freer regime, will organize a new form of production preparatory to Socialism.

What the peasants and workers will destroy first of all, for it oppresses them both economically and politically more than anything else, is the whole machinery of government dictatorship. Owing to the fact that the state finances are unsound, industrial undertakings and the kolkhozy are operating on a deficit and the government treasury no longer receives any surplus funds. When the OGPU, the huge bureaucratic apparatus and the Red Army are no longer well paid their discipline will be destroyed. They will become less dependable, less capable and ready to offer resistance to the growing insubordination of the masses. If in addition there is discord and indecision among the dictators themselves, then that will mean the end of the dictatorship.

The disbanding of the political police, the bureaucracy and the army will be the first result of the overthrow of the Red dictatorship.

Where, then, are the elements that will make a White dictatorship not only possible but inevitable ?

This does not at all mean that the overcoming of Bolshevism will and must assume the form of a democratic idyl. Sixteen years of steady and growing misery and oppression can not help but kindle the fire of hate in the hearts of the people, and we are able to judge of the intensity of this hatred from the unceasing killings of Bolshevik agents in the villages. To this must be added the utter lack of experience and traditions associated with free organization and self-rule among the people. If under these circumstances there should be an outbreak of rebellion among the peasants and workers they are likely at first to lead to a condition that is the very opposite of dictatorship, namely to anarchy and chaos. But ultimately there will be formed new political and social combinations the nature and character of which we can not as yet discern. For in the present condition of Russia everything is abnormal, therefore the overcoming of it may assume abnormal forms. But where the peasants and the workers are given an opportunity for free self-determination, they always tend toward democratic forms of organization. What ground have we for supposing then that the Russian peasants and workers will act differently after they will have overthrown their only overlord—the Bolshevist dictatorship? Or where is that power that is capable of imposing a new dictatorship upon them against their will? Such fears proceed not from a study of the present social structure in Russia, but from historical analogy with events that have taken place under an entirely different set of circumstances.

In my opinion the Socialist International has not the slightest reason or right to brand in advance as a reactionary movement every rebellion of the Russian people against the prevailing dictatorship. The democratic movement among the peasants and workers must count upon our fullest sympathy. Every attempt on the part of the White Guard elements to gain ascendancy in Russia will meet the unanimous resistance of all Socialists without distinction. But it would be extremely erroneous to suspect and denounce as White Guardist every popular movement without investigation, merely because it arouses fear in the hearts of the dictators in the Kremlin.

Our first duty is to watch carefully events in Russia. Then we shall not be deceived by partisans either on the right or on the left. At the present moment there is no more important research work than that of studying conditions in Russia. It is of decisive importance to the labor movement of the entire world.

I agree with Otto Bauer as far as the appraisal of the importance of the study of conditions in Russia is concerned. But I thoroughly disagree with him as to the essence of this appraisal. Otto Bauer thinks that every method of overthrowing the Soviet government would be a reactionary step for the whole of Europe. I expect the very opposite result from such an overthrow.

The old idealists among the dictators in the Kremlin have either died out or been removed from office. The men who are at the helm now have derived from the class struggle of the proletariat, in which they formerly participated as part of the Social-Democratic movement, only the desire to utilize the working class for their own ends, which in practice are no longer the liberation of the laboring masses but the strengthening of their own absolutism. The working classes not alone of Russia but of the entire world have become their cannon fodder. In the eyes of the Kremlin rulers the proletarians of all countries must play the part of wooden soldiers marching to their command. This is really the task of the Comintern. This is what all the illusions about a world revolution have come to. The leaders of the Comintern themselves probably no longer do not believe in this world revolution. But the greater the misery in their own country, the more interested are they in having the workers of other countries drawn into all sorts of senseless adventures. The more wretched the end of these adventures, the more harm they cause the proletariat, the more insignificant by comparison will the troubles in Russia appear.

In this effort to establish their dictatorship over the proletariat of the world and to drag it into adventures regardless of consequences, the Moscow dictators encounter the determined resistance of Social-Democracy. Therefore they regard the Social Democracy as their most dangerous enemy. The rage of the Communists is directed principally not against foreign capitalists but against the workers organized into Social-Democratic parties and free trade unions.

The rulers of Russia seem to be able to get along with the capitalists and capitalist governments and to do business with them. For the capitalists are not in the least embarrassed by dictatorship methods, nor by the omnipotence of a political police, nor by the exploitation of the masses for purposes of "primitive accumulation." They would greatly appreciate having a similar regime in their own countries. Bismark, for example, knew that the best way to control a proletariat attempting to lift its head is by encouraging it to open mutiny against the government and thus to create an opportunity for the bloody suppression of the workers. The fact that from time to time and by the most stupid methods the Communists create such opportunities for blood-letting from which the workers suffer makes them a valuable ally of all the reactionary forces of capitalism.

The fundamental aim of the Communists of every country is not the destruction of capitalism but the destruction of democracy and of the political and economic organizations of the workers.

By their policies they always pave the way for reaction. The capitalists no longer fear Soviet Russia, they help her. The entire Five-Year plan was conceived in the expectation that the capitalists of the entire world would vie with one another in supplying Soviet Russia with improved means of production, and in this the Communists were not deceived. And the capitalists fear Soviet Russia just as little politically as they do economically. Mussolini owes his success in no small measure to the Communists. They made possible the triumph of Hitler in Germany. In France and other countries the reactionaries owe a number of their seats in Parliament to the Communists. Everywhere from the moment the war ended the Communists have been doing the greatest harm to the cause of the working class by bringing discord into its ranks.

Right now one hears louder than ever the demand for a united front which before the war existed in almost every country of the world, with the exception of Russia, and which gave the laboring masses a chance to assert themselves victoriously. The split in the ranks of the proletariat was responsible for the fact that the revolutions of 1918 and 1919 did not accomplish the maximum results possible at that time. Now all our revolutionary gains are threatened, if we do not form a united front. The building of such a front is the most urgent need in the class struggle of the proletariat. In this we all agree. But I am not as optimistic as Otto Bauer and others that the united front could be re-established by negotiations between the Socialist International and the Comintern.

I am far from opposing an honest rapprochement. I should never wish to play the part of an opponent of unity. But I can foresee that nothing worth-while will come of these attempts.

Some say: we are absolutely opposed to the Communist parties outside of but not to the dictatorship in Russia. In reality the reverse is true: cooperation with those Communist parties who are freeing themselves from their dependence on the present rulers of Russia for the purpose of attaining some common goal is possible. This has been proved by experience more than once. On the other hand, those Communists who are ruled by Moscow are implacably hostile to our party not because of their Communist objectives, which are shared also by the Communist opposition, but because what the Moscow rulers want is not independently thinking allies but obedient tools.

The enemy that makes impossible any united front resides in Moscow. The conflict between Moscow and the Socialist International is not based upon a misunderstanding hut is deeply rooted in their respective natures and is just as insoluble as is the contradiction between dictatorship and democracy.

The re-establishment of a united proletarian front is impossible as long as the Socialist parties adhere firmly to democratic ideals, while Russia is ruled by a dictatorship seeking to subordinate to itself the proletariat of the whole world.

A united front will come of itself as soon as this dictatorship has vanished, for without it the Communist parties will be deprived of their life-force. They will speedily disintegrate as soon as slogans and money cease to come from Russia and the iron and golden ring that is holding them has been removed.

With the disappearance of the Bolshevist dictatorship there will begin a period of speedy unification and coordination of all the independent organizations of the proletarian democracy, who will resume their march to victory.

Not the collapse of the dictatorship in Russia but its further continuance in power constitutes the gravest menace and causes the greatest damage to the liberation struggle of the modern working class.

1883:
MARX'S THEORY OF VALUE, AN ARTICLE

Eleanor Marx

Chapter-5

David Ricardo begins his great work, "Principles of Political Economy and Taxation," with these words: "The value of a commodity, or the quantity of any other commodity for which it will exchange, depends upon the relative quantity of labor necessary for its production, and not on the greater or less *compensation* which is paid for that labor." This great discovery of Ricardo's, that there is but *one* real standard of value, *labor,* forms the starting-point of Marx'"Das Kapital." I cannot enter here into a detailed account of the way in which Marx completes, and partly corrects, Ricardo's theory of value, and develops, out of it, a theory of that fearfully contested subject, *currency,* which by its clearness, simplicity, and logical force, has carried conviction even into the heads of many political economists of the ordinary stamp. I must confine myself to the mode, based upon his theory of value, which Marx explains the origin and the continued accumulation of capital in the hands of a, thereby, privileged class.

Suppose all exchanges of commodities to be entirely fair; suppose that every buyer gets the full value in goods for his money, and that every seller receives in money the full value of the necessary labor invested in his produce. If, then, as political economists are in the habit of assuming, every producer sells that which he does not want, and buys with the money thus obtained that which he does want, but which he does not himself produce, then all things are for the best in this best of economical worlds; but the formation of Capital—this word taken, for the present, in its usual meaning—is impossible. A man may save money, or store up goods, but he cannot, as yet, use them as Capital, except perhaps by lending the money on interest. But that is, though a very ancient, yet a very subordinate and primitive form of Capital. The making of profits is impossible on the basis supposed above.

End yet, we see every day that profits, and very large profits, are made by some people. In order to account for this, let us begin by looking at the *form* of the transaction which produces profits. Hitherto we have dealt with independent producers, who, under a system of social division of labor, sell what they do not want, and buy what they do want for their own use. But now the producer appears as a man who enters the market, not with produce, but with money, and who buys, not what he wants, but what he does not want for his own use. He buys, in one word, in order to re-sell what he has bought. But to buy 20 tons of pig-iron, or 10 bales of cotton for £100, and to re-sell them for £100 would be an absurdity. And indeed we find our business man does not commit such an absurdity. Be buys his commodities, say for £100, and re-sells them, on an average, say for £110. But how is this possible? We still assume that all commodities are bought and sold at this full labor value. Then no profit can come out of any amount of such buying and selling. A change in the value of the commodity bought and sold, for instance, the rise in cotton in consequence of the American Civil War, may explain how profits arise in a few solitary instances. But commodities do not always rise in value, they generally fluctuate about a certain average value and price. What is gained now is lost hereafter. With our supposition of equal exchanges, profits are impossible.

Very well. Suppose now, exchanges were not equal—suppose every seller to be able to sell his article 10 per cent above its real value. Then, what every one of them gains as a seller, he loses again as a buyer. Again, let every buyer buy at 10 per cent, below the value of the article bought. What he gains as a buyer, leaves his hands again as soon as he turns seller.

Suppose, finally, profits to be the result of cheating. I sell you a ton of iron for £5, while it is worth no more than £3. In that case, I am £2 richer, and you are £2 poorer. Before the bargain you had £5 in money and I £3 in value of iron—together £8. After the bargain you hold £3 in iron and I £5 in gold—together again £8. Value has changed hands, but it has not been created, and profits to be real most be value newly created. It is self-evident that the totality of the capitalist class of a country cannot cheat itself.

Thus if equivalents are exchanged, profits are impossible; and if non-equivalents are exchanged, profits are equally impossible. Yet they exist. How is this economical enigma to be solved? Now it is evident that the increase of value which appears in the re-sale as profits, and which transforms money into capital, cannot arise from that money, for both in the buying and in the selling the money merely represents the value or the commodity bought and sold (we assume hero again all exchanges to be exchanges of equivalents). Nor can it arise from the value of the commodity which is supposed to be bought and sold at its full value, neither more nor less. The increase of value can, therefore, arise only out of the *actual use* of the commodity in question. But how can new value arise from the use, the consumption of a commodity? This would only be possible if our business-men had the good luck to find in the market a commodity endowed with the special quality that its consumption would be, *ipso facto,* a creation of wealth.

And that commodity exists in the market. That commodity is called by economists *Labor,* but Marx, more correctly, calls it *Labor-power,* and this expression I shall use here.

The existence of Labor-power as a commodity in the market, presupposes that it is sold by its owner, and, therefore, that the latter is a free agent, who sells his Labor-power to another free agent, both dealing with each other voluntarily and on an equal footing. It presupposes, moreover, that the sale is for a limited time only, as otherwise the seller, from a free agent, would become a slave.

And, finally, it presupposes that the owner of the labor-power, the future laborer, is not in a position to sell commodities, the produce of his own labor, but that he is compelled to sell, instead, his capacity to labor. Thus, our business-man lives in a society where he meets the free laborer in the market—free not only to dispose as a free agent of his labor-power, but free also from the possession of all means by which he himself could transform the labor-power into actual labor, into work. A free man—but free also from the ownership of victuals, of raw material, and of tools, unless, perhaps, the simplest end cheapest.

That our two "free agents" are enabled to meet each other in the market, is evidently not a phenomenon produced by simple nature. It is the result of a long historical process, the result of many previous revolutions of society. And, indeed, it is only since the latter half of the fifteenth century that we find the mass of the population being gradually tamed into snob "free" sellers of their own labor-power.

Now labor-power, as a saleable commodity has a value and a price like other commodities. Its value is determined, as in all other cases, by the labor necessary for its production, and therefore its reproduction. The value of labor-power is the value of the necessaries of life required to keep the laborer in a state fit for his work, and as he is subject to natural decay and death, to reproduce and to continue the race of sellers of labor-power. The extent and composition of these necessaries of life varying very much for different epochs and countries, are yet more or less fixed for a single country, and a given period. The standard of life established there among the working class settles it.

Let us now see how our business-man consumes the labor-power he has bought. Suppose the work to be done is cotton-spinning. The hired laborer is introduced into the factory and there finds all the requisites for his work: cotton in the state of preparation which renders it fit for spinning into yarn, machinery, etc. Suppose the normal production of a spinner per hour to be one and two-third pounds of yarn, for which one and two-thirds pounds of cotton are required (leaving unavoidable waste out of the question). Then in six hours our spinner will turn 10 lbs. of cotton into 10 lbs. of yarn. If the value of the cotton be 1s. per lb. the 10 lbs. of yarn will represent in value of cotton l0s. Assuming the wear and tear of machinery, oil, coal, etc., during these six hours to represent a value of 2s., that will raise the value of the yarn to 12s. There remains to be known how much is added to its volume by the labor of the spinner.

Suppose the value of labor-power for one day, that is to say the value of the necessaries of life required to maintain the laborer for one day to be 3s. Suppose, again, that this sum of necessaries, or the 3s. representing it in money, are equivalent to, or embody the labor of one worker for six hours. Our spinner, then, at the end of six hours work has added a value of 3s. to the yarn, so that its total value is 15s. Our businessman, now a master cotton-spinner, has in his yarn the full equivalent of his outlay: 10s. for cotton, 2s. for wear and tear, etc., 3s. for labor-power employed—total 15s. He is repaid in the value of his yarn for every fraction of a farthing he has advanced. But there is no margin for any profits. But our master cotton-spinner or would-be capitalist very soon informs us that this is not the way at all in which he understood his bargain. If six hours labor suffice to *keep* the laborer for a full day, including the night; that is no reason why the laborer should not work a whole day. He, the master, has hired the man's labor-power for a day. He, therefore, is entitled to have a full day's work out of him. The value of the labor-power and the value of the labor it is capable of performing may be different things. If they are, then the worker is entitled to have the first and the employer is equally entitled to pocket the second. Labor is not only the source of wealth, and of value, but it is also the source of more value than that of the labor-power required to perform that labor. And that is the very reason why the employer has hired the laborer.

Instead of discharging his workman after the six hours he makes him work say another six hours, twelve in all (we will not at present mind the Factory Acts). Then after twelve hours work we have the following result:—

20 lbs. of cotton at 1s	£1 0 0
Wear and tear twelve hours, twice 2s.	0 4 0
Labour added in twelve hours	0 6 0
Value of 20 lbs. of yarn	£1 10 0
Outlay of Employer	
20 lbs. of cotton, as above,	£1 0 0
Wear and tear	0 4 0
Wages paid to spinner	0 3 0
	£1 7 0
Margin for profit	3s.

The enigma is solved, the possibility of profits explained. Money has been transformed into capital.

The above simple transaction between employer and workman not only explains the genesis of capital, but it forms the groundwork of our whole system of production (called by Marx *capitalist production).* It forms the gist of Marx' whole book, and is at this moment perfectly understood by the Socialists of the Continent, especially by those of Germany and Russia.

I said the 3s. were not profit, but *margin* for profit. The sum thus entering the pocket of the capitalist Marx calls *surplus value.* It is not all profit, but it includes the employer's profit. He has to share it with others: with the Government in the shape of rates and taxes, with the landlord for rent, with the merchant, etc. The laws that regulate this repartition will be explained in the third Book (2nd volume) of "Das Kapital," which, together with the second, the author has left in manuscript. 'It will be published in German as soon as possible.

Thus, all classes of society not composed of actual and immediate producers of wealth (and these, in England at least, me almost exclusively wages-laborers), all classes, from kings and queens to music-masters and greengrocers, live upon their respective shares of this surplus-value. In other words, they live upon the net produce of the surplus labor which the capitalist extracts from his workpeople, but for which he does not pay. It matters not whether the share of surplus-labor falling to each member of society not actually a producer is granted as a gift by Act of Parliament from the public revenue, or whether it has to be earned by performing some function not actually productive. There is no other fund out of which they can be paid, but the sum total of the surplus value created by the immediate producers, for which they are not paid.

REVOLUTIONARY UNIONISM

E.V. Debs

Chapter-6

The unity of labor, economic and political, upon the basis of the class struggle, is at this time the supreme need of the working class. The prevailing lack of unity implies lack of class consciousness; that is to say, enlightened self-interest; and this can, must and will be overcome by revolutionary education and organization. Experience, long, painful and dearly bought, has taught some of us that craft division is fatal to class unity. To accomplish its mission the working class must be united. They must act together; they must assert their combined power, and when they do this upon the basis of the class struggle, then and then only will they break the fetters of wage slavery.

We are engaged today in a class war; and why? For the simple reason that in the evolution of the capitalist system in which we live, society has been mainly divided into two economic classes—a small class of capitalists who own the tools with which work is done and wealth is produced, and a great mass of workers who are compelled to use those tools. Between these two classes there is an irrepressible economic conflict. Unfortunately for himself, the workingman does not yet understand the nature of the conflict, and for this reason has hitherto failed to accomplish any effective unity of his class.

It is true that workers in the various departments of industrial activity have organized trade unions. It is also true that in this capacity they have from time to time asserted such power as this form of organization has conferred upon them. It is equally true that mere craft unionism, no matter how well it may be organized, is in the present highly developed capitalist system utterly unable to successfully cope with the capitalist class. The old craft union has done its work and belongs to the past. Labor unionism, like everything else, must recognize and bow to the inexorbable law of evolution.

The craft union says that the worker shall receive a fair day's pay for a fair day's work. What is a fair day's pay for a fair day' work? Ask the capitalist and he will give you his idea about it. Ask the worker and, if he is intelligent, he will tell you that a fair day's pay for a fair day's work is all the workingman produces.

While the craft unionist still talks about a fair day's pay for a fair day's work, implyin that the economic interests of the capitalist and the worker can be harmonized upon a basis of equal justice to both, the Industrial Worker says, "I want all I produce by my labor.'

If the worker is not entitled to all he produces, then what share is anybody else entitled to?

Does the worker today receive all he produces? Does he receive anything like a fair (?) share of the product of his labor? Will any trade-unionist of the old school make any such claim, and if he is bold enought to make it, can he verify it?

The student of this question knows that, as a matter of fact, in the capitalist system in which we live today the worker who produces all wealth receives but enough of his product to keep him in working and producing order. His wage, in the aggregate, is fixed by his living necessities. It suffices, upon the average, to maintain him according to the prevailing standard of living and to enable him to reproduce himself in the form of labor power. He receives, as a matter of fact, but about 17 per cent of what his labor produces.

The worker produces a certain thing. It goes from the manufacturer to the jobber, from the jobber to the wholesaler, and from the wholesaler to the retailer—each of these adding a profit, and when it completes the circle and comes back to the worker who produced it and he stands face to face with the product of his own labor, he can buy back, upon the average, with his paltry wage but about 17 per cent of it. In other words, he is exploited, robbed, of about 83 per cent of what his labor produces. And why? For the simple reason that in modern industry, the tool, in the form of a great machine with which he works and produces, is the private property of the capitalist, who didn't make it, and could not, if his life depended upon it, use it.

The evolution is not yet complete.

By virtue of his private ownership of the social tool—made and used by the co-operative labor of the working class—the employer has the economic power to appropriate to himself, as a capitalist, what is produced by the social labor of the working class. This accounts for the fact that the capitalist becomes fabulously rich, lives in a palace where there is music and singing and dancing, and where there is the luxury of all climes, while the workingmen who do the work and produce the wealth and endure the privations and make the sacrifices of health and limb and life, remain in a wretched state of poverty and dependence.

The exploiting capitalist is the economic master and the political ruler in capitalist society, and as such holds the exploited wage worker in utter contempt.

No master ever had any respect for his slave, and no slave eer had, or ever could have, any real love for his master.

I must beg you to indulge the hoarseness of my voice, which has been somewhat strained addressing meetings of the Industrial Workers held in and about Chicago during the last two or three evenings; but, fortunately, my eyesight has not been strained reading the accounts of these meetings in the capitalist papers of Chicago.

Alert, vigilant, argus-eyed as the capitalist dailies of Chicago are, there is not one of them that knows of this meeting of the Industrial Workers. But if this were a meeting of the American Federation of Labor and an old trade union leader were here, you would read tomorrow morning a full account of it and him in every capitalist paper in the city. There is a reason for this that explains itself.

The capitalist papers know that there is such an organization as the Industrial Workers, because they have lied about it. Just now they are ignoring it. Let me serve notice on them through you and the thousands of other who flock to our meetings everywhere, that they will reckon with the Industrial Workers before six months have rolled around.

There are those wage workers who feel their economic dependence, who know that the capitalist for whom they work is the owner of their job, and therefore the master of their fate, who are still vainly seeking by individual effort and through waning craft unions to harmonize the conflicting interests of the exploiting capitalist and the exploited wage slave. They are engaged in a vain and hopeless task. They are wasting time and energy worthy of a better cause. These interests never can and never will be harmonized permanently, and when they are adjusted even temporarily it is always at the expense of the working class.

It is no part of the mission of this revolutionary working class union to conciliate the capitalist class. We are organized to fight that class, and we want that class to distinctly understand it. And they do understand it, and in time the working class will also understand it; and then the capitalist class will have reason to understand it better still. Their newspapers understand it so well even now that they have not a single favorable comment to make upon it.

When the convention of delegates was in session here in June last for the purpose of organizing the Industrial Workers, every report that appeared in a Chicago paper—capitalist paper I mean; every single report was a tissue of perversion, misstatement and downright falsehood. They knew that we had met for a purpose, and that that purpose was to fight the class of which they are the official mouthpieces. Now, it seems to me that this uniform hostility of the capitalist press ought to be significant to even the unthinking workingman. Capitalist papers are, as a rule, quite friendly to the craft unions. They do not misrepresent them; do no lie about them; do not traduce their representatives. They are exceedingly fond of them, because they know enough about their own interests to know that the craft unions are not only not a menace to them, but are in fact bulwarks of defense to them. And why? Because, chiefly, craft unions divide and do not unite the working class. And I challenge contradiction.

There was a time when the craft union expressed in terms of unionism the prevailing mode of industry. That was long ago when production was still mainly carried on by handicraftsmen with hand tools; when one man worked for another to learn his trade that he might become its master. The various trades involved skill and cunning; considerable time was required to master them. This was in the early stages of the capitalist system. Even at that early day the antagonism between employer and employed found expression, although the employer was not at that time the capitalist as he is today. The men who followed these trades found it necessary in order to protect themselves in their trade interests to band together, form a union, so that they might act together in resisting the encroachments of the "boss.' So the trade union came into existence.

The mode of production since that time has been practically revolutionized. The hand tool has all but disappeared. The mammoth machine has taken its place. The hand tool was made and used by the individual worker and was largely within his own control. Today the machine that has supplanted the old tool is not owned nor controlled by the man, or rather the men, who use it. As I have already said, it is the private property of some capitalist who may live at a remote point and never have seen the machine or the wage slaves who operate it.

In other words, the production of wealth, in the evolution of industry, from being an individual act a half century ago has become a social act. The tool, from being an individual tool, has become a social instrument. So that the tool has been socialized and production has also been socialized. But the evolution is yet to complete its work. This social tool, made socially and used socially, must be socially owned.

In the evolution of industry the trade has been largely undermined. The old trade union expresses the old form of industry, the old mode of individual production based upon the use of the individual tool. That tool has about disappeared; that mode of production has also about disappeared, but the trade union built upon that mode of production, springing from the use of the hand tool, remains essentially the same.

The pure and simple trade union, in seeking to preserve its autonomy, is forced into conflict with other trade unions by the unceasing operation of the laws of industrial evolution. How many of the skilled trades that were in operation half a century ago are still practiced?

At the town where I live there used to be quite a number of cooper shops. Barrels were made by hand and a cooper shop consisted wholly of coopers. The coopers' union was organized and served fairly well the purposes of the coopers of that day, but it does not serve the purposes of the workers who make barrels today. They do not make barrels in the way they used to be made. Today we want a union that expresses the economic interests of all the workers in the cooperage plant engaged in making and handling barrels. But a few coopers still remain, a very few. It is no longer necessary to be a cooper to make a barrel. The machine is the cooper today. The machine make the barrel, and almost anyone can operate the machine that makes the barrel.

You will observe that labor has been subdivided and specialized and that the trade has been dissipated; and now a body of men and boys work together co-operatively in the making of a barrel, each making a small part of a barrel. Now we want a union which embraces all the workers engaged in making barrels. We lose sight of the cooper trade as evolution has practically disposed of that. We say that since the trade has completely changed, the union which expressed that trade must also change accordingly. In the new union we shall include not only the men who are actually engaged in the making of barrels directly, but also those who are placing them upon the market. There are the typewriters, the bookkeepers, the teamsters, and all other classes of labor that are involved in the making and delivering of the barrels. We insist that all the workers in the whole of any given plant shall belong to one and the same union.

This is the very thing the workers need and the capitalist who owns the establishment does not want. He believes in labor unionism if it is the 'right kind.' And if it is the right kind for him it is the wrong kind for you. He is more than willing that his employers shall join the craft union. He has not the slightest objection. On the contrary, it is easily proven that capitalists are among the most active upholders of the old craft unions.

The capitalists are perfectly willing that you shall organize, as long as you don't do a thing against them; as long as you don't do a thing for yourselves. You cannot do a thing for yourselves without antagonizing them; and you don't antagonize them through your craft unions nearly as much as you buttress their interests and prolong their mastery.

The average workingman imagines that he must have a leader to look to; a guide to follow, right or wrong. He has been taught in the craft union that he is a very dependent creature; that without a leader the goblins would get him without a doubt, and he therefore instinctively looks to his leader. And even while he is looking at his leader there is someone else looking at the same leader from the other side.

You have depended too much on that leader and not enough on yourself. I don't want you to follow me. I want you to cultivate self-reliance.

If I have the slightest capacity for leadership I can only give evidence of it by leading you to rely upon yourselves.

As long as you can be led by an individual you will be betrayed by an individual. That does not mean that all leaders are dishonest or corrupt. I make no such sweeping indictment. I know that many of them are honest. I know also that many of them are in darkness themselves, blind leaders of the blind. That is the worst that can be said of them. And let me say to you that the most dangerous leader is not the corrupt leader, but the honest, ignorant leader. That leader is just as fatal to your interests as teh one who deliberately sells you out for a paltry consideration.

You are a workingman! Now, at your earliest leisure look yourself over and take an inventory of your resources. Invoice your mental stock; see what you have on hand.

You may be of limited mentality; and that is all you require in the capitalist system. You need only small brains, but huge hands.

Most of your hands are calloused and you are taught by the capitalist politician, who is the political mercenary of the capitalist who fleeces you, you are taught by him to be proud of your horny hands. If that is true he ought to be ashamed of his. He doesn't have any horns on his hands. He has them on his brain. He is as busy with his brain as you are with your hands, and because he is busy with his brain and you neglect yours, he gets a goodly share of what you produce with your hands. He is the gentleman who calls you the horny handed sons of toil. That fetches you every time. I tell you that the time has come for you to use your brains in your own interest, and until you do that you will have to use your hands in the interest of your masters.

Now, after you have looked yourself over; after you have satisfied yourself what you are, or rather, what you are not, you will arrive at the conclusion that as a wage worker in capitalist society you are not a man at all. You are simply a thing. And that thing is bought in the labor market, just as hair, hides and other forms of merchandise are bought.

When the capitalist requires the use of your hands, does he call for men? Why, certainly not. He doesn't want men, he only wants hands. And when he calls for hands, that is what he wants. Have you ever seen a placard posted: "Fifty hands wanted'? Did you ever know of a capitalist to respond to that kind of an invitation?

President Roosevelt would have you believe that there are no classes in the United States. He was made president by the votes of the working class. Did you ever know of his stopping over night in the home of a workingman? Is it by mere chance that he is always sheltered beneath the hospitable roof of some plutocrat? Not long ago he made a visit here and he gave a committee representing the workers about fifteen minutes of his precious time, just time enough to rebuke them with the intimation that organized labor consisted of a set of law-breakers, and then he gave fifteen hours to the plutocrats of Chicago, being wined and dined by them to prove that there are no classes in the United States, and that you, horny handed veteran, with your wage of $1.50 a day, with six children to support on that, are in the same class with John D. Rockefeller! Your misfortune is that you do not know you are in the same class. But on election day it dawns upon you and you prove it by voting the same ticket.

Since you have looked yourself over thoroughly, you realize by this time that, as a workingman, you have been supporting, through your craft unions and through your ballots, a social system that is the negation of your manhood.

The capitalist for whom you work doesn't have to go out and look for you; you have to look for him, and you belong to him just as completely as if he had a title to your body; as if you were his chattel slave.

He doesn't own you under law, but he does under the fact.

Why? Because he owns the tool with which you work, and you have got to have access to taht tool if you work; and if you want to live you have got to work. If you don't work you don't eat; and so, scourged by hunger pangs, you look about for that tool and you locate it, and you soon discover that between yourself, a workingman, and that tool that is an essential part o fyourself in industry, there stands the capitalist who owns it. He is your boss; he owns your job, takes your product and controls your destiny. Before you can touch that tool to earn a dime you must petition the owner of it to allow you to use it, in consideration of your giving to him all you produce with it, except just enough to keep you alive and in working order.

Observe that you are displaced by the surplus product of your own labor; that what you produce is of more value under capitalism than you who produce it; that the commodity which is the result of your labor is of greater value under capitalism than your own life.

You consist of palpitating flesh; you have wants. You have necessities. You cannot satisfy them, and you suffer. Butt he product of your labor, the property of the capitalist, that is sacred; that must be protected at all hazards. After you have been displaced by the surplus product of your labor and you have been idle long enough, you become restive and you begin to speak out, and you become a menace. The unrest culminates in trouble. The capitalist presses a button and the police are called into action. Then the capitalist presses button No. 2 and injunctions are issued by the judges, the judicial allies and servants of the capitalist class. Then button No. 3 is pressed and the state troops fall into line; and if this is not sufficient button No. 4 is pressed and the regular soldiers come marching to the scene. That is what President Roosevelt meant when he said that back of the mayor is the governor, back of the governor the President; or, to use his own words, back of the city, the state and back of the state the nation—the capitalist nation.

If you have been working in a steel mill and you have made more steel than your master can sell, and you are locked out and get hungry, and the soldiers are called out, it is to protect the steel and shoot you who made the steel—to guard the men who steal the steel and kill the men who made it.

I am not asking you to withdraw from the craft unions simply because the Industrial Workers has been formed. I am asking you to think about these matters for yourselves.

I belonged to a craft union from the time I was nineteen years of age. I can remember the very evening I first joined the Brotherhood of Locomotive Firemen. I can recall with what zeal I went to work to organize my craft, and it was the pride of my life to see that union expand. I did what I could to build it up. In time I was made to realize that that union was not sufficient unto itself. I next did what I could to organize other branches of the service and then establish a federation of the various unions of railroad employees, and finally succeeded; but soon after the federation was formed, on account of craft jealousies, it was disrupted. I then, along with a number of others who had had the same experience and had profited by it, undertook to organize the railway men within one organization, known as the American Railway Union. The railroad corporations were the deadly enemies of that organization. They understood that its purpose was to unify all the railroad employees. They knew that the unity of the working class meant their end, and so they set their faces like flint against the American Railway Union. And while they were using all their powers to crush and to stamp out the American Railway Union, they were bestowing all their favors upon the several craft brotherhoods, the engineers and the firemen, the conductors and the brakemen. They knew that so long as these craft unions existed there could be no unification of the men employed in the railway service.

Are the railroad men of this country organized today? No! Not nearly one-half of them are organized at all. And when the railroad corporations from motives of good policy make a concession to the engineers of the conductors, it is gouged out of the poor devils who work for a dollar a day and are compelled to submit.

There are a great many engineers who are perfectly willing to be tied up in a contract. They think they can save themselves at the expense of their fellow-workers. But they are going to reap, sooner or later, just what they have sown. In the next few years they will become motermen.

While we are upon this question, let us consult industrial history a moment. We will begin with the craft union railroad strike of 1888. The Brotherhood of Engineers and the Brotherhood of Firemen on the C., B. & Q. system went out on strike. Some 2,000 engineers and firemen vacated their posts and went out on one of the most bitterly contested railroad, the rest of the employees, especially the conductors, who were organized in craft unions of their own, remained at their posts, and the union conductors piloted the scab engineers over the line. I know whereof I speak. I was there. I took an active part in that strike.

I saw craft union pitted against craft union, and I saw the Brotherhood of Engineers and the Brotherhood of Firemen completely wiped from the C.,B. & Q. system. And now you find these men, seventeen years later, scattered all over the United States. They had to pay the penalty of their ignorance in organizing a craft instead of organizing as a whole.

In 1892 a strike occurred on the Lehigh Valley; the same result. Another on the Toledo, Ann Arbor & North Michigan. Same result. The engineers have had no strike from that time to this. Every time they have had a strike they have been defeated.

The railroad corporations are shrewd enough to recognize the fact that if they can keep certain departments in their employ in a time of emergency they can defeat all the rest. A manager of a railroad who can keep control of 15 per cent of the old men can allow 85 per cent to go out on strike and defeat them every time. That is why they have made some concessions to the engineers and conductors and brakesmen, and now and then to the switchmen, the most militant labor union of them all.

A year and a half ago the telegraph operators on the Missouri, Kansas & Texas went out on strike. The engineer remained at his post; so did the fireman; the conductor at his; and the brakeman at his. And they hauled the scabs that flocked from all pats of the country to the several points along the line, and delivered them in good order to take the places vacated by the strikers; worked all round them and with them until they had mastered the details of their several duties; and having done this, the strike was at an end, and the 1,300 craft unionists out of jobs. You will find them scattered all over the country.

Now, were not these other craft unions scabbing on the telegraphers just as flagrantly as if they had stepped into their positions and discharged their duties? They were acting with the corporation against their union fellow workingmen, helping hte corporation to defeat and crush them. Without their aid the corporation could not have succeeded. With their aid it was very easily done.

Is it possible that a craft unionist can see such an object lesson as this so plainly presented to him and still refuse to profit by it? Still close his eyes and, as it were, shut up his reason, and absolutely decline to see that this is suicidal policy and that its fruit must always be disruption and disaster?

This world only respects as it is compelled to respect; and if you workingmen would be respected you must begin by respecting yourselves. You have had enough of this sort of experience. You have had more than enough of it right here in Chicago.

Why didn't the steel trust annihilate the Amalgamated Steelworkers? Only two years ago they defeated them completely. The trust had its iron heel upon the neck of the Steelworkers' Union, and could have, had it chosen, completely crushed the life out of it. But Morgan was too wily. Schwab was too wise. They used to oppose trade unions. They don't oppose them any longer. They have discovered that a union can be turned the other way; that it can be made useful to them instead of being useful to the working class. Morgan now says he is in favor of trade unions, and Schwab agrees. They didn't crush out the Steelworkers' Union because they knew that another and a better one would spring from its ruins. They were perfectly willing that the old craft union should grow up again and block the way to real union.

You have had a machinists' strike here in Chicago. You are well aware of this without my telling you. There is something pathetic to me about every strike.

I have said and say again that no strike was ever lost; that it has always been worth all it cost. An essential part of a workingman's education is the defeats he encounters. The strikes he loses are after all the only ones he wins. I am heartily glad for myself that I lost the strike. It is the best thing that ever happened to me. I lost the strike of the past that I may win the strike of the future.

I am a discredited labor leader, but I have good staying qualities. The very moment the capitalist press credits me with being a wise labor leader, I will invite you to investigate me upon the charge of treason. I am discredited by the capitalist simply because I am true to his victim. I don't want his favors. I do not court his approbation. I would not have it. I can't afford it. If I had his respect it would be at the price of my own.

I don't care anything about what is called public opinion. I know precisely what that means. It is but the reflect of the interests of the capitalist class. As between the respect of the public and my own, I prefer my own; and I am going to keep it until I can have both.

When I pick up a capitalist newspaper and read a eulogy of some labor leader, I know that that leaderhas at least two afflictions; the one is mental weakness and the other is moral cowardice—and they go together. Put it down that when the capitalist who is exploiting you credits your leader with being safe and conservative and wise, that leader is not serving you. And if you take exception to that statement, just ask me to prove it.

The rank and file of all unions, barring their ignorance, are all right. The working class as a whole is all right. Many of them are misguided, and stand in the light of their own interest.

It is sometimes necessary that we offend you and even shock you, that you may understand that we are your friends and not your enemies. And if we are against your unions it is because we are for you. We know that you have paid your dues into them for years and that you are animated by a spirit of misdirected loyalty to those unions.

I can remember that it was not a very easy matter for me to give up the union in which I had spent my boyhood and all the years of my young manhood. I remember that I felt there was something in it in the nature of a sacrifice, and yet I had to make it in the nature of a sacrifice, and yet I had to make it in the interest of the larger duty that I owned myself and the working class.

Let me say to you, if you are a craft unionist, that infinitely greater than your loyalty to you craft is your loyalty to the working class as a whole. No craft union can fight this great battle successfully alone. The craft is a part, a part only, of the great body of the working class. And the time has come for his class, numerically overwhelming in the majority, to follow in one respect at least the example of its capitalist masters and unite as whole.

In this barbarous competitive struggle in which we are engaged, the workers, the millions, are fighting each other to sell themselves into slavery; the middle class are fighting each other to other to get enough trade to keeep soul and body together, and the professional class are fighting each other like savages for practice. And this is called civilization! What a mockery! What a sham! There is no real civilization in the capitalist system.

Today there is nothing so easily produced as wealth. The whole earth consists of raw materials; and in every breath of nature, in sunshine, and in shower, hidden everywhere, are the subtle forces that may, by the touch of the hand of labor, be set into operation to transmute these raw materials into wealth, the finished products, in all their multiplied forms and in opulent abundance for all. The merest child can press a button that will set in operation a forest of machinery and produce wealth enough for a community.

Whatever may be said of the ignorant, barbarous past, there is no excuse for poverty today. And yet it is the scourge of the race. It is the Nemesis of capitalist civilization. Ten millions, one-eighth of our whole population, are in a state of chronic poverty. Three millions of these have been sunk to unresisting pauperism. The whole working class is in a sadly dependent state, and even the most favored wage-worker is left suspended by a single thread. He does not know what hour a machine may be invented to make his trade useless, displace him and throw him into the increasing army of the unemployed.

And how does labor lvie today? Here in Chicago you may walk along a certain boulevard, say 18th street, and you will find it lined with magnificent palaces. Beyond that you will find a larger district where the still complacent middle class abide. Beyond that is a very much larger territory where the working class exist; and still beyond that, to complete the circle, you see the red lights flickering in the distance.

Prostitution is a part, a necessary part, of capitalist society. The department store empties in the slums.

I have been here enough to know that when the daughter of a workingman is obliged to go up the street to look for employment, when she is fourteen or fifteen years of age, and ought to be in the care and keeping of a loving mother, and have all of the advantages that our civilization makes possible for all—when she is forced to go to a department store, to one of those capitalist emporiums, and there find a place, if she can, and work for a wage of $3 a week, and have to obey a code of cast-iron regulations, appear tidy and neatly dressed and be subjected to a thousand temptations daily, and then takes a misstep, the first, as she is more than apt to do, especially if she has no home in any decent sense of that term—the very instant this is added to her poverty, she is doomed—damned. All the doors of capitalist society are closed in her face. The coals of contumely are poured upon her had. There is for her no redemption, and she takes the next step, and the next, until at last she ends a disgraceful career in a brothel hell.

This may be your child. And if you are a workingman, and this should fall to the lot of the innocent blue-eyed child that you love more than you do your own life—I want you to realize that if such a horror be written in the book of fate, that you are responsible for it, if you use or misuse your power to perpetuate the capitalist system and working class slavery.

You can change this condition—not tomorrow, not next week, nor next year; but in the meantime the next thing to changing it is making up your mind that it shall be changed. That is what we Industrial Unionists have done. And so there has come to us a new state of mind, and in our hearts there is the joy of service and the serenity of triumph.

We are united and we cannot be disunited. We cannot be stampeded. We know that we are confronted by ten thousand difficulties. We know that all the powers of capitalism are to be arrayed against us. But were these obstacles multiplied by a million, it would simply have the effect of multiplying our determination by a million, to overcome them all. And so we are organizing and appealing to you.

The workingman today does not understand his industrial relation to his fellow-workers. He has never been correlated with others in the same industry. He has mechanically done his part. He has simply been a cog, with little reference to, or knowledge of, the rest of the cogs. Now, we teach him to hold up his head and look over the whole mechanism. If he is employed in a certain plant, as an Industrial Unionist, his eyes are opened. He takes a survey of the entire productive mechanism, and he understands his part in it, and his relation to every other worker in that industry. The very instant he does that he is buoyed by a fresh hope and thrilled with a new aspiration. He becomes a larger man. He begins to feel like a collective son of toil.

Then he and his fellows study to fit themselves to take control of this productive mechanism when it shall be transferred from the idle capitalist to the workers to whom it rightfully belongs.

In every mill and every factory, every mine and every quarry, every railroad and every shop, everywhere, the workers, enlightened, understanding their self-interest, are correlating themselves in the industrial and economic mechanism. They are developing their industrial consciousness, their economic and political power; and when the revolution comes, they will be prepared to take possession and assume control of every industry. With the education they will have received in the Industrial Workers they will be drilled and disciplined, trained and fitted for Industrial Mastery and Social Freedom.

SOCIALISM AND THE POLITICAL STRUGGLE

G.V. Plekhanov

Chapter-7

Introduction

The present article may be an occasion for much misunderstanding and even dissatisfaction. People who sympathise with the trend of *Zemlya i Volya* and *Chorny Peredel* (publications in the editing of which I used to take part) may reproach me with having diverged from the theory of what is called Narodism. The supporters of other factions of our revolutionary party may be displeased with my criticism of outlooks which are dear to them. That is why I consider a short preliminary explanation necessary.

The desire to work *among the people* and for the people, the certitude that "the emancipation of the working classes must be conquered by the working classes themselves"—this *practical* tendency of our Narodism is just as dear to me as it used to be. But its *theoretical* propositions seem to me, indeed, erroneous in many respects. Years of life abroad and attentive study of the social question have convinced me that the triumph of a spontaneous popular movement similar to Stepan Razin's revolt or the Peasant Wars in Germany cannot satisfy the social and political needs of modern Russia, that the old forms of our national life carried within them many germs of their disintegration and that they cannot "develop into a higher communist form" except under the immediate influence of a strong and well-organised *workers'* socialist party. For that reason I think that besides fighting absolutism the Russian revolutionaries must strive at least to work out the elements for the establishment of such a party in the future. In this creative work they will necessarily have to pass on to the basis of modern socialism, for the ideals of Zemlyai Volya do not correspond to the condition of the industrial workers. And that will be very opportune now that the theory of Russian exceptionalism is becoming synonymous with stagnation and reaction and that the progressive elements of Russian society are grouping under the banner of judicious

"Occidentalism".

I go on to another point of my explanation. Here I will first of all say in my defence that I have been concerned not with persons but with opinions, and that my personal differences with this or that socialist group do not in the least diminish my respect for all who sincerely fight for the emancipation of the people.

Moreover, the so-called terrorist movement has opened a new epoch in the development of our revolutionary party—the epoch of *conscious political struggle* against the government. This change in the direction of our revolutionaries' work makes it necessary for them to reconsider all views that they inherited from the preceding period. Life demands that we attentively reconsider all our intellectual stock-in-trade when we step on to new ground, and I consider my pamphlet as a contribution which I can make to this matter of criticism which started long ago in our revolutionary literature. The reader has probably not yet forgotten the biography of Andrei Ivanovich Zhelyabov which contained a severe and frequently very correct critical appraisal of the programme and activity of the Zemlya i Volya group. It is quite possible that my attempts at criticism will be less successful, but it would hardly be fair to consider them less timely.

Every class struggle is a political struggle.

—*Karl Marx*

Since the Russian revolutionary movement finally took the path of open struggle against absolutism, the question of the socialists' political tasks has become the most vital and most burning question for our party. Because of it people have drifted apart who had been attached to each other by many years of joint practical work, because of it whole groups and organisations have fallen to pieces. It can even be said that all Russian socialists have temporarily been split into two camps supporting diametrically opposite views on "politics". Extremes were unavoidable in this matter, as always in such cases. Some considered the political struggle as almost tantamount to betrayal of the people's cause, as a manifestation of bourgeois instincts among our revolutionary intelligentsia and a defilement of socialist programme purity. Others not only recognised that struggle as necessary, they were even ready, for the sake of its imaginary interests, to compromise with the liberally-minded oppositional elements of our society. Some even went to the extent of considering any manifestation of class antagonism in Russia as harmful for the present. Such views were held, for instance, by Zhelyahov, who, as his biographer says, "imagined the Russian revolution not exclusively as the emancipation of the peasant or even (?) the workers' estate, but as the political regeneration of the whole Russian people generally". [1] In other words, the revolutionary movement against the absolute monarchy merged in his imagination with the working class's social-revolutionary movement for its economic emancipation; the particular, specially Russian task of the present hid from view the general task of the working class in all civilised countries. The difference could not go any farther, a break became inevitable.

Time, however, smoothed out extremes and resolved a considerable number of the disputed questions to the satisfaction of both sides. Little by little all or nearly all recognised that the political struggle which had been taken up must he pursued until a broad emancipation movement in the people and society destroyed the edifice of absolutism as an earthquake destroys a poultry-house, if Marx's forceful expression can be used here. But to very many of our socialists this struggle still appears as some kind of forced compromise, some temporary triumph of "practice" over "theory", a mockery by life of the impotence of thought. Even the politicians, in justifying themselves against the reproaches showered on them, avoided all appeal to the basic propositions of socialism, and referred only to the incontestible demands of reality. At the bottom of their hearts they themselves apparently also believed that political tendencies were by no means suited to them, but they consoled themselves with the consideration that only in a free state could they let the dead bury the dead and, renouncing all political considerations, devote themselves wholly to the cause of socialism. This vague conviction sometimes led to misunderstandings that were not without their curious side. Analysing the speech of "the Russian guest" at the Chur Congress and attempting to justify itself against the allegation that it dabbled in politics, *Narodnaya Volya* noted, among other things, that its supporters were neither socialists nor political radicals, but simply, Narodovoltsi. The terrorist organ presumed that "in the West" the attention of the radicals was absorbed exclusively by political questions while the socialists would not have anything to do with politics. Anybody who knows the programmers of the West European socialists understands, of course, how erroneous such an idea is as far as the enormous majority of them are concerned. It is well known that Social-Democracy in Europe and America never maintained the principle of political "abstention". Its supporters do not ignore "politics". Only they do not consider the task of the socialist revolution to be "the regeneration of the whole people generally". They try to organise the workers into a separate party in order in order thus to segregate the exploited from the exploiters and give political expression to the economic antagonism. Where in our country did they get the certitude that socialism calls for political indifference—a certitude which is in glaring contradiction with reality? Schiller's Wallenstein tells Max Piccolomini that human reason is broad, whereas the world is narrow, so that thoughts can live at ease together in the former while there are harsh clashes between things in the latter. Must we say that in our brain, on the contrary, concepts of things which in practice not only get on very well together, but are utterly unthinkable without their mutual connection, cannot live side by side? To answer that question we must first of all make clear the conceptions of socialism which our revolutionaries had during the epoch when political tendencies arose among them. Once convinced that these conceptions were erroneous or backward we shall consider what place is given to the political struggle by the doctrine which even its bourgeois opponents do not refuse to call scientific socialism. All that we shall have to do then will be to make in our general conclusions the corrections which are inevitable when we consider the various peculiarities of the contemporary state of affairs in Russia—and our subject will be exhausted; the political struggle of the working class against its enemies belonging to one historical formation or another will finally reveal to us its connection with the general tasks of socialism.

I

Socialist propaganda has enormously influenced the whole course of intellectual development in the civilised countries. There is hardly a single branch of sociology that has not felt its impact in one sense or another. It has in part destroyed old scientific prejudices and in part transformed them from a naive delusion into a sophism. It is understandable that the influence of socialist propaganda must have affected the supporters of the new teaching still more powerfully. All the traditions of previous "political" revolutionaries have been ruthlessly criticised, all methods of social activity have been analysed from the standpoint of the "new Gospel". But as the scientific substantiation of socialism was complete only with the appearance of *Capital,* it is easy to understand that the results of this criticism have by no means always been satisfactory. And as, on the other hand, there were several schools in utopian socialism which had almost equal influence, little by little a kind of medium socialism, as it were, has been worked out, and this has been adhered to by people who did not claim to found a new school and were not among the particularly zealous supporters of previously existing schools. This eclectic socialism, as Frederick Engels says, is "a mish-mash of such critical statements, economic theories, pictures of future society by the founders of different sects, as excite a minimum of opposition; a mish-mash which is the more easily brewed the more the definite sharp edges of the individual constituents are rubbed down in the stream of debate, like rounded pebbles in a brook".[2] This medium socialism, the same author notes, still reigns in the heads of most of the worker socialists in England and in France.[3] We Russians could add that exactly the same mish-mash reigned in the first half of the seventies in the minds of our socialists and represented the general background against which two extreme trends stood out: the so-called Vperyod group and the Bakuninists. The former showed a tendency towards German Social-Democracy, the latter were a Russian version of the anarchist faction of the International. Differing very greatly from each other in almost all respects, the two trends were at one—strange as that is—in their negative attitude to "politics". And it must be confessed that the anarchists were more consistent in this respect than the Russian Social-Democrats of the time.

From the anarchist point of view the political question is the touchstone of any working-class programme. The anarchists not only deny any deal with the modern state, they go so far as to exclude from their notions of "future society" anything that recalls the idea of state in one way or another. "Autonomy of the individual in an autonomous community"—such has been the motto of all consistent supporters of this trend. We know that its founder—Proudhon—in his publication La Voix du peuple set himself the not quite modest task "to do as regards the government" (which he confused with the state) "what Kant did as regards religion"[4] and carried his anti-state zeal so far as to declare that Aristotle himself was "a sceptic in matters of state".[5] The accomplishment of the task he had set himself was very simple and followed, if you like, quite logically from the economic doctrines of the French Kant. Proudhon was never able to imagine the economic system of the future otherwise than in the form of commodity production, corrected and supplemented by a new, "just" form of exchange on the basis of "constituted value". For all its "justice", this new form of exchange does not, of course, preclude the purchase, sale or promissory notes which go with commodity production and circulation. All these transactions naturally presuppose various contracts and it is these that determine the mutual relations between the transacting sides. But in modern society "contracts" are based on common legal standards compulsory for all citizens and safeguarded by the state. In the "future society" everything would supposedly proceed somewhat differently. Revolution, according to Proudhon, was to abolish "laws", leaving only "contracts". "There is no need for laws voted by a majority or unanimously," he says in his Idée générale de la Révolution au XIX siècle, "every citizen, every commune and corporation will establish their own particular laws" (p. 259). With such a view of the matter, the political programme of the proletariat was simplified to the extreme. The state, which recognises only general laws compulsory for all citizens, could not even be a means for attaining socialist ideals. Making use of it for their aims, the socialists only consolidate the evil by the rooting out of which "social liquidation" should begin. The state must "decline", thus affording "every citizen, every commune and corporation" full freedom to decree "their own particular laws" and to conclude the "contracts" which they require. And if the anarchists do not waste time during the period preceding the "liquidation", these "contracts" will be concluded in the spirit of the *System of Economic Contradictions* and the triumph of the *Revolution* will be assured.

The task of the Russian anarchists was simplified still more. "The destruction of the state" (which little by little replaced in the anarchist programme its "decline" recommended by Proudhon) was to clear the way for the development of the "ideals" of the Russian people. And as communal land tenure and organisation of crafts into artels occupy a very prominent place in these "ideals", it was presumed that the "autonomous" Russians of democratic origin would conclude their "contracts" not in the spirit of Proudhon's reciprocity but rather of agrarian communism. As a "born socialist", the Russian people would not be long in understanding that mere communal land tenure and communal ownership of the instruments of production do not guarantee the desired "equality" and would be forced to set about organising "autonomous communes" on completely communist foundations.

The Russian anarchists, however—at least those of the so-called rebel shade—bothered little about the economic consequences of the popular revolution they preached. They considered it their duty to remove those social conditions which, in their opinion, hindered the normal development of national life; but they did not ask themselves which road that development would take once it was freed from external hindrances. That this peculiar refashioning of the famous motto of the Manchester School, laissez faire, laissez passer, to make it look revolutionary, precluded all possibility of seriously appraising the contemporary condition of our social and economic life and did away with every criterion for determining even the concept of the "normal" course of its development—this did not occur either to "rebels" or to the "Narodniks" who appeared later.

At the same time it would be utterly hopeless to attempt such an appraisal as long as Proudhon's teachings remained the point of departure of our revolutionaries' considerations. The weakest point of those teachings, the point in which they offend logic, is the concept of commodity and of exchange value, *i.e.*, those very premises on which alone the correct conclusions about the mutual relations of the producers in the future economic organisation can be based. From the standpoint of Proudhon's theories no special importance attaches to the circumstance that contemporary Russian communal land tenure by no means precludes commodity production. The Proudhonist has no inkling of the "inner, inevitable dialectics", which transforms commodity production at a definite stage of its development into .. capitalist production.[6] And that is why it did not occur to his Russian cousin to ask himself whether the divided efforts of "autonomous" persons, communes and corporations would suffice for the struggle against this tendency of commodity production which threatens one fine day to supply a certain proportion of the "born" Communists with "honourably acquired" capitals and to turn them into exploiters of the remaining masses of the population. The anarchist denies the creative role of the state in the socialist revolution for the very reason that he does not understand the tasks and the conditions of that revolution.

We cannot enter here into a detailed analysis of anarchism in general or of Bakuninism in particular.[7] We wish merely to point out to readers that both Proudhon and the Russian anarchists were completely right from their point of view when they raised "political non-interference" to the position of main dogma in their practical programme. The social and political composition of Russian life in particular, it seemed, justified the negation of "politics" which is compulsory for all anarchists. Before entering the field of political agitation the *"inhabitant"* of Russia has to become a *citizen, i.e.*, to win for himself at least some political rights, and first of all, of course, the right to think as he pleases and to say what he thinks. Such a task amounts in practice to a "political revolution", and the experience of Western Europe has clearly "shown" all anarchists that such revolutions have not brought, do not and cannot bring any benefit to the people. As for the consideration that the people must be educated politically by taking part in their country's public life, that could not be put into practice, if only for the reason that the anarchists consider, as we have already seen, that such participation is not education, but perversion of the popular masses: it develops in them "belief in the state" and therefore the tendency to statehood, or as the late M. A. Bakunin would have said, "infects them with its official and social venom, and, in any case, distracts them at least for a short time from what is now the only useful and salutary matter—from revolt."[8] And at the same time, according to the philosophy of history of our "rebels", it appeared that the Russian people had shown its anti-state tendency by a whole series of large and small movements and could therefore be considered mature enough politically. So down with all "dabbling in politics"! Let us help the people in its anti-state struggle. Let us unite its dispersed efforts in one revolutionary stream—and then the awkward edifice of the state will crash, opening by its fall a new era of social freedom and economic equality! These few words expressed the whole programme of our "rebels".

In this sketchy review of the programmes of the different groups of Russian revolutionaries we must not forget that the views according to which "all constitutions" were only more or less unprofitable contracts with the devil, as old F. H. Jacobi put it—such views, we say, were typical not only of the Narodniks and anarchists. If the reader knows about Frederick Engels' polemic with P. Titachov,[9] he will probably remember that the editor of *Nabat,* a who disagreed with the Bakuninists on the question of practical struggle, was in perfect agreement with them on their basic views about the social and political condition of our country. He looked at it through the same prism of Russian exceptionalism and the "inborn communist tendencies of the Russian people".[10] Like a genuine Blanquist he did not deny "politics", of course, but he understood it exclusively as a plot whose purpose is to seize state power. This purpose, it seems, occupied the whole field of vision of our Blanquists of that time and led them to many contradictions. To remain consistent they had to admit that their activity could be useful to the cause of progress only in the exceptional case that the blow they dealt would not deviate a hair's breadth from its target. If their planned seizure of power is a failure, if their plot is discovered or the revolutionary government is overthrown by the liberal party, the Russian people, far from winning anything, will risk losing much. The last of the supposed cases is particularly disastrous. The liberals will establish a strong government which will be far more difficult to fight than modern "absolutely absurd" and "absurdly absolute" monarchy, while "the fire of economic progress" will destroy the radical bases of the people's life. Under its influence exchange will develop, capitalism will consolidate itself, the very principle of the village commune will be destroyed—in a word, the river of time will wash away the stone from which the communist heaven is within hand's reach. In cases of failure the Russian Blanquists would be bound to do terrible damage to the cause of popular emancipation and thus fall into the tragic position of William Tell, who had to risk the life of his own son. And as they have hardly distinguished themselves by the skill of the mythic Swiss "seditionary", the Russian people would not shout to them:

> Shoot! I fear not!
>
> if it adopted their view on the "radical bases" of its life and had been invited to give its opinion about their programme.

Such a narrow and hopeless philosophy of Russian history was bound to lead logically to the amazing conclusion that Russia's economic backwardness was a most reliable ally of the revolution and that stagnation was to be blazoned as the first and only paragraph of our "minimum programme". "Every day brings us new enemies, creates new social factors hostile to us," we read in the first, November, issue of *Nabat* for 1875. "Fire is creeping up to our state forms, too. Now these are dead, lifeless. Economic progress will stir life in them, will breathe into them a new spirit, will give them the strength and the fortitude which they have so far lacked", and so forth. But if Joshua succeeded as the Bible relates, in stopping the sun "for ten degrees", the time of miracles has passed and there is not a single party which could shout: "Stop, productive forces!

Do not move, capitalism! " History pays as little attention to the fears of revolutionaries as to the jeremiads of reaction. "Economic progress" does its work without waiting for the anarchists or the Blanquists to put their intentions into practice. Every factory founded in Petersburg, every new wage-worker employed by a Yaroslavl handicraftsman strengthens the "flame of progress", which is supposed to be fatal to the revolution, and consequently decreases the probability of popular victory. Can such a view of the mutual relations of the various social forces in Russia be called revolutionary? We do not think so. In order to make themselves revolutionary in substance and not in name alone, the Russian anarchists, Narodniks and Blanquists should first of all have revolutionised their own heads, and to do so they should have learned to understand the course of historical development and been able to lead it instead of asking old mother history to mark time while they laid new, straighter and better beaten roads for her. The Vperyod group understood the immaturity and erroneousness of the outlooks just expounded, and there was a time when it could have obtained dominating intellectual influence among our revolutionaries. That was the time when practical experience had shaken the foundations of the old anarchist Narodism and all its supporters felt that their programme needed to be seriously reconsidered. Then a consistent criticism of all its theoretical and practical principles could have made the impending turn in the movement still more decisive and irrevocable. The Vperyod group could most conveniently have undertaken that criticism; maintaining almost entirely the standpoint of the Social-Democrats, they were completely free from all Narodnik traditions. But in order to be successful, their criticism *should not have condemned, but elucidated and generalised* the vital requirements of Russian life which were more and more driving our revolutionaries on to the road of political struggle. And yet the *Vperyod* group rejected "politics" just as resolutely as the anarchists. I admit that they did not think socialism to be incompatible with interference in the political life of the bourgeois state, and they fully approved of the programme of West European Social-Democracy. But they presumed that in the modern state "founded on law" the possibility of openly organising the working class into a political party of its own is bought at too high a price—by the final victory of the bourgeoisie and the deterioration of the workers' condition corresponding to the epoch of capitalism. They forgot that in appraising this situation one must take into account not only the distribution of the national income, but also *the whole organisation of production and exchange;* not only the *average quantity* of products consumed by the workers, but also the *form* which those products take[11] ; not only the *degree* of exploitation, but also, in particular, *its form;* not only *the fact of the enslavement* of the working masses, but also the *ideas and concepts* which emerge or may emerge in the head of the worker under the influence of this fact.[12] They would hardly have agreed that the factory worker was bound to be more receptive to socialism than the temporarily bound peasant; still less would they have admitted that the transition, for instance, from natural economy to money economy increases the possibility of a conscious movement of the working masses for their own economic emancipation. The philosophical and historical parts of Marx's teaching remained for them an unread chapter in their favourite book; they believed too much in the omnipotent influence of their propaganda to seek support for it in the objective conditions of social life. And like the socialists of the utopian period, they held that the whole future of their country, including the social revolution, could be achieved by that propaganda. Posing the question in this way, they could have said with the anarchists, parodying Proudhon's well-known saying: la révolution est au-dessus de la politique. But that was just the reason why they could not get our movement out of the state of inertia it had got into at the end of the seventies owing to the rejection of all political struggle, on the one hand, and the impossibility, on the other, of creating a working-class party of any strength under contemporary political conditions.

The honour of giving new scope to our movement belongs beyond dispute to Narodnaya Volya. Everybody still recalls the attacks that the Narodnaya Volya trend drew upon itself. The writer of these lines himself belonged to the resolute opponents of this trend, and although he perfectly admits now that the struggle for political freedom has become a burning issue for modern Russia, he is still far from sharing all the views expressed in Narodnaya Volya publications. That does not prevent him, however, from acknowledging that in the disputes which took place in the Zemlya i Volya organisation about the time of its split, the Narodnaya Volya members were perfectly right as long as they did not go beyond our practical experience. That experience was already then leading to amazing and completely unexpected conclusions, although we did not dare to draw them precisely because of their unexpectedness. Attempts at the practical struggle "against the state" should already then have led fundamentally to the thought that the Russian "rebel" was compelled by the insuperable force of circumstances to direct his agitation not against the state generally, but only against the *absolute* state, to fight not the idea of state, but the idea of bureaucracy, not for the full economic emancipation of the people, but for the removal of the burdens imposed on the people by the tsarist autocracy. Of course, the agrarian question lay at the root of all or nearly all manifestations of popular dissatisfaction. It could not be otherwise among an agricultural population, where the "power of the land" is felt in absolutely the whole make-up and needs of private and social life. This agrarian question kept crying out for a solution, but it did not rouse *political* discontent. The peasants waited calm and confident for this question to be solved from above: they "rebelled" not for a redistribution of the land, but against oppression by the administration, against the excessive burdens of the taxation system, against the Asiatic way in which arrears were collected, and so on and so forth. The formula which applied to a large number of the cases of active protest was the "legal state", not "Land and Freedom" (Zemlya i Volya) as it seemed to everybody at the time. But if that was so, and if revolutionaries considered themselves obliged to take part in the scattered and ill-considered struggle of isolated communes against the absolute monarchy, was it not time they understood the meaning of their own efforts and directed them with greater purposefulness? Was it not time for them to call all the progressive virile forces of Russia to the struggle and, having found a more general expression for it, to attack absolutism in the very centre of its organisation? In answering these questions in the affirmative, the members of Narodnaya Volya were only summing up the revolutionary experience of previous years; in raising the banner of political struggle, they only showed that they were not afraid of the conclusions and consciously continued to follow the road which we had taken although we had an erroneous idea of where it led to. "Terrorism" grew quite logically out of our "rebelliousness".

But with the appearance of Narodnaya Volya, the logical development of our revolutionary movement was already entering a phase in which it could no longer be satisfied with the Narodnik theories of the good old time, *i.e.*, a time innocent of political interests. Examples of theory being outgrown by practice are not rare in the history of human thought in general and of revolutionary thought in particular. When revolutionaries introduce some change or other into their tactics or recast their programme one way or another, often they do not even suspect what a serious test they are giving the teachings generally acknowledged among them. Many of them indeed perish in prison or on the gallows, fully confident that they have worked in the spirit of those teachings, whereas in substance they represent new tendencies which took root in the old theories but have already outgrown them and are ready to find new theories to express them. So it has been with us since the Narodnaya Volya trend consolidated. From the standpoint of the old Narodnik theories, this trend could not stand criticism. Narodism had a sharply negative attitude to any idea of the state; Narodnaya Volya counted on putting its social-reform plans into practice with the help of the state machine. Narodism refused to have anything to do with "politics"; Narodnaya Volya saw in "democratic political revolution" the most reliable "means of social reform". Narodism based its programme on the so-called "ideals" and demands of the peasant population; Narodnaya Volya had to address itself mainly to the urban and industrial population, and consequently to give an incomparably larger place in its programme to the interests of that population. Briefly, in reality, the Narodnaya Volya trend was the complete and all-round denial of Narodism, and as long as the disputing parties appealed to the fundamental propositions of the latter, the "innovators" were completely in the wrong: their practical work was in irreconcilable contradiction with their theoretical views. It was necessary completely to reconsider these views, so as to give Narodnaya Volya's programme singleness of purpose and consistency; the practical revolutionary activity of its supporters had to be at least *accompanied* by a theoretical revolution in the minds of our socialists; in blowing up the Winter Palace we had at the same time to blow up our old anarchic and Narodnik traditions. But here, too, the "course of ideas" lagged behind the "course of things" and it is still difficult to foresee when it will catch up at last. Unable to make up their minds to break with Narodism, the new group was obliged to have recourse to fictions which brought with them at least a semblance of a solution of the contradictions inherent in their programme. The idea of Russian exceptionalism received a new elaboration, and whereas previously it had led to the complete rejection of politics, it now turned out that the exceptionalism of Russian social development consisted precisely in economic questions being and having to be solved in our country by means of state interference. The extremely widespread ignorance here in Russia of the economic history of the West provided the reason why nobody was amazed at "theories" of this kind. The period of capitalist accumulation in Russia was contrasted with the period of capitalist production in the West, and the inevitable dissimilarity between these two phases of economic development was cited as a most convincing proof of, first, our exceptionalism and, second, the appropriateness of the "Narodnaya Volya programme" determined by that exceptionalism.

Need it be added that our revolutionary writers, like the majority of Russian writers generally, considered the "West" from the standpoint of the Jewish boy in Weinberg's well-known story. To this poor schoolboy the whole world seemed as though it were divided into two equal parts: "Russia and abroad", notable points of distinction existing for him only between these two "halves" of the globe, but "abroad" seemed to him a completely homogeneous whole. Russian writers, propagandists of "exceptionalism", introduced only one new thing into that clever geographical classification: they divided "abroad" into East and West, and, not stopping long to think, began to compare the latter with our "glorious state", which was ascribed the role of a kind of "Middle Empire". The historical development of Italy was thus identified with that of France and no distinction was seen between England's economic policy and Prussia's; Colbert's activity was lumped together with Richard Cobden's and the peculiarly "patriotic" physiognomy of Friedrich List was lost in the crowd of "West European" political economists who followed Turgot's advice and tried "to forget that in the world there are states separated by frontiers and organised in different ways". Just as all cats appear grey and resemble one another perfectly in the dark, so the social relations of the various states in the "West" lost all distinction in the reflected light of our exceptionalism. One thing was evident: the "Franks" had already "gone bourgeois" long ago, whereas the "brave Russians" had preserved the "primitive" innocence and were advancing to their salvation as a chosen people along the road of exceptionalism. To reach the promised land they only had to keep unswervingly to that path of exceptionalism and not be surprised that the Russian socialists' programmes contradicted the scientific principles of West European socialism and sometimes their own premises!

A typical sample of the fictions quickly thought out to conform Narodnaya Volya's practical programme with Narodnik theories was the famous prophecy that if only we managed to achieve universal suffrage, 90 per cent of the deputies in the future Russian Constituent Assembly would be supporters of the social revolution. Here the theory of our exceptionalism reached the limit beyond which it was threatened with ruin by plain common sense. The Narodniks of the "old faith" firmly held to their dogma of exceptionalism but all the same admitted that this exceptionalism still needed some finishing touches. Some found that the Russian people still had a too embryonic bump...sorry!—feeling of bravery and independence; others strove to put the exceptionalist sentiment of the Russian people into practice in the form of a no less original revolutionary organisation. But they all equally acknowledged the necessity for preliminary work among the people. Narodnaya Volya went further. In the leading articles of the very first issues of its journal it began to develop the thought that such work is, first, fruitless ("wasting our energy beating about the people like a fish on the ice") and, secondly, superfluous, because 90 per cent of the deputies sympathising with the social revolution are more than enough to carry out the aspirations of the Russian Narodniks. Narodnaya Volya's programme could not have given itself a Narodnik character otherwise than by carrying to absurd extremes all the typical features of the Narodnik world outlook.

This is what constitutes the negative service of the fictions of Narodnaya Volya. They aroused the critical thought of the Russian revolutionaries by presenting to them in an exaggerated form the "exceptional" features of their Narodnik programme. But one can hardly say anything about the positive service of these fictions. They temporarily strengthened the energy of the fighters, who needed a theoretical foundation for their practical work, but, being strung hastily together, they did not stand the slightest impact of serious criticism, and by their fall they compromised the cause of the struggle waged under their banner. Having dealt the death-blow to all the traditions of orthodox Narodism by its practical activity and having done so much for the development of the revolutionary movement in Russia, Narodnaya Volya cannot find a justification for itself—nor should it seek one—outside modern scientific socialism. But to adopt this new standpoint it must make a thorough review of its programme, for the theoretical errors and gaps in that programme could not but give it a definite one-sidedness in practice.

Before saying in which sense this review must be undertaken, let us endeavour, according to our plan, to elucidate scientific socialism s attitude to the political movements of the working class.

II

But what is scientific socialism? Under that name we understand the communist teaching which began to take shape at the beginning of the forties out of utopian socialism under the strong influence of Hegelian philosophy on the one side, and of classical economics on the other; the teaching which first really explained the whole course of human cultural development, pitilessly shattered the bourgeois theoreticians' sophisms and, "armed with all the knowledge of its age", came out in defence of the proletariat. This teaching not only showed with complete clarity how unsound scientifically are the opponents of socialism, but pointing out the errors, it at the same time explained them historically and thus, as Haym once said of Hegel's philosophy, "tied to its triumphal chariot every opinion it had defeated". As Darwin enriched biology with his amazingly simple and yet strictly scientific theory of the origin of species, so also the founders of scientific socialism showed us in the development of the productive forces and their struggle against backward "social conditions of production" the great principle of the variation of *species of social organisation.* We hardly need to say whom we consider as the founders of this socialism. This merit belongs indisputably to Karl Marx and Frederick Engels, whose doctrine stands in exactly the same relation to the modern revolutionary movement in civilised humanity as, in the words of one of them, advanced German philosophy stood in its time to the emancipation movement in Germany; it is its *head,* and the proletariat is its *heart.* But it goes without saying that the development of scientific socialism is not complete and can no more stop at the works of Engels and Marx than the theory of the origin of species could be considered as finally elaborated with the publication of the principal works of the English biologist. The establishment of the basic propositions of the new teaching must be followed by the detailed elaboration of questions pertaining to it, an elaboration which will supplement and complete the revolution carried out in science by the authors of the *Manifesto of the Communist Party.* [13] There is not a single branch of sociology which would not acquire a new and extraordinarily vast field of vision by adopting their philosophical and historical views. The beneficial influence of those views is already beginning to be felt in the fields of history, law and so-called primitive culture. But this philosophical and historical aspect of modern socialism is still too little known in Russia, and therefore we do not consider it superfluous to quote a few excerpts here, in order to acquaint our readers with it in Marx's own words.

Incidentally, although scientific socialism traces its genealogy "from Kant and Hegel", it is nevertheless the most deadly and resolute opponent of idealism. It drives it out of its last refuge—sociology—in which it was received with such delight by the positivists. Scientific socialism presupposes the "materialist conception of history", *i.e.*, it explains the spiritual history of humanity by the development of social relations (among other things under the influence of surrounding nature). From this point of view, as also from that of Vico, "the course of ideas corresponds to the course of things", and not inversely. The principal cause of this or that make-up of social relations, this or that direction in their development, is the condition of the productive forces and the economic structure of society corresponding to them. "In the social production of their life," says Marx, [14] "men enter into definite relations that are indispensable and independent of their will, relations of production which correspond to a definite stage of development Of their material productive forces. The sum-total of these relations of production constitutes the economic structure of society, the real foundation on which rises a legal and political super-structure and to which correspond definite forms of social consciousness. The mode of production of material life conditions the social, political and intellectual life process in general. It is not the consciousness of men that determines their being, but, on the contrary, their social being that determines their consciousness... Legal relations as well as forms of state are to be grasped neither from themselves nor from the so-called general development of the human mind, but rather have their roots in the material conditions of life, the sum-total of which Hegel, following the example of the Englishmen and Frenchmen of the eighteenth century, combines under the name of 'civil society', that, however, the anatomy of civil society is to be sought in political economy...At a certain stage of their development, the material productive forces of society come in conflict with the existing relations of production, or—what is but a legal expression for the same thing—with the property relations within which they have been at work hitherto. From forms of development of the productive forces these relations turn into their fetters. Then begins an epoch of social revolution. With the change of the economic foundation the entire immense superstructure is more or less rapidly transformed...No social order ever perishes before all the productive forces for which there is room in it have developed; and new, higher relations of production never appear before the material conditions of their existence have matured in the womb of the old society itself.

> "Therefore mankind always sets itself only such tasks as it can solve; since, looking at the matter more closely, it will always be found that the task itself arises only when the material conditions for its solution already exist or are at least in the process of formation."

It is now understandable why Marx and Engels reacted with such scornful derision to the "true socialists" in Germany at the end of the forties, who adopted a negative attitude to the German bourgeoisie's struggle against absolutism, "preaching to the masses that they had nothing to gain, and everything to lose, by this bourgeois movement". The historical teaching of Marx and Engels is the genuine "algebra of the revolution", as Herzen once called Hegel's philosophy. That is why Marx and Engels sympathised with "every revolutionary movement against the existing social and political order of things"; and for the same reason they warmly sympathised with the Russian movement, which made Russia, as they said, the vanguard of the revolution in Europe. But despite all their clarity and unambiguousness, Marx's views gave occasion for many misunderstandings in the field of revolutionary theory and practice. Thus, it is often said in our country that the theories of scientific socialism, are inapplicable to Russia because they have their root in West European economic relations. To Marx's teaching is attributed the absurd conclusion that Russia must go through exactly the same phases of historical and economic development as the West. Influenced by the conviction that this conclusion is inevitable, more than one Russian philosopher, familiar neither with Marx nor with the history of Western Europe, entered the lists against the author of *Capital* and accused him of narrow and stereotyped views. This, of course, was tilting at windmills. Our Don Quixotes did not understand that the history of West European relations was used by Marx only as the basis of the *history of capitalist production,* which emerged and developed precisely in that part of the world. Marx's general philosophical and historical views stand in exactly the same relation to modern Western Europe as to Greece and Rome, India and Egypt. They embrace the entire cultural history of humanity and can be inapplicable to Russia only if they are generally untenable. It goes without saying that neither the author of *Capital* nor his famous friend and colleague lost sight of the economic peculiarities of any particular country; only in those peculiarities do they seek the explanation of all a country's social, political and intellectual movements. That they do not ignore the significance of our village commune is revealed by the fact that as recently as January 1882 they did not consider it possible to make any decisive forecast concerning its destiny. In the preface to our translation of the *Manifesto of the Communist Party* (Geneva, 1882) they even say explicitly that under certain conditions the Russian village commune may "pass directly to the higher form of communist common ownership". These circumstances are, in their opinion, closely connected with the course of the revolutionary movement in the west of Europe and in Russia. "If the Russian revolution," they say, "becomes the signal for a proletarian revolution in the West, so that both complement each other, the present Russian common ownership of land may serve as the starting-point for a communist development." *(Manifesto of the Communist Party,* VIII.) It will hardly occur to a single Narodnik to deny that the solution of the village commune question depends on such a condition. Hardly anybody will assert that the oppression by the modern state is favourable to the development or even to the mere maintenance of the commune. And in exactly the same way hardly anyone who understands the significance of international relations in the economic life of modern civilised societies can deny that the development of the Russian village commune "into a higher form of communist common ownership" is closely linked with the destiny of the working-class movement in the West. It thus turns out that nothing in Marx's views on Russia contradicts the most obvious reality, and the absurd prejudices concerning his extreme "Occidentalism" have not the slightest trace of reasonable foundation.

But there is another misunderstanding which directly concerns a question interesting us—the significance of political struggle in the reorganisation of social relations—and takes root in an erroneous understanding of Marx s view of the role of the economic factor in the human cultural development. This view has often been interpreted by many in the sense that the author of *Capital* attributes only the slightest importance to the political structure of society, considering it as a secondary detail not worth attention and which, far from being the aim, cannot even be a means of fruitful activity. Even now, one not infrequently meets "Marxists" who ignore the political tasks of socialism on these very grounds. Economic relations, they say, are the basis of all social organisation. Changes in these relations are the cause of all political reorganisation. In order to free itself from capitalist oppression, the working class must bear in mind not the effect, but the cause, not the political, but the economic organisation of society. Political organisation will not bring the workers nearer to their goal, since political enslavement will continue as long as their economic dependence on the propertied classes is not removed. The *means* of struggle which the workers use must be brought into line with the *aim* of the struggle. An economic revolution can be achieved only by struggle on economic ground.

With a certain amount of consistency, "Marxism" understood in that way should have changed the socialists' views of the aims and the means of the social revolution and brought them back to Proudhon's famous formula: "political revolution is the aim, economic revolution, the means". In exactly the same way it should have brought the socialist-revolutionaries considerably nearer—at least in theory—to the followers of "conservative socialism" which so resolutely opposes independent political action on the part of the working class. Rodbertus, the last honest and intelligent representative of this socialism, was unable to agree with Lassalle precisely because that celebrated agitator endeavoured to advance the German workers along the path of independent political activity. Not Marx, but Rodbertus, not *revolutionary,* but *conservative, monarchist* socialism denies the significance of "political admixtures to the economic aims" of the working class. And the conservatives know full well why they do so; but those who wish to conciliate the revolutionary movement of the working class with the rejection of "politics", those who attribute to Marx the practical tendencies of Proudhon or even of Rodbertus, show clearly that they do not understand the author of *Capital* or that they deliberately distort his teaching. We speak of deliberate distortion because a certain book by the Moscow Professor Ivanyukov is nothing but such a deliberate distortion of the consequences following from the basic propositions of scientific socialism. This book shows that our Russian *police* socialists are not averse to exploiting for their reactionary aims even a theory under whose banner the most revolutionary movement of our age is proceeding. This alone could make a detailed elucidation of modern socialism's *political* programme indispensable. We will now begin that elucidation, without, however, entering into a controversy with Messrs. Ivanyukov, for it is sufficient to bring out the true sense of a given theory in order to refute deliberate distortions of it. And besides, we are far more interested here in those revolutionaries who, for all the sincerity of their aspirations, are still permeated, although perhaps unconsciously, with anarchist teachings and are therefore prepared to see in Marx's works thoughts which are in place only in *The General Idea of the Revolution in the Nineteenth Century.* The criticism of the conclusions they draw from Marx's philosophical and historical views will logically take us on to the question of the so-called *seizure of power* and will show us how far they are right who see in that act a crime against the idea of human liberty, and also those who, on the contrary, see it as the Alpha and the Omega of the whole social-revolutionary movement.

Let us first consider what the concepts of cause and effect signify when applied to social relations.

If we push a billiard ball with the hand or a cue, it is set in motion; if we strike steel against a flint, a spark appears. In each of these cases it is very easy to determine which phenomenon acts as the cause and which is the effect. But the task is easy only because it is extremely simple. If instead of two isolated phenomena we take a process in which several phenomena or even several series of phenomena are observed simultaneously, the matter is more complicated. Thus, the burning of a candle is, relatively speaking, a fairly complicated process as a result of which light and heat are produced. Hence it would seem that we run no risk of error if we call the heat given off by the flame one of the effects of this chemical process. That is, indeed, the case to a certain extent. But if we contrived in some way to deprive the flame of the heat which it gives off, the combustion would immediately cease, for the process we are considering cannot take place at the ordinary temperature. Therefore, it would also be right to a certain extent to say that heat is the cause of combustion. In order not to deviate from the truth in one direction or the other we should say that heat, while it is the *effect* of combustion at a particular moment, is its cause the moment following. This means that when we speak Of a combustion process lasting a certain time we must say that heat is *both* its *effect* and its *cause,* or, in other words, *neither effect nor cause*, but simply one of the phenomena arising from that process and constituting, in turn, a necessary condition for it. Let us take another example. Everybody, "even if he has not been trained in a seminary", knows that what are called the vegetative processes of the human organism exert great influence on psychic phenomena. One mental disposition or other proves to be the effect of a particular physical condition of the organism. But once a certain mental disposition exists, the same vegetative processes are often influenced by it, and it thus becomes the cause of the particular changes in the physical condition of the organism. In order not to go wrong here in one direction or the other, we should say that the psychic phenomena and the vegetative life of the organism constitute two series of coexisting processes, each of which is influenced by the other. If a doctor were to ignore psychic influences on the grounds that man's mental disposition is the effect of the physical condition of his organism, we would infer that schoolboy logic had made him unfit for rational medical practice.

Social life is distinguished by still greater intricacy than the life of the individual organism. That is why the relativity of the concepts of cause and effect is more noticeable here. According to the teaching of classical economics, the size of wages is determined, on the average, by the level of the worker's primary requirements. This means that a given size of wages is the *effect* of a given condition of the worker's requirements. But these requirements, in turn, can grow only if there is a rise in wages, because otherwise there would not be sufficient cause to change their level. Consequently, a given size of wages is the *cause* of a given condition of the worker's requirements. One cannot get out of this logical circle by means of the schoolboy categories of cause and effect. We shall fall into it at every step in our sociological considerations if we forget that "cause and effect are conceptions which only hold good in their application to individual cases; but as soon as we consider the individual cases in their general connection with the universe as a whole, they run into each other, and they become confounded when we contemplate that universal action and reaction in which causes and effects are eternally changing places, so that what is effect here and now will be cause there and then, and vice versa". (Frederick Engels.)[15]

Having made this reservation, let us endeavour to determine in what sense the causal connection between the economic relations and the political structure of a given society must be understood.

What does history teach us in this respect? It shows that whenever and wherever the process of economic development gave rise to a splitting of society into classes, the contradictions between the interests of those classes invariably led them to struggle for political domination. This struggle arose not only between the various strata of the dominating classes, but also between those classes, on the one hand, and the people, on the other, provided the latter was given conditions at all favourable to intellectual development. In the states of the ancient Orient we see the struggle between the soldiers and the priests; all the drama in the history of the ancient world is in the struggle between the aristocracy and the *demos,* the patricians and the plebeians; the Middle Ages bring forth the burghers, who strive to conquer political mastery within the bounds of their communes; finally, the present-day working class wages a political struggle against the bourgeoisie, which has achieved complete domination in the modern state. Always and everywhere, political power has been the lever by which a class, having achieved domination, has carried out the social upheaval necessary for its welfare and development. So as not to go too far afield, let us consider the history of the "third estate", the class that can look with pride at its past, full of brilliant achievements in all branches of life and thought. It will hardly occur to anybody to reproach the bourgeoisie with lack of tact or ability to attain its aims by the most appropriate means. Nor will anybody deny that its strivings have always had a quite definite economic character. But that did not prevent it from following the path of political struggle and political gains. Now by arms, now by peace treaties, sometimes for the republican independence of its towns, sometimes for the strengthening of royal power, the rising bourgeoisie waged a hard, uninterrupted struggle against feudalism for whole centuries, and long before the French Revolution it could proudly draw its enemies' attention to its successes. "The chances were different and the success varying in the great struggle of the burghers against the feudal lords," the historian says,[16] "and not only was the sum of privileges wrested from them by force or obtained by agreement not the same everywhere, but even when the political forms were the same there were different degrees of liberty and independence for the towns." Nevertheless, the sense of the movement was identical everywhere—it meant the beginning of the social emancipation of the third estate and the decline of the aristocracy, secular and ecclesiastical.[17] In general this movement brought the burghers "municipal independence, the right to elect all the local authorities, the exact fixing of duties", guaranteed the rights of the individual inside the town communes,[18] gave the bourgeoisie a more elevated position in the estate-based states of the "ancien regime", and finally, by a series of continuous gains, brought it to complete domination in modern society. Setting itself social and economic aims which were perfectly defined although they changed with time, and drawing means to continue the struggle from the advantages of the economic position which it had already attained, the bourgeoisie did not miss an opportunity of giving legal expression to the stages in economic progress which it had reached; on the contrary, it made just as skilful a use of each political gain for new conquests in the economic field. No further back than in the middle forties of this century the English Anti-Corn Law League, following Richard Cobden's clever plan, aimed at increasing its *political* influence in the shires in order to secure the abolition of the "monopoly" it hated and which, apparently, was exclusively *economic*.

History is the greatest of dialecticians. If in the course of its progress, reason, as Mephistopheles says, is changed into irrationality and blessings become a plague, not less often in the historical process does an effect become a cause and a cause prove to be an effect. Arising from the economic relations of its time, the political might of the bourgeoisie in its turn served, and still serves, as an indispensable factor for the further development of those relations.

Now that the bourgeoisie is nearing the end of its historical role and that the proletariat is becoming the only representative of progressive strivings in society, we can observe a phenomenon similar to the one referred to above, but taking place in changed conditions. In all the advanced states of the civilised world, in Europe as well as America, the working class is entering the arena of political struggle and the more it is conscious of its economic tasks, the more resolutely it separates into a political party of its own. "As the existing political parties have always acted only in the interests of property-owners for the preservation of their economic privileges," we read in the programme of the North American Socialist Workers' Party, "the working class must organise into a big workers' party to *achieve political power in the state* and gain economic independence; for the emancipation of the working class can be effected only by the workers themselves."[19] The French Workers' Party expresses itself in the same spirit and in complete agreement with the programme of German Social-Democracy, acknowledging that the proletariat must aspire to an economic revolution "by all means in its power, including universal franchise, thus transformed from a weapon of deceit, which it has been up to now, into a *weapon of emancipation*". The Spanish Workers' Party also strives to "conquer political power" in order to remove the obstacles in the way of the emancipation of the working class.[20]

In England, where, with the ending of the chartist movement, the struggle of the proletariat has been concentrated exclusively on the economic field, the political aspirations of the workers have begun to revive of late. Only a few years ago, the German economist Lujo Brentano noted with triumph in his book *Das Arbeitsverhaltniss, etc.* the complete disappearance of the Social-Democratic trends in England, and philosophised profoundly and with true bourgeois self-satisfaction on the subject that "at present England again constitutes a *single* nation", that "the English workers of our time again form part of the great Liberal Party" and do not strive to seize state power in order, by means of it, "to reorganise society in their own interests" (p. 110). The recently published *Manifesto* of the British Democratic Federation shows that the bourgeois economist's joy was somewhat premature. The Democratic Federation aims at causing the exploited to break away politically from the exploiters and calls from the first of these "nations" precisely to seize state power for the purpose of reconstructing society in the interests of the workers. "The time has come," says the *Manifesto,* "when the mass of the people must necessarily take the management of matters which concern it in its own hands; at present, political and social power is the monopoly of people who live by the labour of their fellow-citizens.

The landowners and capitalists who have control of the Upper House and have filled the Lower House aspire only to safeguard their own interests. Take your fate in your own hands, remove the rich parasites of these two groups and rely only on yourselves! " The *Manifesto* demands *"full franchise for all adult men and women"* in the United Kingdom, and other political reforms which "would only show that the men and women of this country have become the masters at home" Then comes a list—representing the immediate demands of the British Democratic Federation—of measures necessary for the development of a "healthy, independent and soundly educated generation, ready to organise the labour of each for the good of all and to *take control, ultimately, Of the entire social and political machine of the state,* in which class differences and privileges will then cease to exist".

Thus, the British proletariat, too, is again entering on the path which the workers of other civilised states entered upon long ago.

But, as the bourgeoisie not only fought the aristocracy on the basis of already existing political relations, but aspired to reshape those relations in its own interests, so also the proletariat does not restrict its political programme to the seizure of the modern state machine. The conviction is more and more spreading among its members that "every order of things which determines the relations of citizens to one another and governs their labour and property relations corresponds to a particular form of government which is at the same time the means of implementing and preserving that order".[21] While the representative (monarchic or republican) system was the progeny of the bourgeoisie, the proletariat demands *direct popular legislation* as the only political form under which its social aspirations can be put into effect. This demand of the working class is among the first in the programme of Social-Democracy in all countries and is very closely related to all the other points in its programme.[22] In spite of Proudhon, the proletariat continues to see in the "political revolution" the most powerful means of achieving an economic revolution.

This testimony of history alone should incline us to think that the political tendencies of the various social classes are based on a correct practical instinct, and not on an erroneous theory. If, despite the complete dissimilarity in all other respects, all classes which wage a conscious struggle against their opponents begin at a definite stage in their development to strive to ensure for themselves political influence and later domination, it is clear that the political structure of society is a far from indifferent condition for their development. If, moreover, we see that not a single class which has achieved political domination has had cause to regret its interest in "politics", but on the contrary, that each one of them attained the highest, the culminating point of its development only after it had acquired political domination, then we must admit that the political struggle is an instrument of social reconstruction whose effectiveness is proved by history. Every teaching which runs counter to this historical induction loses a considerable part of its power of conviction, and if modern socialism were in fact to condemn the political striving of the working class as inexpedient, that would be sufficient reason not to call it scientific.

Let us now check our induction by the deductive method, taking Marx's philosophical and historical views as the premises for our conclusions.

Imagine a society in which a particular class is completely dominant. It secured this domination thanks to the advantages of its economic position which, according to our premises, open before it the path to all other successes in social life. In its capacity as the *ruling* class it naturally reshapes social organisation to provide the most favourable conditions for its own existence and carefully removes from it all that can in any way weaken its influence. "Those in power, the mighty, in every period," Schäffle correctly notes, "are also the ones who create law and morality. They only apply the urge of self-preservation inherent in all when they exploit the consequences of their victory, install themselves as rulers at the top and endeavour to maintain domination hereditary as long as possible, as the means to a privileged situation and the exploitation and subjection of those who are not free...There is hardly another section of positive law for which the dominating estates in every period have such great respect and for which they vindicate so much the character of 'eternal' institutions or even 'sacred' foundations of society as that which has consolidated and safeguards the right of their estate and the domination of their class."[23] And as long as the dominating class is the vehicle of the most progressive social ideals, the system it has set up will satisfy all the demands of social development. But as soon as the economic history of a particular society brings forward new elements of a progressive movement, as soon as the "productive forces of society come in conflict with the existing relations of production, or—what is but a legal expression for the same thing—with the property relations within which they have been at work hitherto", the progressive role of the ruling class in question will be over. From a representative of progress it will become its sworn enemy and, of course, it will make use of the state machine for self-defence. In its hands political power will become the most powerful weapon of reaction. To free the road for the development of the productive forces of society it is necesSary to remove the property relations which hinder that development, *i.e.*, as Marx says, to carry out a social revolution. But that is impossible as long as legislative power is in the hands of the old order, in other words, as long as it safeguards the interests of the ruling class. It is therefore not astonishing that innovators, *i.e.*, representatives of the oppressed class or classes, will strive to wrest this terrible weapon out of the hands of their opponents and turn it against them. The very logic of things will bring them out on to the road of political struggle and seizure of state power, although they set themselves the task of an economic revolution. Lassalle uttered a profound truth when he said in the preface to his *System of Acquired Rights:* "...where juridical right as private right seems to become entirely detached from the political element, *it is far more political than the political element,* for there it is the *social* element".[24]

In practical life, of course, things are far from going as fast as one might suppose, judging *a priori.* Only gradually does the oppressed class become clear about the connection between its economic position and its *political* role in the state. For a long time it does not understand even its economic task to the full. The individuals composing it wage a hard struggle for their daily subsistence without even thinking which aspects of the social organisation they owe their wretched condition to. They try to avoid the blows aimed at them without asking where they come from or by whom, in the final analysis, they are aimed. As yet they have no class consciousness and there is no guiding idea in their struggle against individual oppressors. The oppressed class does not yet exist *for itself;* in time it *will* be the advanced class in society, but it is not yet *becoming* such. Facing the consciously organised power of the ruling class are separate individual strivings of isolated individuals or isolated groups of individuals. Even now, for example, we frequently enough meet a worker who hates the particularly intensive exploiter but does not yet suspect that the whole class of exploiters must be fought and the very possibility of exploitation of man by man removed.

Little by little, however, the process of generalisation takes effect, and the oppressed begin to be conscious of themselves as a class. But their understanding of the specific features of their class position still remains too one-sided: the springs and motive forces of the social mechanism as a whole are still hidden from their mind's eye. The class of exploiters appears to them as the simple sum of individual employers, not connected by the threads of political organisation. At this stage of development it is not yet clear in the minds of the oppressed—any more than in Professor Lorenz von Stein's—what connection exists between "society" and "state". State power is presumed to stand above the antagonisms of the classes; its representatives appear to be the natural judges and conciliators of the hostile sides. The oppressed class has complete trust in them and is extremely surprised when its requests for help remain unanswered by them. Without dwelling on particular examples, we will merely note that such confusion of concepts was displayed even recently by the British workers, who waged quite an energetic struggle in the economic field and yet considered it possible to belong to one of the bourgeois political parties.

Only in the next and last stage of development does the oppressed class come to a thorough realisation of its position. It now realises the connection between society and state, and it does not appeal for the curbing of its exploiters to those who constitute the political organ of that exploitation. It knows that the state is a fortress serving as the bulwark and defence of its oppressors, a fortress which the oppressed can and must capture and reorganise for their own defence and which they cannot bypass, counting on its neutrality. Relying only on themselves, the oppressed begin to understand that "*political* self-help", as Lange says, "is the most important of all forms of *social* self-help". They then fight for political domination in order to help themselves by changing the existing social relations and adapting the social system to the conditions of their own development and welfare. Neither do they, of course, achieve domination immediately; they only gradually become a formidable power precluding all thought of resistance by their opponents. For a long time they fight only for concessions, demand only such reforms as would give them not domination, but merely the possibility to develop and mature for future domination; reforms which would satisfy the most urgent and immediate of their demands and extend, if only slightly, the sphere of their influence over the country's social life. Only by going through the hard school of the struggle for separate little pieces of enemy territory does the oppressed class acquire the persistence, the daring, and the development necessary for the decisive battle. But once it has acquired those qualities it can look at its opponents as at a class finally condemned by history; it need have no doubt about its victory. What is called the revolution is only the last act in the long drama of revolutionary class struggle which becomes conscious only insofar as it becomes a *political* struggle.[25]

The question is now: would it be expedient for the socialists to hold the workers back from "politics" on the grounds that the Political structure of society is determined by its economic relations? Of course not! They would be depriving the workers of a fulcrum in their struggle, they would be depriving them of the possibility of concentrating their efforts and aiming their blows at the social organisation set up by the exploiters. Instead, the workers would have to wage guerrilla warfare against individual exploiters, or at most separate groups of those exploiters, who would always have on their side, the organised power of the state. This was the kind of mistake the Russian socialists from among the so-called intelligentsia made when they censured the Northern Union of Russian Workers (in No.4 of *Zemlya i Volya*) for having included certain political demands in its programme. The same mistake was repeated by Zerno when it recommended that the workers should wage the struggle on economic ground, fight for a shorter working day, higher wages, etc., that they should kill spies and particularly hated foremen and employers, but did not say a word about the *political* tasks of the Russian workers. This lack of synthesis in our socialists' revolutionary views and programmes could not fail to have the most damaging effect on the results of their work. By preserving the political indifference of the workers as a most important sign of the radical nature of their economic demands, we gave indirect support to modern absolutism. Moreover, by cutting short our programmes at the very point where we should have summed up politically the social demands of the working class, we were diminishing the practical significance of those programmes in the eyes of the workers, who understood better than we did the utter futility of the divided struggle against individual exploiters. Fortunately, our working-class movement very soon outgrew this first phase of its development. The answer given by the Northern Union of Russian Workers to the editors of *Zemlya i Volya* (see No. 5 of that publication) showed that at least the members of the Union had understood earlier than our "intelligentsia" how inappropriate was this "political non-interference" of the working class.

All that is very well, some readers may say, but your arguments are not to the point. We do not deny, they may argue, that it would be *useful* for the working class to gain political influence and take state power in its own hands; we only maintain that at present that is *impossible* for many reasons. Your reference to the history of the bourgeoisie proves nothing, for the position of the proletariat in bourgeois society is nothing like that of the third estate in the states of the "ancien regime"! Even Marx admits the difference and formulates it as follows in the *Manifesto of the Communist Party:* "The serf, in the period of serfdom, raised himself to membership in the commune, just as the petty bourgeois, under the yoke of feudal absolutism, managed to develop into a bourgeois. The modern labourer, on the contrary, instead of rising with the progress of industry, sinks deeper and deeper below the conditions of existence of his own class. He becomes a pauper, and pauperism develops more rapidly than population and wealth in bourgeois countries." There is nothing surprising in the fact that every progressive step made by the bourgeoisie in the domain of production and exchange was accompanied by the "corresponding political conquests"; everybody knows that improvement in the material welfare of any particular class is accompanied by the growth of its political influence. But the very fact that the political gains of the bourgeoisie presupposed an increase in its wealth makes us abandon any hopes in the political movements of the working class. Falling deeper and deeper into "pauperism", the workers apparently must lose even the little influence which they won in the struggle for the interests of the bourgeoisie, "fighting the enemies of their enemies—the remnants of absolute monarchy, the landowners, the non-industrial bourgeois", and so on. The political struggle of the working class is purposeless because it is doomed to failure by virtue of the economic position of the workers.

For all its inner untenability, this objection seems at first glance so decisive as not to be passed over in silence. It is the last argument of those supporters of the theory of political non-interference who consider themselves followers of Marx.[26] Therefore, if it is disposed of, the theory of non-interference falls away altogether and the political tasks of modern socialism stand out in their true light.

The working class's share in the national product is constantly diminishing—there is not a shade of doubt about that. The working class is becoming poorer not only relatively, but absolutely too; its income, far from increasing in the same progression as those of other classes in society, is falling; the real wages of the modern proletarian (the quantity of consumer goods falling to his share) are less than the worker's pay was five hundred years ago—this has been proved by the studies of Rogers, Du Chatelet and others.[27] But it by no means follows from this that the economic conditions are at present less favourable to the political movement of the working class than they were in the fourteenth century. We have already said that in thus appraising the economic conditions in a particular country one must take into account not only the distribution of the national income, but mainly the organisation of production and the mode of exchange of products. The strength of the rising bourgeoisie lay not so much in its wealth as in the social and economic progress of which it was once the vehicle. It was not the increase in its income that impelled it to take the path of revolutionary struggle and guaranteed the growth of its political influence; it was the contradiction between the productive forces it brought into existence and the conditions under which the production and exchange of products took place in feudal society. Having once become the representative of progressive demands in that society, the bourgeoisie rallied all the dissatisfied elements under its banner and led them to fight against a regime which the overwhelming majority of the people hated. Not money, but the immaturity of the working class gave the bourgeoisie the leading role in that emancipation movement. Its wealth and its already fairly high social position were naturally indispensable for the fulfilment of this role; but what was that indispensability determined by? First of all by the fact that the bourgeoisie could not destroy the old order without assistance from the lower strata of the population. In this its wealth helped it by giving it influence over the masses which were to fight for its domination. Had the bourgeoisie not been rich it would have had no influence, and without influence over the people it would not have defeated the aristocracy; for the bourgeoisie was strong not of itself, but by virtue of the power which it had already mastered and which it commanded thanks to its capital. The question now arises, *is it possible* for the proletariat to have such influence over another class of the population, and *does it need* such influence to be victorious? It is enough to ask the question and we hear a resolute "No!" from everybody who understands the present position of the working class. It is *impossible* for the proletariat to influence lower classes in the way the bourgeoisie once influenced it, for the simple reason that there are no classes below it; the proletariat itself is the very lowest economic group in modern society. *Nor is there any need* for it to aim at such influence, because it is at the same time the *most numerous* section in society, because precisely the proletariat, with other sections of the working population, has always been the agent whose intervention has decided political issues. We say the most numerous class because all "the other classes decay and finally disappear in the face of modern industry; the proletariat is its special and essential product. The lower middle class, the small manufacturer, the shopkeeper, the artisan, the peasant, all these fight against the bourgeoisie, to save from extinction their existence as fractions of the middle class. They are therefore...conservative. Nay more, they are reactionary, for they try to roll back the wheel of history. If by chance they are revolutionary, they are so only in view of their impending transfer into the proletariat, they thus defend not their present, but their future interests, they desert their own standpoint to place themselves at that of the proletariat".

Formerly the working class was victorious under the command of the bourgeoisie, and it only naively wondered at the strange fact that nearly all the difficulties in the struggle fell to its lot while nearly all the advantages and honours of victory went to its ally. Now it is not satisfied with this auxiliary role and it turns against the bourgeoisie the very strength which once secured the latter's victory. But that strength is now much greater. It has grown and is continuing to grow in the same measure as the concentration of capital and the spread of large-scale production. Besides, it has grown in the same measure as the political experience of the working class, which the bourgeoisie itself brought into the social arena. Can there be any doubt that the proletariat, which, when led by the bourgeoisie, was once strong enough to destroy feudal absolutism, will in time be strong enough to smash the political domination of the bourgeoisie on its own initiative? The bourgeoisie was able to defeat feudalism only thanks to its wealth, the proletariat will defeat the bourgeoisie for the very reason that its lot—"pauperism"—is becoming the lot of an ever-increasing portion of modern society.

But in the history of its development the bourgeoisie received from its wealth another and indeed extremely "*productive* service", as its economists would say. It received knowledge and became the most advanced and educated section of society at that time. Can the proletariat acquire that knowledge, can it be at the Same time the poorest and the most advanced of all classes in society? Without this condition political domination is out of the question for the proletariat, for without knowledge there is no strength.

We have already said that the bourgeoisie itself began the political education of the proletariat. It took care of the education of the proletariat as much as this was necessary for the struggle against its own enemies. It shattered the proletariat's religious beliefs whenever this was required to weaken the political significance of the clergy; it broadened the proletariat's legal outlook wherever it needed to oppose "natural" law to the written law of the estate-based state.

Now the economic question is on the agenda and political economy now plays—as a very clever German[28] said—just as important a role as natural law played in the eighteenth century. Will the bourgeoisie agree to be the working class's leader in the investigation of the relations between labour and capital, that question of questions of the whole of social economy? It is reluctant to take upon itself even that role, advantageous as it is to itself, because merely to raise that question means to threaten the bourgeoisie's domination. But *can* it fulfil that role, if only in the way it once did in regard to religion and law? No, it cannot. Blinded by their class interests, its representatives in science lost long ago all ability to investigate social questions objectively, scientifically. Therein lies the whole secret of the present decay of bourgeois economics. Ricardo was the last economist who, though still a bourgeois in heart and soul, was intelligent enough to understand the diametrical opposition of interests between labour and capital. Sismondi was the last bourgeois economist who had enough feeling to deplore that antagonism sincerely. After them, the *general* theoretical studies of bourgeois economists in the main lost all scientific significance. To convince oneself of this it is sufficient to recall the history of political economy since Ricardo and to look through the works of Bastiat, Carey, Leroy-Beaulieu or the modern Katheder Sozialisten. From peaceful and objective thinkers the bourgeois economists have become militant guardians and watchdogs of capital who devote all their efforts to reconstructing the very edifice of science for the purpose of war. But in spite of these warlike exertions, they continually retreat and leave in their enemies' hands the scientific territory over which they once had uncontrolled sway. Nowadays people who display no "demagogic" strivings whatever try to assure us that the workers are "better able than any Smith or Faucher to master the most abstract concepts" in the science of economics. Such was the opinion, for instance, of a man who has the highest authority among German economists but who, for his part, had the deepest scorn for them. "We look upon the workers as children," this man added, "whereas they are already head and shoulders above us."[29]

But is there no exaggeration in what he says? Can the working class understand "abstract" questions of social economics and socialism at least as well as, if not better than, people who have spent years and years on their education?

What are the principles of modern scientific socialism founded on? Are they the concoctions of some leisurely benefactor of humanity, or are they the summing up of those very phenomena which we all come up against, one way or another, in our daily life, the explanation of the very laws which determine our participation in the production, the exchange, or simply the distribution of products? Whoever answers this question will agree that the working class has many chances of understanding correctly the "most abstract" laws of social economics and of mastering the most abstract principles of scientific socialism. The difficulty in understanding the laws of some particular science is caused by incomplete knowledge of the data underlying those laws. Wherever it is only a question of everyday phenomena in which the scientific law only generalises facts that everybody knows, people in the practical field not only understand perfectly the theoretical principles, they can sometimes even teach the theoreticians themselves. Ask the farmer about the influence that the distance to the market has on the price of his products or the effect the fertility of the soil has on the size of the land rent. Ask the manufacturer how the expansion of the market influences the cheapening of production. Or ask the worker where the employer gets his profits from...You will see that all these people know Ricardo, although they have never even seen the cover of his works. Yet these questions are reputed to be very intricate and "abstract", whole seas of ink have been used upon them and such a tremendous number of volumes have been written about them that they are enough to terrify you when you begin to study economics. The same in each and every part of social economics. Take the theory of exchange value. You can explain to the worker in a couple of words what it is determined by and how but many of Messrs. the bourgeois economists are still unwilling or unable to understand this perfectly simple theory, and in their disputes about it they fall into gross errors of logic for which no teacher of arithmetic would hesitate to give an elementary school pupil a bad mark. That is why we think that the writer we quoted was correct and that the only understanding audience today on urgent social problems is one of proletarians or of people who have adopted the proletarian stand point. Once the fundamental principles of social economics are mastered, the understanding of scientific socialism no longer presents any difficulty: here too the worker will only follow the directions of his practical experience. This aspect of the question was magnificently explained by Marx. "By heralding the dissolution of the *hitherto existing world order*," we read in *A Contribution to the Critique of Hegel's Philosophy of Law,* "the proletariat merely proclaims the secret of its own existence, for it is the *factual dissolution* of that world order. By demanding the *negation of private property,* the proletariat merely raises to the rank of *a principle of society* what society has raised to the rank of *its* principle, what is already embodied in it as the negative result of society without its own participation."[30] So we see that the proletariat needs no material wealth to attain to an understanding of the conditions of its emancipation. Its pauperism, determined *not by the poverty of the barbarism of society, but by defects in the social organisation*—this pauperism, far from making the understanding of these conditions more difficult, makes it easier.

The laws governing the distribution of products in capitalist society are extremely unfavourable to the working class. But the organisation of production and the form of exchange characteristic of capitalism provide for the first time both the objective and the subjective possibility for the emancipation of the working people. Capitalism broadens the worker's outlook and removes all the prejudices he inherited from the old society; it impels him to fight and at the same time ensures his victory by increasing his numbers and putting at his disposal the economic possibility of organising the kingdom of labour. Technical progress increases man's power over nature and raises labour productivity to such a degree that the necessity of labour cannot become a hindrance, but, on the contrary, will be an indispensable condition for the all-round development of the members of socialist society. At the same time, the socialisation of *production* characteristic of capitalism paves the way for the conversion of its *instruments and products* into common property. The joint-stock company, the highest form of organisation for industrial enterprises at the present time, excludes the capitalists from any active role in the economic life of society and turns them into drones whose disappearance cannot cause the slightest disorganisation in the course of that life. "If the energetic race of major-demos once succeeded without difficulty in deposing a royal dynasty which had grown indolent," the conservative Rodbertus says, "why should a living and energetic organisation of workers (the staff of companies is composed of qualified workers), why should not such an organisation in time remove owners who have become mere *rentiers*?...And yet capital cannot turn off this road! Having outlived its period of prosperity, capital is becoming its own grave-digger!

"Why, we ask, in our turn, should not the same organisation of workers which will be in a position "to remove owners who have become mere *rentiers*"—why should not such an organisation be in a position to seize state power and thus achieve political domination? For the former presumes the latter: only such an organisation can "remove" the owners as can overcome their *political* resistance.

But that is not all: there are other social phenomena which also increase the probability of the proletariat's *political* victory.

> "...Entire sections of the ruling classes are, by the advance of industry, precipitated into the proletariat, or are at least threatened in their conditions of existence. These also supply the proletariat with fresh elements of enlightenment and progress.
>
> "Finally, in times when the class struggle nears the decisive hour, the process of dissolution going on within the ruling class, in fact within the whole range of old society, assumes such a violent, glaring character, that a small section of the ruling class cuts itself adrift, and joins the revolutionary class, the class that holds the future in its hands. Just as, therefore, at an earlier period, a section of the nobility went over to the bourgeoisie, so now a portion of the bourgeoisie goes over to

the proletariat, and in particular, a portion of the bourgeois ideologists, who have raised themselves to the level of comprehending theoretically the historical movement as a whole."

There is a very remarkable legend among the Negroes of North Guinea. "One day," it says, "God summoned the two sons of the first human couple. One of them was white, the other dark-skinned. Placing before them a heap of gold and a book, God ordered the dark-skinned brother, as being the elder, to choose one of the two. He chose the gold, so the younger brother received the book. An unknown force immediately transported the younger one with the book to a cold, distant country. But thanks to his book he became learned, terrifying and strong. As for the elder brother, he remained in his native country and lived long enough to see how superior science is to wealth."

The bourgeoisie once had both knowledge and wealth. Unlike the dark-skinned brother in the Negro legend, it obtained possession of both gold and book, because history, the god of human societies, does not recognise the right of classes which are under age, and commits them to the guardianship of their elder brothers. But the time came when the working class, slighted by history, grew out of childhood and the bourgeoisie had to share with it. The bourgeoisie kept the gold, while the younger brother received the "book", thanks to which, despite the darkness and cold of his cellars, he has now become "strong and terrifying". Little by little, scientific socialism is ousting the bourgeois theories from the pages of this magic book, and soon the proletariat will read in the book how they can gain material sufficiency. Then they will throw off the shameful yoke of capitalism and show the bourgeoisie "how superior science is to wealth".

III

In the first chapter we endeavoured to explain historically the origin of the conviction that socialism is incompatible with any politics". We saw that this conviction was based on Proudhon's and Bakunin's teaching on the state, on the one hand, and on a certain inconsistency in our Social-Democrats of the seventies, on the other.

Moreover, it was supported by the general tone of the background against which both the tendencies mentioned above stood out. That background consisted, as we said quoting Engels, in a mish-mash of manifold theories of the founders of different socialist sects. The utopian socialists, we know, had an entirely negative attitude to the political movements of the working class, seeing in them nothing but "blind unbelief in the new Gospel". This negative view of "politics" came to us with the teachings of the utopians. Long before revolutionary movement of any strength began in Russia, our socialists, like the "true" socialists in Germany at the end of the forties (see the *Manifesto of the Communist Party,* p. 32), were ready "to hurl the traditional anathemas against liberalism, against representative government, against bourgeois competition, bourgeois freedom of the press, bourgeois legislation, bourgeois liberty and equality", forgetting entirely that all these attacks "presupposed the existence of modern bourgeois society, with its corresponding economic conditions of existence, and the political constitution adapted thereto", *i.e.*, the very conditions that it should still have been a question of assuring in our country.[31]

As a result of all these influences there arose such a firm conviction of the inexpediency of any political struggle except the revolutionary struggle in the narrow and vulgar sense of the wòrd, that we began to regard with prejudice the socialist parties in Western Europe which saw electoral campaigns, for instance, as a powerful means of educating and organising the working masses. All the political and economic gains those campaigns brought seemed to us unpardonable opportunism, a ruinous deal with the demon of the bourgeois state, tantamount to renouncing bliss in future socialist life. We ourselves did not even notice that our theories were involving us in a vicious circle of insoluble contradictions. We regarded the village commune as the point of departure of Russia's social and economic development and, at the same time, renouncing political struggle, we voluntarily deprived ourselves of all possibility of safeguarding that commune against the present destructive influences by state interference. We were thus forced to remain indifferent spectators of a process which was destroying the very foundation on which we wished to erect the edifice of the future.

We saw, however, that the logic of events had led the Russian movement on to another road and forced the Russian revolutionaries, as represented by the Narodnaya Volya party, to fight for political influence and even dominance as one of the most powerfactors of economic revolution. We also saw that having entered upon that road our movement was growing to such an extent that the social and political theories of different varieties of Proudhonism were too narrow and cramping for it. The course of events peculiar to Russian social life clashed with the course of the ideas dominating among our revolutionaries and thus provoked a new trend of thought.

This trend, we said further, will not rid itself of its characteristic contradictions until it merges with the incomparably deeper and wider current of modern socialism. The Russian revolutionaries must adopt the standpoint of Western Social-Democracy and break with "rebel" *theories* just as a few years ago they renounced "rebel" *practice,* introducing a new, *political* element into their programme. This will not be difficult for them to do if they endeavour to adopt the correct view of the political side of Marx s teaching and are willing to reconsider the methods and immediate aims of their struggle by applying this new criterion to them.

We saw as early as in the second chapter what false conclusions were prompted by the philosophical and historical premises of modern socialism. *Narodnaya Volya* itself apparently did not notice the erroneousness of those conclusions and was inclined "even to defend Dühring's sociological standpoint on the predominant influence of the political and legal element in the social structure over the economic", as P. L. Lavrov put it in describing the most recent tendencies in the Russian revolutionary movement.[32] And it is only by this inclination that we can explain the polemic contained in the home review of Narodnaya Volya No. 6 against some kind of "immediate interpreters of Marx's historical theory", who, according to the author, based their views "mainly on Hegel's famous triad", not having "any other inductive material" for their conclusions and explaining "Hegel's law in the sense evil, merely in its extreme development, will lead to good".[33] It is sufficient to acquaint oneself with the programme of the German Social-Democrats or the French collectivists to see how "Marx's historical theory" is understood by his West European followers and, if you like, by his "immediate interpreters". We, for our part, can assure our Russian comrades that these "interpreters" understand "Hegel's law" by no means "in the sense that evil, merely in its extreme development, will lead to good", and, besides, that they use it as "*inductive* material" only when they study the history of German philosophy, in which this law has a very prominent place and which, *in any case,* it cannot be left out of, just as, according to the popular saying, you cannot leave words out of a song. The passage we quoted is an almost word-for-word repetition of the reproach addressed by Dühring to Marx that in his historical scheme "the Hegelian negation of negation plays, for want of better and clearer means, the role of a midwife with whose help the future emerges from the womb of the present".[34] But this trick has already received the punishment it deserved from Engels, who showed the utter scientific worthlessness of the former Berlin *Dozent's* works. Why, then, repeat other people's errors and adopt, on such shifting grounds, a negative attitude towards the greatest and most revolutionary social theory of the nineteenth century? For without revolutionary theory there is no revolutionary movement in the true sense of the word. Any class which strives for its emancipation, any political party which aims at dominance, is revolutionary only insofar as it represents the most progressive social trends and consequently is a vehicle of the most progressive ideas of its time. An idea which is inherently revolutionary is a kind of dynamite which no other explosive in the world can replace. And as long as our movement is under the banner of backward or erroneous theories it will have revolutionary significance only by some, but by no means all of its aspects. At the same time, without its members knowing it, it will bear in itself the germs of reaction which will deprive it even of that little significance in the more or less near future, because, as Heine said,

New time needs a new garment
For the new job it's got to do.

And indeed that really new time will come at last—for our country too.

Incorrect understanding of some principles of modern socialism is not, however, the main obstacle preventing our revolutionary movement from taking the road paved by the working class in the West. A closer acquaintance with the literature of "Marxism" will show our socialists what a powerful weapon they have deprived themselves of by refusing to understand and master the theory of the great teacher of the "workers of all countries". They will then see that our revolutionary movement, far from losing anything, will gain a lot if the Russian Narodniks and the Russian Narodnaya Volya at last become Russian Marxists and a new, higher standpoint reconciles all the groups existing among us, which are all right each in its own way, because despite their one-sidedness each of them expresses a definite vital need of Russian social life.

Another obstacle prevents our movement from developing in the direction just indicated. It consists in our lacking sense of proportion in politics. Since the very beginning of our movement this has prevented our revolutionaries from bringing their immediate tasks into line with their strength and it is due to nothing else than lack of political experience on the part of Russian public figures. Whether we went among the people to disseminate socialist publications, settled in the villages to organise the protesting elements of our peasantry or joined directly in the fight against the representatives of absolutism, we repeated one and the same mistake everywhere. We always overestimated our strength and never fully took account of the resistance that would be offered by the social environment, wc hastened to raise a method of action temporarily favoured by circumstances into a universal principle precluding ail other ways and means. As a result, all our programmes were in a state of absolutely unstable equilibrium which could be upset by the most insignificant change in the surrounding atmosphere. We changed those programmes almost every couple of years and could not keep to anything *lasting* because we always kept to something *narrow* and *one-sided.* Just as, according to Belinsky's words, Russian society had experience of all literary trends even before it had any literature, so the Russian socialist movement managed to try out all possible shades of West European socialism despite the fact that it had not yet become a movement of our working class.

The struggle against absolutism that Narodnaya Volya has undertaken will undoubtedly help greatly to eliminate the onesidedness of the study *groups* by bringing our revolutionaries out on to a broader path and compelling them to strive to set up a real *party*. But in order to put a stop to the continual changing of programmes, to rid themselves of these habits of political nomads and to acquire intellectual stability at last, the Russian revolutionaries must complete the criticism which began with the rise of conscious political trends among them. They must adopt a critical attitude to the very programme which has made necessary the criticism of *all* previous programmes and theories. The "Narodnaya Volya party" is the child of a time of transition. Its programme is the last produced in the conditions which made our one-sidedness inevitable and therefore legitimate. Although it broadens the political horizon of the Russian socialists, this programme in itself is not yet free from one-sidedness. The lack of sense of proportion in politics, of the ability to line up the immediate aims of the party with its actual or potential strength is also still conspicuous in it. The Narodnaya Volya party reminds one of a man who is going along a real road but has no idea of distances and therefore feels sure that he can leave "miles and leagues behind—twenty thousand leagues, ere night, covered in a single flight". Practice will, of course, shatter his illusion, but that shattering may cost him a great deal. It would be better for him to ask himself whether seven-league strides do not belong to the realm of fantasy.

By seven-league strides we mean the element of fantasy whose existence in the programme referred to we have already pointed out and which was manifested in the second issue of *Narodnaya Volya* by assurances concerning the social-revolutionary (we do not say *socialist)* majority in the future Russian Constituent Assembly, 55 and in No. 8-9 by considerations on "the seizure of power by the provisional revolutionary government". We are profoundly convinced that this element of fantasy is highly dangerous for the "Narodnaya Volya party" itself. Dangerous to it as a socialist party because it diverts attention of the working class from the immediate tasks in Russia; dangerous to it as a party which has assumed the initiative of our emancipation movement because it will alienate from the party great resources and forces which, in other circumstances, would accrue to it out of the socalled society. Let us explain this in greater detail.

To whom does Narodnaya Volya appeal, to whom can it and should it appeal in fighting absolutism? "The enlistment in the organisation"—Narodnaya Volya—"of *individuals from the peasantry* capable of joining it," we read in Kalendar Narodnoi Voli,[35] "has naturally always been acknowledged as very desirable...But as for a mass peasant organisation at present, that was considered completely fantastic when our programme was drawn up, and, if we are not mistaken, subsequent practice was unable to change the opinion of our socialists on this subject." Perhaps the "Narodnaya Volya party" intends to rely on the more progressive section of our labouring population, *i.e.*, on the town workers? It does actually attach great importance to propaganda and organisation among them, it considers that "the urban working population must be the object of the party's serious attention". But the very reason on which it bases this necessity shows that in the party's conception the town workers must be only one of the elements in our revolutionary movement. They "are of particular significance for the revolution, both by their position and by their relatively greater maturity", the same document explains; "the success of the first attack depends entirely on the conduct of the workers and the troops". So the impending revolution will not be a working-class revolution in the full sense of the term, but the workers must take part in it because they "are of particular significance *for it*". Which other elements, then, will be included in this movement? We have already seen that one of these elements will be the "troops". but in the army "in present conditions propaganda among the men is so difficult that great hope can hardly be placed upon It. Action on *the officer corps* is far more convenient: being more educated and having greater liberty they are more susceptible to influence"! That is quite correct, of course, but we will not stop at that for the moment, we will go further. Besides the workers and "the officer corps", the Narodnaya Volya party has in mind the liberals and "Europe", in relation to which "the policy of the party must strive to ensure the sympathy of the peoples for the Russian revolution, to rouse sympathy for the revolution among the European public". To attain this aim "the party must make known to Europe all the disastrous significance of Russian absolutism for European civilisation itself, and also the party's true aims and the significance of our revolutionary movement as the expression of the protest of the whole nation". As far as the "liberals" are concerned, "we must point out, without concealing our radicalism, that given the present setting of our party tasks, our interests and theirs compel us to act jointly against the government".

Thus we see that the Narodnaya Volya party relies not only, nor even mainly, on the working and peasant classes. It also has in mind society and the officer corps, which, in substance, is the very flesh and bone" of that society. It wants to convince the liberal part of that society that "given the present setting of our party tasks" the interests of Russian liberalism coincide with those of the Russian social-revolutionary party. What, then, does it do to that conviction upon the Russian liberals? First of all it publishes the programme of the Executive Committee which Says that "the *people's will* would be sufficiently well expressed and Implemented by a Constituent Assembly freely elected by universal suffrage and receiving instructions from the electors". In its famous "Letter to Alexander III" the Executive Committee also demanded "the convocation of representatives of the whole Russian people to reconsider the existing forms of statehood and public life and to refashion them according to the desires of the people". That programme does indeed coincide with the interests of the Russian liberals, and in order to carry it out they would probably be reconciled even to universal suffrage, which the Executive Committee cannot fail to demand. In all this, the programme of the said Committee displays far greater maturity than all those which preceded it. But, not to mention such a huge blunder as to demand freedom of assembly, of speech, of the press and of electoral programmes only "as a temporary measure", let us recall other statements of the Narodnaya Volya party. The party organ hastened to warn its readers that the majority of the deputies to the Constituent Assembly would be supporters of radical economic revolution. We have already said above that this assurance was no more than a fiction invented to conciliate incompatible elements in the Narodnaya Volya programme. Let us now consider the printed expression of that assurance from the stand-point of tactics. The question is: does an economic revolution suit the interests of Russian liberalism? Does our liberal society sympathise with the agrarian revolution which Narodnaya Volya says the peasant deputies will aim at? West European history tells us most convincingly that whenever the "red spectre" took at all threatening forms the "liberals" were ready to seek protection in the embraces of the most unceremonious military dictatorship. Did the terrorist organ think that our Russian liberals would be an exception to this general rule? If so, on what did it base its conviction? Did it also think that contemporary "public opinion in Europe" was so imbued with socialist ideas that it would sympathise with the convocation of a social-revolutionary Constituent Assembly? Or did it think that although the European bourgeoisie trembled at the red sprectre in their own countries they would cheer its appearance in Russia? It goes without saying that it thought nothing of the sort and forgot nothing of the sort. But why, in that case, make such a risky statement? Or was the Narodnaya Volya party organ so convinced of the inevitable realisation of its prophecy that it considered it necessary to rouse the members of the organisation to take steps corresponding to the importance of the anticipated event? Bearing in mind the fact that the same organ declared work among the people useless, we think the statement was intended rather to calm than to rouse: a social-revolutionary majority in the Constituent Assembly was expected *despite* the fact that the work referred to now recalls the "Danaides filling bottomless barrels".

In itself the statement could have been regarded as unimportant, especially as *Narodnaya Volya* itself had apparently given up its exaggeratedly optimistic hopes about the future composition of the Russian Constituent. We think so, because the leading article in No. 8-9 speaks of the economic revolution which, in the absence of social-revolutionary initiative among the people themselves, must be accomplished by the "provisional revolutionary government" before the convocation of the Constituent Assembly. The author of the article quite rightly sees such a revolution as the only guarantee that "the Zemsky Sobor which is convoked will be attended by true representatives of the people". Thus, *Narodnaya Volya's* former illusion has been shattered completely. But, unfortunately, it has only disappeared to give place to a new one, still more harmful for the cause of the Narodnaya Volya party. The element of fantasy in the programme has not been removed but has only assumed a new form, being now called that very *"seizure of power by the provisional revolutionary government"* which is supposed to give the party the possibility to carry out the economic revolution referred to. It is obvious that the new "setting of the party tasks" can on no account impress upon either Russian liberalism or bourgeois Europe the idea that they have common interests with the Russian revolutionary movement. However downtrodden and crushed Russian society may be it is by no means deprived of the instinct of self-preservation and in no case will it voluntarily meet the "red spectre" half-way; to point out to it such a formulation of the party tasks means to deprive oneself of its support and to rely only on one's own strength. But is that strength great enough to warrant the risk of alienating such an ally? Can our revolutionaries really seize power and retain it, if only for a short time, or is all talk of this nothing else than cutting the skin of a bear that has not been killed and which, by force of circumstances, is not even going to be killed? That is a question which has recently become an urgent one for revolutionary Russia...

Let us hasten to make a reservation. The previous pages must already have convinced the reader that we do not belong to the opponents in principle of such an act as the seizure of power by a revolutionary party. In our opinion that is the last, and what is more, the absolutely inevitable conclusion to be drawn from the political struggle which every class striving for emancipation must undertake at a definite stage in social development. Having gained political domination, a revolutionary class will retain that domination and be relatively secure against the blows of reaction only when it uses against reaction the mighty weapon of state power. "Den Teufel halte, wer ihn halt!" says Faust.

But there is no more difference between heaven and earth than between the dictatorship of a class and that of a group of revolutionary *raznochintsi.* This applies in particular to the dictatorShip of the working class, whose present task is not only to overthrow the political domination of the unproductive classes in society, but also to do away with the anarchy now existing in production and consciously to organise all functions of social and economic life. The mere *understanding* of this task calls for an advanced working class with political experience and education, a working class free from bourgeois prejudices and able to discuss its situation by itself. In addition to this, its *solution* presupposes that socialist ideas are spread among the proletariat and that the proletariat is conscious of its own strength and confident in victory. But *such* a proletariat *will not allow* even the sincerest of its well-wishers to seize power. It will not allow it for the simple reason that it has been to the school of political education with the firm intention of finishing it at some time and coming forward as an independent figure in the arena of historical life, instead of passing eternally from one guardianship to another; it will not allow it because such a guardianship would be unnecessary, as the proletariat could then solve the problem of the socialist revolution itself; and finally it will not allow it because such a guardianship would be harmful, for the conscious participation of the producers in organising production cannot be replaced by any conspiratorial skill, any daring or self-sacrifice on the part of the conspirators. The mere thought that the social problem can be solved in practice by anybody but the workers themselves shows complete misunderstanding of this problem, irrespective of whether the idea is held by an "Iron Chancellor" or a revolutionary organisation. Once the proletariat has understood the conditions of its emancipation and is mature to emancipate itself, it will take state power in its own hands in order to finish off its enemies and build up social life, not, of course, on thc basis of *an*-archy, which would bring new disasters, but of *pan*-archy, which will give all adult members of society the possibility to take part in the discussion and settlement of social matters. And until the working class is sufficiently developed to be able to fulfil its great historical task, the duty of its supporters is to accelerate the process of its development, to remove the obstacles preventing its strength and its consciousness from growing, and not to invent social experiments and vivisection, the outcome of which is always more than doubtful.

That is how we understand the seizure of power in the socialist revolution. Applying this point of view to Russian reality we must admit that we by no means believe in the early possibility of a socialist government in Russia.

Narodnaya Volya considers the contemporary "relation of political and economic factors on Russian soil" particularly "advantageous" to the socialists. We agree that it is more advantageous for them in Russia than in India, Persia or Egypt, but it cannot be compared, of course, with the social relations in Western Europe. And if Narodnaya Volya arrives at its convictions by comparing our system not with the Egyptian or the Persian, but with the French or the English system, then it has made a very big mistake. The contemporary "relation" of social factors "on Russian soil" is the cause of the ignorance and indifference of the popular masses; when were such qualities advantageous for their emancipation? Narodnaya Volya apparently presumes that this indifference has already begun to disappear because among the people "there is growing hatred of the privileged ruling estates and persistent striving for a radical change in economic relations". But what comes of that striving? "Hatred of the privileged estates" proves nothing at all; it is often not accompanied by a single ray of political consciousness. Furthermore, at the present time we must clearly distinguish between *estate* consciousness and *class* consciousness, for the old division into estates no longer corresponds to the economic relations in Russia and is preparing to give place to formal equality of citizens in a "legal state" If Narodnaya Volya considers the contemporary outlook of our peasantry from the standpoint of the development of their *class* and *political* consciousness, it will hardly persist in saying that the relation between our social factors is advantageous to the cause of the social revolution. For it certainly cannot consider "advantageous" to that cause the rumours, for instance, circulating among the peasantry about their own struggle against the government. No matter how strongly "hatred of the ruling classes" is shown in these rumours, the fact that the revolutionary movement itself is attributed by the peasants to scheming by the serfdom-minded nobility and the officials is evidence that the "provisional revolutionary government" will be in great danger when the people begins "winning economic equality from those who have been exploiting and oppressing it for centuries". Then the relation between the factors now interesting us will perhaps display rather disadvantageous qualities for the temporarily victorious conspirators. And then, what is meant by "winning economic equality"?

Is it enough for that to expropriate the big landowners, capitalists and businessmen? Does it not require production itself to be organised in a definite manner? If so, are Russia's present economic relations favourable to such organisation? In other words, does the "economic factor" offer us much chance of success? We do not think so, and for the following reason. Any organisation presupposes in what is to be organised certain qualities determined by the purpose and character of the organisation. The socialist organisation of production implies such a character of the economic relations as will make that organisation the logical conclusion of the entire previous development of the country and is therefore distinguished by an extremely significant definiteness. In other words socialist organisation, like any other, requires the appropriate basis. But that basis does not exist in Russia. The old foundations of national life are too narrow, heterogeneous and one-sided, and moreover too shaky, and new ones are as yet only being formed. The objective social conditions of production necessary for socialist organisation have not yet matured, and that is why the producers themselves have not yet either the striving or the ability for such organisation: our peasantry can yet neither understand nor fulfil this task. Therefore, the "provisional government" will have not to "sanction", but to *carry out* "the economic revolution", granted that it is not swept away by a wave of the popular movement, granted that the producers are obedient enough.

You cannot create by decrees conditions which are alien to the very character of the existing economic relations. The "provisional government" will have to reconcile itself to what exists, to take as the basis of its reforming activity what it is given by present Russian reality. And on that narrow and shaky foundation the edifice of socialist organisation will be built by a government which will include: first, town workers, as yet little prepared for such a difficult task; second, representatives of our revolutionary youth, who have always kept aloof from practical life; third, the "officer corps", whose knowledge of economics is certainly subject to doubt. We do not want to make the quite probable supposition that, besides all these elements, liberals will also find their way into the provisional government, and they will not sympathise with, but hinder the social-revolutionary "setting of the party tasks". We suggest that the reader merely weigh up the circumstances we have just enumerated and then ask himself: has an "economic revolution" which begins in such circumstances much chance of success? Is it true that the present "relation of political and economic factors on Russian soil" is favourable to the cause of the socialist revolution? Is not the confidence that this relation is advantageous one of the fictions borrowed from the old anarchist and rebel outlook and carried to impossible extremes in the programme of the new *political* party? Yet it is this fiction that determines the most "immediate tasks" of the party and underlies the desire for the immediate "seizure of power" a striving that terrifies our society and makes the entire activity of our revolutionaries one-sided!

Perhaps it will be objected that Narodnaya Volya does not even think of undertaking the socialist organisation of society immediately after seizing power, that the "economic revolution" it plans is intended only to educate the people for a future socialist revolution. Let us see whether this supposition is possible, and if so, what conclusions follow from it.

The leading article of No. 8-9 of *Narodnaya Volya* speaks of the economic equality which will be "won" by the people itself, or, if the people lacks initiative, created by the provisional government. We have already said that so-called economic equality is possible only with a socialist organisation of production. But let us assume that *Narodnaya Volya* considers it possible under other circumstances too, that economic equality, in its opinion, will be sufficiently guaranteed by the transfer of the land and the instruments of production to the ownership of the working people. Such an opinion would be nothing but a return to the old Narodnik ideals of Zemlya i Volya, and from the economic standpoint it would show the same weaknesses that characterised those ideals. The mutual relations of individual village communes, the conversion of the product of the commune members' labour into commodities and the capitalist accumulation connected with it would threaten to make that "equality" extremely precarious! With the independence of the *mir* "as an economic and administrative unit", with "broad territorial self-government guaranteed by the electivity of all offices", and "the ownership of the land by the people" which the Executive Committee's programme demands, the central government *would not be able* to take steps to consolidate that equality, even if we assume that it would devise measures to abrogate not only the written laws of the Russian Empire, but the laws of commodity production itself. And anyhow, it would be reluctant to take such measures, for it would consist of representatives of the "economically and politically emancipated people" whose ideals would be expressed, at the best, by the words "Land and Freedom" and would leave no room for any organisation of national (let alone *international)* production.

Let us suppose that in view of this danger Narodnaya Volya's "provisional government" will not hand over the power it has seized to the representatives of the people but will become a permanent government. Then it will be faced with the following alternative: either it will have to remain an indifferent spectator of the slow decay of the "economic equality" it has established, or it will be obliged to *organise* national production. It will have to fulfil this difficult task either in the spirit of modem socialism, in which it will be hindered by its own unpracticality as well as by the present stage of development of national labour and the workers' own habits; or it will have to seek salvation in the ideals of patriarchal and authoritarian communism", only modifying those ideals so that national production is managed not by the Peruvian "sons of the sun" and their officials but by a socialist caste. But even now the Russian people is too far developed for anybody to flatter himself with the hope that such experiments on it could be successful. Moreover, there is no doubt that under such a guardianship the people, far from being educated for socialism, would even lose all capacity for further progress or would retain that capacity only thanks to the appearance of the very economic *in*equality which it would be the revolutionary government's immediate aim to abolish. Not to mention the influence of international relations or the impossibility of Peruvian communism even in Eastern Europe in the nineteenth or the twentieth century.

Anyhow, why speak so much of the *results* of the seizure of power by our revolutionaries? Is that seizure itself probable or even possible? In our opinion the probability is very small, so small that the seizure of power may be considered as absolutely impossible. Our "thinking proletariat" has already done much for the emancipation of its motherland. It has shaken absolutism, aroused political interest among society, sown the seed of socialist propaganda among our working class. It is intermediary between the higher classes of society and the lower, having the education of the former and the democratic instincts of the latter. This position has eased for it the diversified work of propaganda and agitation. But this same position gives it very little hope of success in a conspiracy to seize power. For such a conspiracy talent, energy and education are not enough: the conspirators need connections, wealth and an influential position in society. And that is what our revolutionary intelligentsia lacks. It can make good these deficiencies only by allying itself with other dissatisfied elements of Russian society. Let us suppose that its plans actually meet with the sympathy of those elements, that rich landowners, capitalists, officials, staff and senior officers join in the conspiracy. There will then be more probability of the conspiracy being a success, although that probability will still be very small—just remember the outcome of most of the famous conspiracies in history. But the main danger to the *socialist* conspiracy will come not from the existing government, but from the members of the conspiracy itself. The influential and high-placed personages who have joined it may be sincere socialists only by a "fortunate coincidence". But as regards the majority of them, there can be no guarantee that they will not wish to use the power they have seized for purposes having nothing in common with the interests of the working class. And once the conspirators deviate from the socialist aim of the conspiracy it can be considered not only useless but even harmful for the social development of the country; for hatred of absolutism does not warrant sympathy for the successes of the "most modern Seyans", as Stepnyak puts it in his well-known book, who would wish to use the conspiracy in their own interests. Thus, the more sympathy a conspiracy of the socialist intelligentsia to seize power in the immediate future meets among influential spheres, *i.e.*, the greater the probability of its outward success, the more open to doubt its results will be; contrariwise, the more such a conspiracy is confined to our socialist "intelligentsia", *i.e.*, the less the probability of its success, the less doubt there will be about its results, as far as the conspirators' intentions are concerned. Everything leads us to think that at present a Russian socialist conspiracy would be threatened with a failure of the second kind rather than of the first.

Considering all that has been said we think that only one aim of the Russian socialists would not be fantastic now: to achieve free political institutions, on the one hand, and to create elements for the setting up of the future *workers' socialist party* of Russia, on the other. They must put forward the demand for a democratic constitution which shall guarantee the workers the "rights of citizen" as well as the "rights of man" and give them, by universal suffrage, the possibility to take an active part in the political life of the country. Without trying to scare anybody with the yet remote "red spectre", such a political programme would arouse sympathy for our revolutionary party among all those who are not systematic enemies of democracy; it could be subscribed to by very many representatives of our liberalism as well as by the socialists.[37] And whereas the seizure of power by some secret revolutionary organisation will always be the work only of that organisation and of those who are initiated in its plans, agitation for the programme mentioned would be a matter for the whole of Russian society, in which it would intensify the conscious striving for political emancipation. Then the interests of the liberals would indeed "force" them to "act jointly with the socialists against the government", because they would cease to meet in revolutionary publications the assurance that the overthrow of absolutism would be the signal for a social revolution in Russia. At the same time another less timid and more sober section of liberal society would no longer see revolutionaries as unpractical youths who set themselves unrealisable and fantastic plans. This view, which is disadvantageous for revolutionaries, would give place to the respect of society not only for their heroism but also for their political maturity. This sympathy would gradually grow into active support, or more probably into an independent social movement, and then the hour of absolutism's fall would strike at last. The socialist party would play an extremely honourable and beneficial role in this emancipation movement. Its glorious past, its selflessness and energy would give weight to its demands and it would at least stand chances of thus winning *for the people* the possibility of political development and education, and *for itself* the right to address its propaganda openly to the people and to organise them openly into a separate party.

But that is not enough: Or more exactly, it is unachievable without simultaneous action of another kind and in another sphere. Without might there is no right. Every constitution—according to Lassalle's splendid expression—corresponds or strives to correspond to the *"real, factual relation of forces in the country"*. That is why our socialist intelligentsia must concern itself with changing the factual relations of Russian social forces in favour of the working class even in the pre-constitutional period. Otherwise the fall of absolutism will by no means justify the hopes placed in it by the Russian socialists or even democrats. Even in a constitutional Russia, the demands of the people may be left completely unattended to or satisfied only as far as is necessary to allow them to pay more taxes which they are now almost unable to do as a result of the rapacity of the state economic management. The socialist party itself, having won for the liberal bourgeoisie freedom of speech and action, may find itself in an "exceptional" position similar to that of German Social-Democracy today. In politics, only he may count on the gratitude of his allies of yesterday, now his enemies, who has nothing more serious to count on.

Fortunately, the Russian socialists can base their hopes on a firmer foundation. They can and must place their hopes first and foremost in the working class. The strength of the working class—as of any other class—depends, among other things, on the clarity of its political consciousness, its cohesion and its degree of organisation. It is these elements of its strength that must be influenced by our socialist intelligentsia. The latter must become the leader of the working class in the impending emancipation movement, explain to it its political and economic interests and also the interdependence of those interests and must prepare it to play an independent role in the social life of Russia. They must exert all their energy so that in the very opening period of the constitutional life of Russia our working class will be able to come forward as a separate party with a definite social and political programme. The detailed elaboration of that programme must, of course, be left to the workers themselves, but the intelligentsia must elucidate for them its principal points, for instance, a radical review of the present agrarian relations, the taxation system and factory legislation, state help for producers' associations, and so forth. All this can be done only by intensive work among at least the most advanced sections of the working class, by oral and printed propaganda and the organisation of workers' socialist study groups. It is true that these tasks have always held a more or less prominent place in the programmes of our socialists, and *Kalendar Narodnoi Voli* can convince us that they were not forgotten even in the heat of the bitterest fight against the government (see "Preparatory Work of the Party" in section *C, Urban Workers)*. But we suggest that everybody who is acquainted with our revolutionary movement should recall and compare how much energy and money was wasted on destructive work and how much was devoted to training elements for the future *workers' socialist party.* We are not accusing anybody, but we think that the distribution of our revolutionary forces was too one-sided. Yet it would be vain for us to try to explain this by the quality of the revolutionary forces themselves or of the elements of the working class which, according to their own programme, they should have influenced. The appearance and success of such publications as *Zerno* and *Rabochaya Gazeta* show that our revolutionaries have not lost their inclination for propaganda, and our working people are not indifferent to it. Of course these publications made mistakes, at times serious ones, but only he who does nothing makes no mistakes. The main trouble is that in their publications one does not see any of the energy with which printed propaganda is conducted among "intellectual" sections of society, that when a print-shop is closed by the police a new one is not opened in its stead, that when it is impossible to publish them in Russia they are not transferred abroad, and so forth. Of all the journals from abroad—and we had a fair number of them—*Rabotnik* alone wrote for the people and that was the great merit of its publishers. But *Rabotnik* has already been closed for a long time and we have heard nothing of new attempts of this kind, with, say, a new programme, better suited to the changed views of the Russian socialists. What has been published here, in Russia, for the workers besides *Zerno* and *Rabochaya Gazeta?* Absolutely nothing. Not a single booklet, not a single pamphlet.[38] And that at a time when the revolutionary movement has centred universal attention upon itself, and the people, grasping avidly at the rumours and opinions, have been wondering anxiously: What do these people want? Can one be astonished, after this, at the absurd answers to this question with which for lack of better ones, they are sometimes satisfied? We repeat: we are not accusing *anybody,* we advise *everybody* to pay attention to this aspect of the matter so as to make up for the omission in time.[39]

Thus, the struggle for political freedom, on the one hand, and the preparation of the working class for its future independent and offensive role, on the other, such, in our opinion, is the only possible "setting of party tasks" at present. To bind together in one two so fundamentally different matters as the overthrow of absolutism and the socialist revolution, to wage revolutionary struggle in the belief that these elements of social development will *coincide* in the history of our country *means to put off the advent of both.* But it depends on us to *bring* these two elements *closer together.* We must follow the splendid example of the German Communists who, as the *Manifesto* says, fight "with the bourgeoisie whenever it acts in a revolutionary way, against the absolute monarchy", and yet "never cease, for a single instant, to instil into the working class the dearest possible recognition of the hostile antagonism between bourgeoisie and proletariat". Acting thus, the Communists wanted "the bourgeois revolution in Germany" to "be but the prelude to an immediately following proletarian revolution".

The present position of bourgeois societies and the influence of international relations on the social development of each civilised country entitle us to hope that the social emancipation of the Russian working class will follow very quickly upon the fall of absolutism. If the German bourgeoisie *"came too late"*, the Russian has come still later, and its domination cannot be a long one. Only the Russian revolutionaries should not, in their turn, begin "too late" the preparation of the working class, a matter which has now become of absolute urgency.

Let us make a reservation to avoid misunderstandings. We do not hold the view, which as we have seen was ascribed to Marx's school rather than it existed in reality, and which alleges that the socialist movement cannot obtain support from our peasantry until the peasant has been turned into a landless proletarian and the village commune has disintegrated under the influence of capitalism. We think that on the whole the Russian peasantry would show great sympathy for any measure aiming at the so-called "nationalisation of the land". Given the possibility of any at all free agitation among the peasants,"[40] they would also sympathise with the socialists, who naturally would not be slow in introducing into their programme the demand for a measure of that kind. But we do not exaggerate the strength of our socialists or ignore the obstacles, the opposition which they will inevitably encounter from that quarter in their work. For that reason, and *for that reason only,* we think that for the beginning they should concentrate their main attention on the industrial centres. The rural population of today, living in backward social conditions is not only less capable of conscious political *initiative* than the industrial workers, it is also less *responsive* to the movement which our revolutionary intelligentsia has begun. It has greater difficulty in mastering the socialist teachings, because its living conditions are too much unlike the conditions which gave birth to those teachings. And besides, the peasantry is now going through a difficult, critical period. The previous "ancestral foundations" of its economy are crumbling, "the ill-lated village commune itself is being discredited in its eyes", as is admitted even by such "ancestral" organs of Narodism as *Nedelya* (see No. 39, the article by Mr. N.Z. "*In Our Native Parts*"); and the new forms of labour and life are only in the process of formation, and this creative process is more intensive in the industrial centres. Like water which washes away the soil in one place and forms new sediments and deposits in others, the process of Russian social development is creating new social formations by destroying the age-old forms of the peasants' relation to the land and to one another. These new social formations contain the embryo of a new social movement which alone can end the exploitation of Russia's working population. The industrial workers, who are more developed and have higher requirements and a broader outlook than the peasantry, will join our revolutionary intelligentsia in its struggle against absolutism, and when they have won political freedom they will organise into a workers' socialist party whose task will be to begin systematic propaganda of socialism among the peasantry. We say *systematic propaganda* because isolated opportunities of propaganda must not be missed even at present. It is hardly necessary to add that our socialists would have to change the distribution of their forces among the people if a strong independent movement made itself felt among the peasantry.

That is the "programme" which life itself suggests to the Russian revolutionary socialist party. Will the party be able to carry out of this programme? Will it be prepared to give up its fantastic plans and notions, which, it must be admitted, have a great appeal to sentiment and imagination? It is as yet difficult to answer that question with certitude. The "Announcement of the Publication of *Vestnik Narodnoi Voli*" speaks of the political tasks of the revolutionary party only in the most general terms. *Vestnik's* editorial board describes those aims as "absolutely definite" and apparently does not consider it necessary to define them again in its announcement. That is why there is ground for fear that it will not consider it necessary either to ask itself whether the "absolutely definite conditions" of present Russian actuality correspond to the "absolutely definite aims" of the Narodnaya Volya party. In that case the new publication will leave unsatisfied the most urgent need of our revolutionary literature, the need for a critical reconsideration of obsolete programmes and traditional methods of action. But we hope that the future will dissipate our fears. We wish to hope that the new publication will take a sober view of our revolutionary party's tasks, on whose fulfilment the party's future depends. Social life will be just as pitiless to the party's present illusions as it was to those of our "rebels" and propagandists. *It is better to follow its directions now than to pay for its stern lessons later by splits and new disappointments.*

FOOT NOTES:

1. See the pamphlet Andrei Ivanovich Zhelyabov, p. 10.
2. See *Entwicklung des Sozialismus,* S. 18.
3. Note to the 1905 edition.] Now Marxism has definitely triumphed in France; its basic propositions are acknowledged, in a more or less distorted form, even by "opportunists" of Jaurès' camp.
4. See Confessions d'un te'volutionnaire. Preface, p. 4. 12
5. To what extent Aristotle was "a sceptic in matters of state" is obvious from the first chapter of the first volume of his *Politics,* in which he says that "the state is the most accomplished form of community", that its purpose is "the supreme good", and that it is therefore a phenomenon "natural in the highest sense of the word, and man is an animal predestined by his very nature to the state form of community". (Book I, Chap. 1, #I-XI of the German Sussemil edition of 1879.) The author of *Politics* is just as much a "sceptic" in questions of state as Proudhon in questions of commodity production; the former could not imagine any other, higher form of community, the latter did not suspect that products could be distributed among the members of society without taking the form of commodities.
6. See Das Kapital, 2. Auflage, S. 607-08.
7. Let us simply remind our reader of the objection made to Proudhon by Rittinghausen. "Power, government and all its forms," said the tireless propagandist of the theory of direct popular legislation, "are only *varieties of the species that is called: interference by society in people's relations with things and, consequently, with one another*...I call on M. Proudhon to throw into my face, as the result of his intellectual labour, the following conclusion: 'No, there must be no such interference by society in people's relations with things and, consequently, with one another!' " See *Legislation directe par le peuple et ses adversaires,* pp. 194-95. Rittinghausen thought that "to pose the question in this way means to solve it", for "M. Proudhon himself admits the *necessity for such interference"*. But he did not foresee that the pupils would go much further than the teacher and that the theory of anarchy would degenerate, finally, into a theory of "social amorphism". The anarchists of today recognise no interference by society in the relations of individuals, as they have repeatedly stated in certain of their publications.
8. See M.A.Bakunin's extremely interesting and typical pamphlet *Science and the Vital Cause of the Revolution.*
9. See "Offener Brief an Herm Fr. Engels".

10. To be persuaded of this one needs but to compare the "Letter to Frederick Engels" just referred to with Bakunin's pamphlet quoted above.
11. *i.e.*, whether they appear as commodities or are directly consumed by the producer's family, his master, and finally, the state, without ever reaching the market.
12. We request that it be borne in mind that we are talking not of the editorial board of the journal *Vperyod,* but of the supporters of that publication working in Russia.
13. Note to the 1905 edition.. Later, Messrs. the "critics of Marx" reproached us, the "orthodox", of revolting against every attempt to develop Marx's views further. The reader sees that I showed no tendency to such a revolt. But it goes without saying that, as a pupil of Marx who understands the great significance of his theory, I had to revolt against every attempt to replace some propositions of Marxism by old, long obsolete bourgeois "dogmas". And I fulfilled that obligation to the best of my ability.
14. *See Zur Kritik der politischen Oekon.,* Vorwort. S. IV-VI.
15. See Herrn Eugen Dühring's Umwälz. der Wissensch, S. 6.
16. See Essai sur l'histoire du Tiers Etat, par. Aug. Thierry, pp. 33-34.
17. The supporters of feudalism understood full well the aims of the burghers and the connection between their political and their economic demands. "Commune is a new and detestable word," said Guibert, abbe de Nogent, "and here is what it means: those who have to pay tithes pay only once a year to their lord the rent they owe him. If they commit some offence, they are quit for the payment of a fine fixed by law, and as for the money levies usually made from serfs, they are entirely exempt from them." Laurent, La féodalité et l'église, p. 546.
18. The Statute of Liege established the principle of the inviolability of the home in the following forceful expression: *"The poor man is king in his home."* Laurent, ibid, p. 548.
19. Von Studnitz, *Nordamerikanische Arbeiterverhaltnisse,* S. 353.
20. We quote this from B. Melon's *Le nouveau parti,* t. I, p. 15.
21. See *Sozialdemokratische Abhandlungen,* von M. Rittinghausen, drittes Heft, "Uber die Nothwendigkeit der direkten Gesetzgebung durch das Volk", S. 3.
22. See the programmes of the German and the North American Workers parties. The *Manifesto* of the British Democratic Federation also demands "direct voting on all important questions".
23. See Schäffle, Bau und Leben des sozialen Körpers, B.III, S. 91 Und

102. 24. See *Das System der erworbenen Rechte,* Leipzig, 1880, erster Theil, Vorrede, S. VII.

25. Note to the 1905 edition. These lines were written 15 years before Bernstein came forward as a "critic" of Marx. Let the reader judge for himself whether the "critic" and his numerous fellow-thinkers are right when they reproach us, the "orthodox" with understanding the revolution of the proletariat as a simple and almost instantaneous "catastrophe".

26. Note to the 1905 edition. This will seem paradoxical, but in actual fact the theory of political non-interference of the working class was formulated by Bakunin *as a conclusion from the materialist explanation of history.* Bakunin, who was an ardent supporter of this explanation, reasoned as follows: if the political system of every given society is based on its economy, then *political* revolution is unnecessary, it will itself be the result of the *economic* revolution. This man, once a pupil of Hegel and who, it seems, should have refined his logic, just could not understand that not only every particular *ready-made* political system is a result of economics, but so is every new political movement which, springing from the given economic relations, serves in turn as a necessary *instrument* for their reconstruction. All the *most serious objections* of the *anarchists* against the *Social-Democrats* are still founded on this *misunderstanding.*

27. Note to the 1905 edition. This concerns the "theory of impoverishment" which caused such a stir at the heyday of *Bernsteinians.* On this subject, see my "Criticism of Our Critics." in Nos. 2 and 3 of *Zarya.*

28. Note to the 1905 edition. *i.e.*, Rodbertus.

29. Note to the 1905 edition. I again mean Rodbertus.

30. See Deutsch-Französische Jahrbücher, 1. und 2. Lieferung, S. 81-85.

31. What is said here does not apply, however, to the group which published *Narodnoye Dyelo* in Geneva, a group which repeatedly affirmed its negative attitude to the "theory of political non-interference".

32. *See the article "View of the Past and the Present of Russian Socialism", *Kalendar Narodnoi Voli, 1883,* p. 109.

33. Note to the 1905 edition. Subsequently, our "legal" N. Mikhailovsky and Bros., repeated this nonsense in all keys. It must be noted in general that in their disputes with us these gentlemen could think of nothing new in comparison with what was written against us in *illegal* literature. Let anybody who wants to convince himself of this read Tikhomirov's article "What Can We Expect from the Revolution? " in the second issue of *Vestnik Narodnoi Voli* and compare it with the

arguments Beltov had to refute much later in his book. "Illegal" thought long ago outstripped "legal" thought in our country.

34. See *Kritische Geschichte der Nationaloekonomie und des Sozialismus,* dritte Auflage, S. 498.
35. "Preparatory Work of the Party", p. 129, note. Plekhanov's italics.
36. See "Letter to Alexander III", *Kalendar Narodnoi Voli,* p. 14.
37. Note to the 1905 edition. The sympathy of "society" is very important for us and we can—or more exactly we had many chances to—win it without changing one iota of our programme. But, of course, it requires tact to make the possibility a reality, and that is what we have not always got. For instance, we sometimes allow ourselves to abuse "capital" about, though, or course, not because of, its "rebellion". Marx would never have made such a gross tactical blunder. He would have considered it worthy of Karl Grun and other "true socialists".
38. Note to the 1905 edition. From this we see that the idea of a popular Publication is by no means a novelty in our literature. But this did not prevent it from seeming a dangerous novelty to many comrades *no further back than on the eve of out Second Congress,* when I was almost its only supporter on the staff of *Iskra.* This idea has now been practically realised—with greater or lesser success. Better late than never. But if you could hear, reader, what amazing arguments were brought out against this idea in the not-far-off time just mentioned, you would exclaim, like Faust: Wie weh, wie weh, wie weh!
39. "This year," we read in the Supplement to Listok of N. V. No. 1 (1883, p. 61), "there was a whole series of strikes which, thanks to the workers' lack of organisation, were mostly failures! "
40. Note to the 1905 edition. *i.e.*, under a constitution.

THE RIGHT OF NATIONS TO SELF-DETERMINATION

Vladimir Lenin

Chapter-8

Clause 9 of the Russian Marxists' Programme, which deals with the right of nations to self-determination, has (as we have already pointed out in *Prosveshcheniye*) given rise lately to a crusade on the part of the opportunists. The Russian liquidator Semkovsky, in the St. Petersburg liquidationist newspaper, and the Bundist Liebman and the Ukrainian nationalist-socialist Yurkevich in their respective periodicals have violently attacked this clause and treated it with supreme contempt. There is no doubt that this campaign of a motley array of opportunists against our Marxist Programme is closely connected with present-day nationalist vacillations in general. Hence we consider a detailed examination of this question timely. We would mention, in passing, that none of the opportunists named above has offered a single argument of his own; they all merely repeat what Rosa Luxemburg said in her lengthy Polish article of 1908-09, "The National Question and Autonomy". In our exposition we shall deal mainly with the "original" arguments of this last-named author.

What is Meant By The Self-Determination Of Nations?

Naturally, this is the first question that arises when any attempt is made at a Marxist examination of what is known as self-determination. What should be understood by that term? Should the answer be sought in legal definitions deduced from all sorts of "general concepts" of law? Or is it rather to be sought in a historico-economic study of the national movements?

It is not surprising that the Semkovskys, Liebmans and Yurkeviches did not even think of raising this question, and shrugged it off by scoffing at the "obscurity" of the Marxist Programme, apparently unaware, in their simplicity, that the self-determination of nations is dealt with not only in the Russian [Social-Democratic] Programme of 1903, but in the resolution of the London International Congress of

1896 (with which I shall deal in detail in the proper place). Far more surprising is the fact that Rosa Luxemburg, who declaims a great deal about the supposedly abstract and metaphysical nature of the clause in question, should herself succumb to the sin of abstraction and metaphysics. It is Rosa Luxemburg herself who is continually lapsing into generalities about self-determination (to the extent even of philosophising amusingly on the question of how the will of the nation is to be ascertained), without any where clearly and precisely asking herself whether the gist of the matter lies in legal definitions or in the experience of the national movements throughout the world.

A precise formulation of this question, which no Marxist can avoid, would at once destroy nine-tenths of Rosa Luxemburg's arguments. This is not the first time that national movements have arisen in Russia, nor are they peculiar to that country alone. Throughout the world, the period of the final victory of capitalism over feudalism has been linked up with national movements. For the complete victory of commodity production, the bourgeoisie must capture the home market, and there must be politically united territories whose population speak a single language, with all obstacles to the development of that language and to its consolidation in literature eliminated. Therein is the economic foundation of national movements. Language is the most important means of human intercourse. Unity and unimpeded development of language are the most important conditions for genuinely free and extensive commerce on a scale commensurate with modern capitalism, for a free and broad grouping of the population in all its various classes and, lastly, for the establishment of a close connection between the market and each and every proprietor, big or little, and between seller and buyer.

Therefore, the tendency of every national movement is towards the formation of *national states*, under which these requirements of modern capitalism are best satisfied. The most profound economic factors drive towards this goal, and, therefore, for the whole of Western Europe, nay, for the entire civilised world, the national state is *typical* and normal for the capitalist period.

Consequently, it we want to grasp the meaning of self-determination of nations, not by juggling with legal definitions, or "inventing" abstract definitions, but by examining the historico-economic conditions of the national movements, we must inevitably reach the conclusion that the self-determination of nations means the political separation of these nations from alien national bodies, and the formation of an independent national state.

Later on we shall see still other reasons why it would be wrong to interpret the right to self-determination as meaning anything but the right to existence as a separate state. At present, we must deal with Rosa Luxemburg's efforts to "dismiss" the inescapable conclusion that profound economic factors underlie the urge-towards a national state.

Rosa Luxemburg is quite familiar with Kautsky's pamphlet *Nationality and Internationality*. (Supplement to Die Neue Zeit No. 1, 1907-08; Russian translation in the journal Nauchnaya Mysl, Riga, 1908.) She is aware that, after carefully analysing the question of the national state in §4 of that pamphlet, Kautsky arrived at the conclusion that Otto Bauer "*underestimates* the strength of the urge towards a national state" (p. 23 of the pamphlet). Rosa Luxemburg herself quotes the following words of Kautsky's: "The national state is the form *most suited* to present-day conditions, [*i.e.*, capitalist, civilised, economically progressive conditions, as distinguished from medieval, pre-capitalist, etc.]; it is the form in which the state can best fulfil its tasks" (*i.e.*, the tasks of securing the freest, widest and speediest development of capitalism). To this we must add Kautsky's still more precise concluding remark that states of mixed national composition (known as multi-national states, as distinct from national states) are "always those whose internal constitution has for some reason or other remained abnormal or underdeveloped" (backward). Needless to say, Kautsky speaks of abnormality exclusively in the sense of lack of conformity with what is best adapted to the requirements of a developing capitalism.

The question now is: How did Rosa Luxemburg treat these historico-economic conclusions of Kautsky's? Are they right or wrong? Is Kautsky right in his historico-economic theory, or is Bauer, whose theory is basically psychological? What is the connection between Bauer's undoubted "national opportunism", his defence of cultural-national autonomy, his nationalistic infatuation ("an occasional emphasis on the national aspect", as Kautsky put it), his "enormous exaggeration of the national aspect and complete neglect of the international aspect" (Kautsky)—and his underestimation of the strength of the urge to create a national state?

Rosa Luxemburg has not even raised this question. She has not noticed the connection. She has not considered the *sum total* of Bauer's theoretical views. She has not even drawn a line between the historico-economic and the psychological theories of the national question. She confines herself to the following remarks in criticism of Kautsky:

"This 'best' national state is only an abstraction, which can easily be developed and defended theoretically, but which does not correspond to reality." (*Przeglad Socjaldemokratyczny*, 1908, No. 6, p. 499.)

And in corroboration of this emphatic statement there follow arguments to the effect that the "right to self-determination" of small nations is made illusory by the development of the great capitalist powers and by imperialism. "Can one seriously speak," Rosa Luxemburg exclaims, "about the 'self-determination' of the formally independent Montenegrins, Bulgarians, Rumanians, Serbs, Greeks, partly even the Swiss, whose independence is itself a result of the political struggle and the diplomatic game of the 'concert of Europe'?!" (P. 500.) The state that best suits these conditions is "not a national state, as Kautsky believes, but a predatory one". Some dozens of figures are quoted relating to the size of British, French and other colonial possessions.

After reading such arguments, one cannot help marvelling at the author's ability to misunderstand *the how and the why of things*. To teach Kautsky, with a serious mien, that small states are economically dependent on big ones, that a struggle is raging among the bourgeois states for the predatory suppression of other nations, and that imperialism and colonies exist—all this is a ridiculous and puerile attempt to be clever, for none of this has the slightest bearing on the subject. Not only small states, but even Russia, for example, is entirely dependent, economically, on the power of the imperialist finance capital of the "rich" bourgeois countries. Not only the miniature Balkan states, but even nineteenth-century America was, economically, a colony of Europe, as Marx pointed out in Capital. Kautsky, like any Marxist, is, of course, well aware of this, but that has nothing whatever to do with the question of national movements and the national state.

For the question of the political self-determination of nations and their independence as states in bourgeois society, Rosa Luxemburg has substituted the question of their economic independence. This is just as intelligent as if someone, in discussing the programmatic demand for the supremacy of parliament, *i.e.*, the assembly of people's representatives, in a bourgeois state, were to expound the perfectly correct conviction that big capital dominates in a bourgeois country, whatever the regime in it.

There is no doubt that the greater part of Asia, the most densely populated continent, consists either of colonies of the "Great Powers", or of states that are extremely dependent and oppressed as nations. But does this commonly known circumstance in any way shake the undoubted fact that in Asia itself the conditions for the most complete development of commodity production and the freest, widest and speediest growth of capitalism have been created only in Japan, *i.e.*, only in an independent national state? The latter is a bourgeois state, and for that reason has itself begun to oppress other nations and to enslave colonies. We cannot say whether Asia will have had time to develop into a system of independent national states, like Europe, before the collapse of capitalism, but it remains an undisputed fact that capitalism, having awakened Asia, has called forth national movements everywhere in that continent, too; that the tendency of these movements is towards the creation of national states in Asia; that it is such states that ensure the best conditions for the development of capitalism. The example of Asia speaks *in favour* of Kautsky and *against* Rosa Luxemburg.

The example of the Balkan states likewise contradicts her, for anyone can now see that the best conditions for the development of capitalism in the Balkans are created precisely in proportion to the creation of independent national states in that peninsula.

Therefore, Rosa Luxemburg notwithstanding, the example of the whole of progressive and civilised mankind, the example of the Balkans and that of Asia prove that Kautsky's proposition is absolutely correct: the national state is the rule and the "norm" of capitalism; the multi-national state represents backwardness, or is an exception. From the standpoint of national relations, the best conditions for the development of capitalism are undoubtedly provided by the national state. This does not mean, of course, that such a state, which is based on bourgeois relations can eliminate the exploitation and oppression of nations. It only means that Marxists cannot lose sight of the powerful *economic* factors that give rise to the urge to create national states. It means that "self-determination of nations" in the Marxists' Programme *cannot*, from a historico-economic point of view, have any other meaning than political self-determination, state independence, and the formation of a national state.

The conditions under which the bourgeois-democratic demand for a "national state" should be supported from a Marxist, *i.e.*, class-proletarian, point of view will be dealt with in detail below. For the present, we shall confine ourselves to the definition of the *concept* of "self-determination", and only note that Rosa Luxemburg *knows* what this concept means ("national state"), whereas her opportunist partisans, the Liebmans, the Semkovskys, the Yurkeviches, *do not even know that*!

The Historically Concrete Presentation Of The Question

The categorical requirement of Marxist theory investigating any social question is that it be examined within *definite* historical limits, and, if it refers to a particular country (*e.g.*, the national programme for a given country), that account be taken of the specific features distinguishing that country from others in the same historical epoch.

What does this categorical requirement of Marxism imply in its application to the question under discussion?

First of all, it implies that a clear distinction must be drawn between the two periods of capitalism, which differ radically from each other as far as the national movement is concerned. On the one hand, there is the period of the collapse of feudalism and absolutism, the period of the formation of the bourgeois-democratic society and state, when the national movements for the first time become mass movements and in one way or another draw *all* classes of the population into politics through the press, participation in representative institutions, etc. On the other hand, there is the period of fully formed capitalist states with a long-established constitutional regime and a highly developed antagonism between the proletariat and the bourgeoisie—a period that may be called the eve of capitalism's downfall.

The typical features of the first period are: the awakening of national movements and the drawing of the peasants, the most numerous and the most sluggish section of the population, into these movements, in connection with the struggle for political liberty in general, and for the rights of the nation in particular. Typical features of the second period are: the absence of mass bourgeois-democratic movements and the fact that developed capitalism, in bringing closer together nations that have already been fully drawn into commercial intercourse, and causing them to intermingle to an increasing degree, brings the antagonism between internationally united capital and the international working-class movement into the forefront.

Of course, the two periods are not walled off from each other; they are connected by numerous transitional links, the various countries differing from each other in the rapidity of their national development, in the national makeup and distribution of their population, and so on. There can be no question of the Marxists of any country drawing up their national programme without taking into account all these general historical and concrete state conditions.

It is here that we come up against the weakest point in Rosa

Luxemburg's arguments. With extraordinary zeal she embellishes her article with a collection of hard words directed against §9 of our Programme, which she declares to be "sweeping", "a platitude", "a metaphysical phrase", and so on without end. It would be natural to expect an author who so admirably condemns metaphysics (in the Marxist sense, *i.e.*, anti-dialectics) and empty abstractions to set us an example of how to make a concrete historical analysis of the question. The question at issue is the national programme of the Marxists of a definite country—Russia in a definite period—the beginning of the twentieth century. But does Rosa Luxemburg raise the question as to *what historical* period Russia is passing through, or *what are the concrete* features of the national question and the national movements of that *particular* country in that *particular* period?

No. she does not! *She says absolutely nothing about it*! In her work you will not find even the shadow of an analysis of how the national question stands in *Russia* in the present historical period, or of the specific features of *Russia* in this particular respect!

We are told that the national question in the Balkans is presented differently from that in Ireland; that Marx appraised the Polish and Czech national movements in the concrete conditions of 1848 in such and such a way (a page of excerpts from Marx); that Engels appraised the struggle of the forest cantons of Switzerland against Austria and the Battle of Morgarten which took place in 1315 in such and such a way (a page of quotations from Engels with the appropriate comments from Kautsky), that Lassalle regarded the peasant war in Germany of the sixteenth century as reactionary, etc.

It cannot be said that these remarks and quotations have any novelty about them, but at all events it is interesting for the reader to be occasionally reminded just how Marx, Engels and Lassalle approached the analysis of concrete historical problems in individual countries. And a perusal of these instructive quotations from Marx and Engels reveals most strikingly the ridiculous position Rosa Luxemburg has placed herself in. She preaches eloquently and angrily the need for a concrete historical analysis of the national question in different countries at different times, but she *does not make the least* attempt to determine *what* historical stage in the development of capitalism *Russia* is passing through at the beginning of the twentieth century, or what the *specific features* of the national question in this country are. Rosa Luxemburg gives examples of how *others* have treated the question in a Marxist fashion, as if deliberately stressing how often the road to hell is paved with good intentions and how often good counsel covers up unwillingness or inability to follow such advice in practice.

Here is one of her edifying comparisons. In protesting against the demand for the independence of Poland, Rosa Luxemburg refers to a pamphlet she wrote in 1898, proving the rapid "industrial development of Poland", with the latter's manufactured goods being marketed in Russia. Needless to say, no conclusion whatever can be drawn from this on the question of the *right* to self-determination; it only proves the disappearance of the old Poland of the landed gentry, etc. But Rosa Luxemburg always passes on imperceptibly to the conclusion that among the factors that unite Russia and Poland, the purely economic factors of modern capitalist relations now predominate.

Then our Rosa proceeds to the question of autonomy, and though her article is entitled "The National Question and Autonomy" *in general*, she begins to argue that the Kingdom of Poland has an *exclusive* right to autonomy (see *Prosveshcheniye*, 1913, No. 12. To support Poland's right to autonomy, Rosa Luxemburg evidently judges the state system of Russia by her economic, political and sociological characteristics and everyday life—a totality of features which, taken together, produce the concept of "Asiatic despotism". (*Przeglad* No. 12, p. 137.)

It is generally known that this kind of state system possesses great stability whenever completely patriarchal and pre-capitalist features predominate in the economic system and where commodity production and class differentiation are scarcely developed. However, if in a country whose state system is distinctly *pre*-capitalist in character there exists a nationally demarcated region where capitalism is rapidly developing, then the more *rapidly* that capitalism develops, the greater will be the antagonism between it and the *pre*-capitalist state system, and the more likely will be the separation of the progressive region from the whole—with which it is connected, not by "modern capitalistic", but by "Asiatically despotic" ties.

Thus, Rosa Luxemburg does not get her arguments to hang together even on the question of the social structure of the government in Russia with regard to bourgeois Poland; as for the concrete, historical, specific features of the national movements in Russia—she does not even raise that question.

That is a point we must now deal with.

The Concrete Features of the National Question in Russia, and Russia's Bourgeois-Democratic Reformation

> "Despite the elasticity of the principle of 'the right of nations to self-determination', which is a mere platitude, and, obviously, equally applicable, not only to the nations inhabiting Russia, but also to the nations inhabiting Germany and Austria, Switzerland and Sweden, America and Australia, we do not find it in the programmes of any of the present-day socialist parties..." (*Przeglad* No. 6, p. 483.)

This is how Rosa Luxemburg opens her attack upon §9 of the Marxist programme. In trying to foist on us the conception that this clause in the programme is a "mere platitude", Rosa Luxemburg herself falls victim to this error, alleging with amusing boldness that this point is, "obviously, equally applicable" to Russia, Germany, etc.

Obviously, we shall reply, Rosa Luxemburg has decided to make her article a collection of errors in logic that could be used for schoolboy exercises. For Rosa Luxemburg's tirade is sheer nonsense and a mockery of the historically concrete presentation of the question.

If one interprets the Marxist programme in Marxist fashion, not in a childish way, one will without difficulty grasp the fact that it refers to bourgeois-democratic national movements. That being the case, it is "obvious" that this programme "sweepingly", and as a "mere platitude", etc., covers *all* instances of bourgeois-democratic national movements. No less obvious to Rosa Luxemburg, if she gave the slightest thought to it, is the conclusion that our programme refers *only* to cases where such a movement is actually in existence.

Had she given thought to these obvious considerations, Rosa Luxemburg would have easily perceived what nonsense she was talking. In accusing *us* of uttering a "platitude" she has used *against us* the argument that no mention is made of the right to self-determination in the programmes of countries where there are *no* bourgeois-democratic national movements. A remarkably clever argument!

A comparison of the political and economic development of various countries, as well as of their Marxist programmes, is of tremendous importance from the standpoint of Marxism, for there can be no doubt that all modern states are of a common capitalist nature and are therefore subject to a common law of development. But such a comparison must be drawn in a sensible way. The elementary condition for comparison is to find out whether the historical periods of development of the countries concerned are at all *comparable*. For instance, only absolute ignoramuses (such as Prince Y. Trubetskoi in *Russkaya Mysl*) are capable of "comparing" the Russian Marxists' agrarian programme with the programmes of Western Europe, since our programme replies to questions that concern the *bourgeois-democratic* agrarian reform, whereas in the Western countries no such question arises.

The same applies to the national question. In most Western countries it was settled long ago. It is ridiculous to seek an answer to non-existent questions in the programmes of Western Europe. In this respect Rosa Luxemburg has lost sight of the most important thing—the difference between countries where bourgeois-democratic reforms have long been completed, and those where they have not.

The crux of the matter lies in this difference. Rosa Luxemburg's complete disregard of it transforms her verbose article into a collection of empty and meaningless platitudes.

The epoch of bourgeois-democratic revolutions in Western, continental Europe embraces a fairly definite period, approximately between 1789 and 1871. This was precisely the period of national movements and the creation of national states. When this period drew to a close, Western Europe had been transformed into a settled system of bourgeois states, which, as a general rule, were nationally uniform states. Therefore, to seek the right to self-determination in the programmes of West-European socialists at this time of day is to betray one's ignorance of the ABC of Marxism.

In Eastern Europe and Asia the period of bourgeois-democratic revolutions did not begin until 1905. The revolutions in Russia, Persia, Turkey and China, the Balkan wars—such is the chain of world events of *our* period in our "Orient". And only a blind man could fail to see in this chain of events the awakening of a *whole series* of bourgeois-democratic national movements which strive to create nationally independent and nationally uniform states. It is precisely and solely because Russia and the neighbouring countries are passing through this period that we must have a clause in our programme on the right of nations to self-determination.

But let us continue the quotation from Rosa Luxemburg's article a little more. She writes:

> "In particular, the programme of a party which is operating in a state with an extremely varied national composition, and for which the national question is a matter of first-rate importance—the programme of the Austrian Social-Democratic Party—does not contain the principle of the right of nations to self-determination." (*Ibid.*)

Thus, an attempt is made to convince the reader by the example of Austria "in particular". Let us examine this example in the light of concrete historical facts and see just how sound it is.

In the first place, let us pose the fundamental question of the completion of the bourgeois-democratic revolution. In Austria, this revolution began in 1848 and was over in 1867. Since then, a more or less fully established bourgeois constitution has dominated, for nearly half a century, and on its basis a legal workers' party is legally functioning.

Therefore, in the internal conditions of Austria's development (*i.e.*, from the standpoint of the development of capitalism in Austria in general, and among its various nations in particular), there are *no* factors that produce leaps and bounds, a combination of which might be the formation of nationally independent states. In assuming, by her comparison, that Russia is in an analogous position in this respect, Rosa Luxemburg not only makes a fundamentally erroneous and anti-historical assumption, but also involuntarily slips into liquidationism.

Secondly, the profound difference in the relations between the nationalities in Austria and those in Russia is particularly important for the question we are concerned with. Not only was Austria for a long time a state in which the Germans preponderated, but the Austrian Germans laid claim to hegemony in the German nation as a whole. This "claim", as Rosa Luxemburg (who is seemingly so averse to commonplaces, platitudes, abstractions . . .) will perhaps be kind enough to remember, was shattered in the war of 1866. The German nation predominating in Austria found itself *outside the pale* of the independent German state which finally took shape in 1871. On the other hand, the Hungarians' attempt to create an independent national state collapsed under the blows of the Russian serf army as far back as 1849.

A very peculiar situation was thus created—a striving on the part of the Hungarians and then of the Czechs, not for separation from Austria, but, on the contrary, for the preservation of Austria's integrity, precisely in order to preserve national independence, which might have been completely crushed by more rapacious and powerful neighbours! Owing to this peculiar situation, Austria assumed the form of a dual state, and she is now being transformed into a triple state (Germans, Hungarians, Slavs).

Is there anything like this in Russia? Is there in our country a striving of the "subject peoples" for unity with the Great Russians in face of the danger of *worse* national oppression?

One need only pose this question in order to see that the comparison between Russia and Austria on the question of self-determination of nations is meaningless, platitudinous and ignorant.

The peculiar conditions in Russia with regard to the national question are just the reverse of those we see in Austria. Russia is a state with a single national centre—Great Russia. The Great Russians occupy a vast, unbroken stretch of territory, and number about 70,000,000. The specific features of this national state are: first, that "subject peoples" (which, on the whole, comprise the majority of the entire population—57 per cent) inhabit the border regions; secondly, the oppression of these subject peoples is much stronger here than in the neighbouring states (and not even in the European states alone); thirdly, in a number of cases the oppressed nationalities inhabiting the border regions have compatriots across the border, who enjoy greater national independence (suffice it to mention the Finns, the Swedes, the Poles, the Ukrainians and the Rumanians along the western and southern frontiers of the state); fourthly, the development of capitalism and the general level of culture are often higher in the non-Russian border regions than in the centre. Lastly, it is in the neighbouring Asian states that we see the beginning of a phase of bourgeois revolutions and national movements which are spreading to some of the kindred nationalities within the borders of Russia.

Thus, it is precisely the special concrete, historical features of the national question in Russia that make the recognition of the right of nations to self-determination in the present period a matter of special urgency in our country.

Incidentally, even from the purely factual angle, Rosa Luxemburg's assertion that the Austrian Social-Democrats' programme does not contain any recognition of the right of nations to self-determination is incorrect. We need only open the Minutes of the Brünn Congress, which adopted the national programme, to find the statements by the Ruthenian Social-Democrat Hankiewicz on behalf of the entire Ukrainian (Ruthenian) delegation (p. 85 of the Minutes), and by the Polish Social-Democrat Reger on behalf of the entire Polish delegation (p. 108), to the effect that one of the aspirations of the Austrian Social-Democrats of both the above-mentioned nations is to secure national unity, and the freedom and independence of their nations. Hence, while the Austrian Social-Democrats did not include the right of nations to self-determination directly in their programme, they did nevertheless allow the demand for national independence to be advanced by *sections* of the party. In effect, this means, of course, the recognition of the right of nations to self-determination! Thus, Rosa Luxemburg's reference to Austria speaks *against* Rosa Luxemburg in *all* respects.

"Practicality" In The National Question

Rosa Luxemburg's argument that §9 of our Programme contains nothing "practical" has been seized upon by the Opportunists. Rosa Luxemburg is so delighted with this argument that in some parts of her article this "slogan" is repeated eight times on a single page.

She writes: §9 "gives no practical lead on the day-by-day policy of the proletariat, no practical solution of national problems".

Let us examine this argument, which elsewhere is formulated in such a way that it makes §9 look quite meaning less, or else commits us to support all national aspirations.

What does the demand for "practicality" in the national question mean?

It means one of three things: support for all national aspirations; the answer "yes" or "no" to the question of secession by any nation; or that national demands are in general immediately "practicable".

Let us examine all three possible meanings of the demand for "practicality".

The bourgeoisie, which naturally assumes the leadership at the start of every national movement, says that support for all national aspirations is practical. However, the proletariat's policy in the national question (as in all others) supports the bourgeoisie only in a certain direction, but it never coincides with the bourgeoisie's policy. The working class supports the bourgeoisie only in order to secure national peace (which the bourgeoisie cannot bring about completely and which can be achieved only with *complete* democracy), in order to secure equal rights and to create the best conditions for the class struggle. Therefore, it is *in opposition to the practicality* of the bourgeoisie that the proletarians advance their *principles* in the national question; they always give the bourgeoisie *only conditional* support. What every bourgeoisie is out for in the national question is either privileges for its *own* nation, or exceptional advantages for it; this is called being "practical". The proletariat is opposed to all privileges, to all exclusiveness. To demand that it should be "practical" means following the lead of the bourgeoisie, falling into opportunism.

The demand for a "yes" or "no" reply to the question of secession in the case of every nation may seem a very "practical" one. In reality it is absurd; it is metaphysical in theory, while in practice it leads to subordinating the proletariat to the bourgeoisie's policy. The bourgeoisie always places its national demands in the forefront, and does so in categorical fashion. With the proletariat, however, these demands are subordinated to the interests of the class struggle. Theoretically, you cannot say in advance whether the bourgeois-democratic revolution will end in a given nation seceding from another nation, or in its equality with the latter; *in either case*, the important thing for the proletariat is to ensure the development of its class. For the bourgeoisie it is important to hamper this development by pushing the aims of its "own" nation before those of the proletariat. That is why the proletariat confines itself, so to speak, to the negative demand for recognition of the *right* to self-determination, without giving guarantees to any nation, and without undertaking to give anything at the *expense* of another nation.

This may not be "practical", but it is in effect the best guarantee for the achievement of the most democratic of all possible solutions. The proletariat needs *only* such guarantees, whereas the bourgeoisie of every nation requires guarantees for *its own* interest, regardless of the position of (or the possible disadvantages to) other nations.

The bourgeoisie is most of all interested in the "feasibility" of a given demand—hence the invariable policy of coming to terms with the bourgeoisie of other nations, to the detriment of the proletariat. For the proletariat, however, the important thing is to strengthen its class against the bourgeoisie and to educate the masses in the spirit of consistent democracy and socialism.

This may not be "practical" as far as the opportunists are concerned, but it is the only real guarantee, the guarantee of the greater national equality and peace, despite the feudal landlords and the *nationalist* bourgeoisie.

The whole task of the proletarians in the national question is "unpractical" from the standpoint of the *nationalist* bourgeoisie of every nation, because the proletarians, opposed as they are to nationalism of every kind, demand "abstract" equality; they demand, as a matter of principle, that there should be no privileges, however slight. Failing to grasp this, Rosa Luxemburg, by her misguided eulogy of practicality, has opened the door wide for the opportunists, and especially for opportunist concessions to Great-Russian nationalism.

Why Great-Russian? Because the Great Russians in Russia are an oppressor nation, and opportunism in the national question will of course find expression among oppressed nations otherwise than among oppressor nations.

On the plea that its demands are "practical", the bourgeoisie of the oppressed nations will call upon the proletariat to support its aspirations unconditionally. The most practical procedure is to say a plain "yes" in favour of the secession of a *particular* nation rather than in favour of all nations having the *right* to secede!

The proletariat is opposed to such practicality. While recognising equality and equal rights to a national state, it values above all and places foremost the alliance of the proletarians of all nations, and assesses any national demand, any national separation, *from the angle* of the workers' class struggle. This call for practicality is in fact merely a call for uncritical acceptance of bourgeois aspirations.

By supporting the right to secession, we are told, you are supporting the bourgeois nationalism of the oppressed nations. This is what Rosa Luxemburg says, and she is echoed by Semkovsky, the opportunist, who incidentally is the only representative of liquidationist ideas on this question, in the liquidationist newspaper!

Our reply to this is: No, it is to the bourgeoisie that a "practical" solution of this question is important. To the workers the important thing is to distinguish the *principles* of the two trends. *Insofar* as the bourgeoisie of the oppressed nation fights the oppressor, we are always, in every case, and more strongly than anyone else, *in favour*, for we are the staunchest and the most consistent enemies of oppression. But insofar as the bourgeoisie of the oppressed nation stands for *its own* bourgeois nationalism, we stand against. We fight against the privileges and violence of the oppressor nation, and do not in any way condone strivings for privileges on the part of the oppressed nation.

If, in our political agitation, we fail to advance and advocate the slogan of the *right* to secession, we shall play into the hands, not only of the bourgeoisie, but also of the feudal landlords and the absolutism of the *oppressor* nation. Kautsky long ago used this argument against Rosa Luxemburg, and the argument is indisputable. When, in her anxiety not to "assist" the nationalist bourgeoisie of Poland, Rosa Luxemburg rejects the *right* to secession in the programme of the Marxists *in Russia*, she is *in fact* assisting the Great-Russian Black Hundreds. She is in fact assisting opportunist tolerance of the privileges (and worse than privileges!) of the Great Russians.

Carried away by the struggle against nationalism in Poland, Rosa Luxemburg has forgotten the nationalism of the Great Russians, although it is *this* nationalism that is the most formidable at the present time. It is a nationalism that is more feudal than bourgeois, and is the principal obstacle to democracy and to the proletarian struggle. The bourgeois nationalism of *any* oppressed nation has a general democratic content that is directed *against* oppression, and it is this content that we *unconditionally* support. At the same time we strictly distinguish it from the tendency towards national exclusiveness; we fight against the tendency of the Polish bourgeois to oppress the Jews, etc., etc.

This is "unpractical" from the standpoint of the bourgeois and the philistine, but it is the only policy in the national question that is practical, based on principles, and really promotes democracy, liberty and proletarian unity.

The recognition of the right to secession for all; the appraisal of each concrete question of secession from the point of view of removing all inequality, all privileges, and all exclusiveness.

Let us consider the position of an oppressor nation. Can a nation be free if it oppresses other nations? It cannot. The interests of the freedom of the Great-Russian population[1] require a struggle against such oppression. The long, centuries-old history of the suppression of the movements of the oppressed nations, and the systematic propaganda in favour of such suppression coming from the "upper" classes have created enormous obstacles to the cause of freedom of the Great-Russian people itself, in the form of prejudices, etc.

The Great-Russian Black Hundreds deliberately foster these prejudices and encourage them. The Great-Russian bourgeoisie tolerates or condones them. The Great-Russian proletariat cannot achieve *its own* aims or clear the road to its freedom without systematically countering these prejudices.

In Russia, the creation of an independent national state remains, for the time being, the privilege of the Great-Russian nation alone. We, the Great-Russian proletarians, who defend no privileges whatever, do not defend this privilege either. We are fighting on the ground of a definite state; we unite the workers of all nations living in this state; we cannot vouch for any particular path of national development, for we are marching to our class goal along *all* possible paths.

However, we cannot move towards that goal unless we combat all nationalism, and uphold the equality of the various nations. Whether the Ukraine, for example, is destined to form an independent state is a matter that will be determined by a thousand unpredictable factors. Without attempting idle "*guesses* ", we firmly uphold something that is beyond doubt: the right of the Ukraine to form such a state. We respect this right; we do not uphold the privileges of Great Russians with regard to Ukrainians; we *educate* the masses in the spirit of recognition of that right, in the spirit of rejecting *state* privileges for any nation.

In the leaps which all nations have made in the period of bourgeois revolutions, clashes and struggles over the right to a national state are possible and probable. We proletarians declare in advance that we are *opposed* to Great-Russian privileges, and this is what guides our entire propaganda and agitation.

In her quest for "practicality" Rosa Luxemburg has lost sight of the *principal* practical task both of the Great-Russian proletariat and of the proletariat of other nationalities: that of day-by-day agitation and propaganda against all state and national privileges, and for the right, the equal right of all nations, to their national state. This (at present) is our principal task in the national question, for only in this way can we defend the interests of democracy and the alliance of all proletarians of all nations on an equal footing.

This propaganda may be "unpractical" from the point of view of the Great-Russian oppressors, as well as from the point of view of the bourgeoisie of the oppressed nations (both demand a *definite* "yes" or "no", and accuse the Social-Democrats of being "vague"). In reality it is this propaganda, and this propaganda alone, that ensures the genuinely democratic, the genuinely socialist education of the masses. This is the only propaganda to ensure the greatest chances of national peace in Russia, should she remain a multinational state, and the most peaceful (and for the proletarian class struggle, harmless) division into separate national states, should the question of such a division arise.

To explain this policy—the only proletarian policy—in the national question more concretely, we shall examine the attitude of Great-Russian liberalism towards the "self-determination of nations", and the example of Norway's secession from Sweden.

The Liberal Bourgeoisie and the Socialist Opportunists In The National Question

We have seen that the following argument is one of Rosa Luxemburg's "trump cards" in her struggle against the programme of the Marxists in Russia: recognition of the right to self-determination is tantamount to supporting the bourgeois nationalism of the oppressed nations. On the other hand, she says, if we take this right to mean no more than combating all violence against other nations, there is no need for a special clause in the programme, for Social-Democrats are, in general, opposed to all national oppression and inequality.

The first argument, as Kautsky irrefutably proved nearly twenty years ago, is a case of blaming other people for one's own nationalism, in her fear of the nationalism of the bourgeoisie of oppressed nations, Rosa Luxemburg is *actually* playing into the hands of the Black-Hundred nationalism of the Great Russians! Her second argument is actually a timid evasion of the question whether or not recognition of national equality includes recognition of the right to secession. If it does, then Rosa Luxemburg admits that, in principle, §9 of our Programme is correct. If it does not, then she does not recognise national equality. Shuffling and evasions will not help matters here!

However, the best way to test these and all similar arguments is to study the attitude of the *various classes* of society towards this question. For the Marxist this test is obligatory. We must proceed from what is objective; we must examine the relations between the classes on this point. In failing to do so, Rosa Luxemburg is guilty of those very sins of metaphysics, abstractions, platitudes, and sweeping statements, etc., of which she vainly tries to accuse her opponents.

We are discussing the Programme of the Marxists *in Russia*, *i.e.*, of the Marxists of all the nationalities in Russia. Should we not examine the position of the *ruling* classes of Russia?

The position of the "bureaucracy" (we beg pardon for this inaccurate term) and of the feudal landlords of our united-nobility type is well known. They definitely reject both the equality of nationalities and the right to self-determination. Theirs is the old motto of the days of serfdom: autocracy, orthodoxy, and the national essence—the last term applying only to the Great-Russian nation. Even the Ukrainians are declared to be an "alien" people and their very language is being suppressed.

Let us glance, at the Russian bourgeoisie, which was "called upon" to take part—a very modest part, it is true, but nevertheless some part—in the government, under the "June Third" legislative and administrative system. It will not need many words to prove that the Octobrists are following the Rights in this question. Unfortunately, some Marxists pay much less attention to the stand of the Great-Russian liberal bourgeoisie, the Progressists and the Cadets. Yet he who fails to study that stand and give it careful thought will inevitably flounder in abstractions and groundless statements in discussing the question of the right of nations to self-determination.

Skilled though it is in the art of diplomatically evading direct answers to "unpleasant" questions, *Rech*, the principal organ of the Constitutional-Democratic Party, was compelled, in its controversy with *Pravda* last year, to make certain valuable admissions. The trouble started over the All-Ukraine Students' Congress held in Lvov in the summer of 1913.[A] Mr. Mogilyansky, the "Ukrainian expert" or Ukrainian correspondent of *Rech*, wrote an article in which he poured vitriolic abuse ("ravings", "adventurism", etc.) on the idea that the Ukraine should secede, an idea which Dontsov, a nationalist-socialist, had advocated and the above-mentioned congress approved.

While in no way identifying itself with Mr. Dontsov, and declaring explicitly that he was a nationalist-socialist and that many Ukrainian Marxists did not agree with him, *Rabochaya Pravda* stated that the *tone of Rech*, or, rather, the *way it formulated the question in principle*, was improper and reprehensible for a Great-Russian democrat, or for anyone desiring to pass as a democrat. Let *Rech* repudiate the Dontsovs if it likes, but, *from the standpoint of principle*, a Great-Russian organ of democracy, which it claims to be, cannot be oblivious of the *freedom* to secede, the *right* to secede.

A few months later, *Rech*, No. 331, published an "explanation" from Mr. Mogilyansky, who had learned from the Ukrainian newspaper Shlyakhi, published in Lvov, of Mr. Dontsov's reply, in which, incidentally, Dontsov stated that "the chauvinist attacks in *Rech* have been properly sullied [branded?] only in the Russian Social-Democratic press". This "explanation" consisted of the thrice repeated statement that "criticism of Mr. Dontsov's recipes" "has nothing in common with the repudiation of the right of nations to self-determination".

"It must be said," wrote Mr. Mogilyansky, "that even 'the right of nations to self-determination' is not a fetish [mark this!] beyond criticism: unwholosome conditions in the life of nations may give rise to unwholesome tendencies in national self-determination, and the fact that these are brought to light does not mean that the right of nations to self-determination has been rejected.'?

As you see, this liberal's talk of a "fetish" was quite in keeping with Rosa Luxemburg's. It was obvious that Mr. Mogilyansky was trying to evade a direct reply to the question whether or not he recognised the right to political self-determination, *i.e.*, to secession.

The newspaper *Proletarskaya Pravda*, issue No. 4, for December 11, 1913, also put this question point-blank to Mr. Mogilyansky and to the Constitutional-Democratic *Party*.

Thereupon *Rech* (No. 340) published an unsigned, *i.e.*, official, editorial statement replying to this question. This reply boils down to the following three points:

1) §11 of the Constitutional-Democratic Party's programme speaks bluntly, precisely and clearly of the "right of nations to free *cultural* self-determination".

2) Rech affirms that *Proletarskaya Pravda* "hopelessly confuses" self-determination with separatism, with the secession of a given nation.

3) "*Actually, the Cadets have never pledged themselves to advocate the right of 'nations to secede'* from the Russian state." (See the article "National-Liberalism and the Right of Nations to Self-Determination", in *Proletarskaya Pravda* No. 12, December 20, 1913.)

Let us first consider the second point in the *Rech* statement. How strikingly it shows to the Semkovskys, Liebmans, Yurkeviches and other opportunists that the hue and cry they have raised about the alleged "vagueness", or "indefiniteness", of the term "self-determination" is *in fact*, *i.e.*, from the standpoint of objective class relationships and the class struggle in Russia, *simply a rehash* of the liberal-monarchist bourgeoisie's utterances!

Proletarskaya Pravda put the following *three* questions to the enlightened "Constitutional-Democratic" gentlemen of *Rech*: (1) do they deny that, throughout the entire history of international democracy, and especially since the middle of the nineteenth century, self-determination of nations has been understood to mean precisely political self-determination, the right to form an independent national state? (2) do they deny that the well-known resolution adopted by the International Socialist Congress in London in 1896 has the same meaning? and (3) do they deny that Plekhanov, in writing about self-determination as far back as 1902, meant precisely political self-determination? When *Proletarskaya Pravda* posed these three questions, *the Cadets fell silent*!

Not a word did they utter in reply, for they had nothing to say. They had to admit tacitly that *Proletarskaya Pravda* was absolutely right.

The liberals' outcries that the term "self-determination" is vague and that the Social-Democrats "hopelessly confuse" it with separatism are nothing more than attempts to *confuse* the issue, and evade recognition of a universally established democratic principle. If the

Semkovskys, Liebmans and Yurkeviches were not so ignorant, they would be ashamed to address the workers in a *liberal* vein.

But to proceed. *Proletarskaya Pravda* compelled *Rech* to admit that, in the programme of the Constitutional Democrats, the term "cultural" self-determination means in effect the *repudiation of political* self-determination.

"Actually, the Cadets have never pledged themselves to advocate the right of 'nations to secede' from the Russian state"—it was not without reason that *Proletarskaya Pravda* recommended to Novoye Vremya and *Zemshchina* these words from *Rech* as an example of our Cadets' "loyalty". In its issue No. 13563, *Novoye Vremya*, which never, of course, misses an opportunity of mentioning "the Yids" and taking digs at the Cadets, nevertheless stated:

> "What, to the Social-Democrats, is an axiom of political wisdom [*i.e.*, recognition of the right of nations to self-determination, to secede], is today beginning to cause disagreement even among the Cadets."

By declaring that they "have never pledged themselves to advocate the right of nations to secede from the Russian state", the Cadets have, in principle, taken exactly the same stand as *Novoye Vremya*. This is precisely one of the fundamentals of Cadet *national-liberalism*, of their kinship with the Purishkeviches, and of their dependence, political, ideological and practical, on the latter. *Proletarskaya Pravda* wrote: "The Cadets have studied history and know only too well what—to put it mildly—pogrom-like actions the practice of the ancient right of the Purishkeviches to 'grab' em and hold 'em' has often led to." Although perfectly aware of the feudalist source and nature of the Purish keviches' omnipotence, the Cadets are, nevertheless, taking their stand *on the basis* of the relationships and frontiers created by that very class. Knowing full well that there is much in the relationships and frontiers created or fixed by this class that is un-European and anti-European (we would say Asiatic if this did not sound undeservedly slighting to the Japanese and Chinese), the Cadets, nevertheless, accept them as the utmost limit.

Thus, they are adjusting themselves to the Purishkeviches, cringing to them, fearing to jeopardise their position, protecting them from the people's movement, from the democracy. As *Proletarskaya Pravda* wrote: "In effect, this means adapting oneself to the interests of the feudal-minded landlords and to the worst nationalist prejudices of the dominant nation, instead of systematically combating those prejudices."

Being men who are familiar with history and claim to be democrats, the Cadets do not even attempt to assert that the democratic movement, which is today characteristic of both Eastern Europe and Asia and is striving to change both on the model of the civilised capitalist countries, is bound to leave intact the boundaries fixed by the feudal epoch, the epoch of the omnipotence of the Purishkeviches and the disfranchisement of wide strata of the bourgeoisie and petty bourgeoisie.

The fact that the question raised in the controversy between *Proletarskaya Pravda* and *Rech* was not merely a literary question, but one that involved a real political issue of the day, was proved, among other things, by the last conference of the Constitutional-Democratic Party held on March 23-25, 1914; in the official report of this conference in *Rech* (No. 83, of March 26, 1914) we read:

> "A particularly lively discussion also took place on national problems. The Kiev deputies, who were supported by N. V. Nekrasov and A. M. Kolyubakin, pointed out that the national question was becoming a key issue, which would have to be faced up to more resolutely than hitherto. F. F. Kokoshkin pointed out, however [this "however" is like Shchedrin's "but"—"the ears never grow higher than the forehead, never!"] that both the programme and past political experience demanded that 'elastic formulas' of 'political self-determination of nationalities' should be handled very carefully."

This most remarkable line of reasoning at the Cadet conference deserves serious attention from all Marxists and all democrats. (We will note in parentheses that *Kievskaya Mysl*, which is evidently very well informed and no doubt presents Mr. Kokoshkin's ideas correctly, added that, of course, as a warning to his opponents, he laid special stress on the danger of the "disintegration" of the state.)

The official report in *Rech* is composed with consummate diplomatic skill designed to lift the veil as little as possible and to conceal as much as possible. Yet, in the main, what took place at the Cadet conference is quite clear. The liberal-bourgeois delegates, who were familiar with the state of affairs in the Ukraine, and the "Left" Cadets raised the question *precisely of the political* self-determination of nations. Otherwise, there would have been no need for Mr. Kokoshkin to urge that this "formula" should be "handled carefully".

The Cadet programme, which was of course known to the delegates at the Cadet conference, speaks of "cultural", *not* of political self-determination. Hence, Mr. Kokoshkin was *defending* the programme *against* the Ukrainian delegates, and *against* the Left Cadets; he was defending "cultural" self-determination *as opposed to* "political" self-determination. It is perfectly clear that in opposing "political" self-determination, in playing up the danger of the "disintegration of the state", and in calling the formula "political self-determination" an "*elastic* " one (quite in keeping with Rosa Luxemburg!), Mr. Kokoshkin was defending Great-Russian national-liberalism against the more "Left" or more democratic elements of the Constitutional-Democratic Party and also against the Ukrainian bourgeoisie.

Mr. Kokoshkin won the day at the Cadet conference, as is evident from the treacherous little word "however" in the *Rech* report; Great-Russian national-liberalism has triumphed among the Cadets. Will not this victory help to clear the minds of those misguided individuals among the Marxists in Russia who, like the Cadets, have also begun to fear the "elastic formulas of political self-determination of nationalities"?

Let us, "however", examine the substance of Mr. Kokoshkin's line of thought. By referring to "past political experience" (*i.e.*, evidently, the experience of 1905, when the Great-Russian bourgeoisie took alarm for its national privileges and scared the Cadet Party with its fears), and also by playing up the danger of the "disintegration of the state", Mr. Kokoshkin showed that he understood perfectly well that political self-determination can mean nothing else but the right to secede and form an independent national state. The question is—how should Mr. Kokoshkin's fears be appraised in the light of democracy in general, and the proletarian class struggle in particular?

Mr. Kokoshkin would have us believe that recognition of the right to secession increases the danger of the "disintegration of the state". This is the viewpoint of Constable Mymretsov, whose motto was "grab 'em and hold 'em". From the viewpoint of democracy in general, the very opposite is the case: recognition of the right to secession *reduces* the danger of the "disintegration of the state".

Mr. Kokoshkin argues exactly like the nationalists do. At their last congress they attacked the Ukrainian "Mazeppists". The Ukrainian movement, Mr. Savenko and Co. exclaimed, threatens to weaken the ties between the Ukraine and Russia, since Austrian Ukrainophilism is strengthening the Ukrainians' ties with Austria! It remains unexplained why Russia cannot try to "strengthen" her ties with the Ukrainians *through the same method* that the Savenkos blame Austria for using, *i.e.*, by granting the Ukrainians freedom to use their own language, self-government and an autonomous Diet.

The arguments of the Savenkos and Kokoshkins are exactly alike, and from the purely logical point of view they are equally ridiculous and absurd. Is it not clear that the more liberty the Ukrainian nationality enjoys in any particular country, the stronger its ties with that country will be? One would think that this truism could not be disputed without totally abandoning all the premises of democracy. Can there be greater freedom of nationality, as such, than the freedom to secede, the freedom to form an independent national state?

To clear up this question, which has been so confused by the liberals (and by those who are so misguided as to echo them), we shall cite a very simple example. Let us take the question of divorce. In her article Rosa Luxemburg writes that the centralised democratic state, while conceding autonomy to its constituent parts, should retain the most important branches of legislation, including legislation on divorce, under the jurisdiction of the central parliament. The concern that the central authority of the democratic state should retain the power to allow divorce can be readily understood. The reactionaries are opposed to freedom of divorce; they say that it must be "handled carefully", and loudly declare that it means the "disintegration of the family". The democrats, however, believe that the reactionaries are hypocrites, and that they are actually defending the omnipotence of the police and the bureaucracy, the privileges of one of the sexes, and the worst kind of oppression of women. They believe that in actual fact freedom of divorce will not cause the "disintegration" of family ties, but, on the contrary, will strengthen them on a democratic basis, which is the only possible and durable basis in civilised society.

To accuse those who support freedom of self-determination, *i.e.*, freedom to secede, of encouraging separatism, is as foolish and hypocritical as accusing those who advocate freedom of divorce of encouraging the destruction of family ties. Just as in bourgeois society the defenders of privilege and corruption, on which bourgeois marriage rests, oppose freedom of divorce, so, in the capitalist state, repudiation of the right to self-determination, *i.e.*, the right of nations to secede, means nothing more than defence of the privileges of the dominant nation and police methods of administration, to the detriment of democratic methods.

No doubt, the political chicanery arising from all the relationships existing in capitalist society sometimes leads members of parliament and journalists to indulge in frivolous and even nonsensical twaddle about one or another nation seceding. But only reactionaries can allow themselves to be frightened (or pretend to be frightened) by such talk. Those who stand by democratic principles, *i.e.*, who insist that questions of state be decided by the mass of the population, know very well that there is a "tremendous distance" [quoting from Griboyedov's comedy *Wit Works Woe*] between what the politicians prate about and what the people decide. From their daily experience the masses know perfectly well the value of geographical and economic ties and the advantages of a big market and a big state. They will, therefore, resort to secession only when national oppression and national friction make joint life absolutely intolerable and hinder any and all economic intercourse. In that case, the interests of capitalist development and of the freedom of the class struggle will be best served by secession.

Thus, from whatever angle we approach Mr. Kokoshkin's arguments, they prove to be the height of absurdity and a mockery of the principles of democracy. And yet there is a modicum of logic in these arguments, the logic of the class interests of the Great-Russian bourgeoisie. Like most members of the Constitutional-Democratic Party, Mr. Kokoshkin is a lackey of the money-bags of that bourgeoisie. He defends its privileges in general, and its *state* privileges in particular. He defends them hand in hand and shoulder to shoulder with Purishkevich, the only difference being that Purishkevich puts more faith in the feudalist cudgel, while Kokoshkin and Co. realise that this cudgel was badly damaged in 1905, and rely more on bourgeois methods of fooling the masses, such as frightening the petty bourgeoisie and the peasants with the spectre of the "disintegration of the state", and deluding them with phrases about blending "people's freedom" with historical tradition, etc.

The liberals' hostility to the principle of political self-determination of nations can have one, and only one, real class meaning: national-liberalism, defence of the state privileges of the Great-Russian bourgeoisie. And the opportunists among the Marxists in Russia, who today, under the Third of June regime, are against the right of nations to self-determination—the liquidator Semkovsky, the Bundist Liebman, the Ukrainian petty-bourgeois Yurkevich—are *actually* following in the wake of the national-liberals, and corrupting the working class with national-liberal ideas.

The interests of the working class and of its struggle against capitalism demand complete solidarity and the closest unity of the workers of all nations; they demand resistance to the nationalist policy of the bourgeoisie of every nationality. Hence, Social-Democrats would be deviating from proletarian policy and subordinating the workers to the policy of the bourgeoisie if they were to repudiate the right of nations to self-determination, *i.e.*, the right of an oppressed nation to secede, or if they were to support all the national demands of the bourgeoisie of oppressed nations. It makes no difference to the hired worker whether he is exploited chiefly by the Great-Russian bourgeoisie rather than the non-Russian bourgeoisie, or by the Polish bourgeoisie rather than the Jewish bourgeoisie, etc. The hired worker who has come to understand his class interests is equally indifferent to the state privileges of the Great-Russian capitalists and to the promises of the Polish or Ukrainian capitalists to set up an earthly paradise when they obtain state privileges. Capitalism is developing and will continue to develop, anyway, both in integral states with a mixed population and in separate national states.

In any case the hired worker will be an object of exploitation. Successful struggle against exploitation requires that the proletariat be free of nationalism, and be absolutely neutral, so to speak, in the fight for supremacy that is going on among the bourgeoisie of the various nations. If the proletariat of any one nation gives the slightest support to the privileges of its "own" national bourgeoisie, that will inevitably rouse distrust among the proletariat of another nation; it will weaken the international class solidarity of the workers and divide them, to the delight of the bourgeoisie. Repudiation of the right to self-determination or to secession inevitably means, in practice, support for the privileges of the dominant nation.

We will get even more striking confirmation of this if we take the concrete case of Norway's secession from Sweden.

Norway's Secession From Sweden

Rosa Luxemburg cites precisely this example, and discusses it as follows:

> "The latest event in the history of federative relations, the secession of Norway from Sweden—which at the time was hastily seized upon by the social-patriotic Polish press (see the Cracow Naprzód) as a gratifying sign of the strength and progressive nature of the tendency towards state secession—at

once provided striking proof that federalism and its concomitant, separation, are in no way an expression of progress or democracy. After the so-called Norwegian 'revolution', which meant that the Swedish king was deposed and compelled to leave Norway, the Norwegians coolly proceeded to choose another king, formally rejecting, by a national referendum, the proposal to establish a republic. That which superficial admirers of all national movements and of all semblance of independence proclaimed to be a 'revolution' was simply a manifestation of peasant and petty-bourgeois particularism, the desire to have a king 'of their own' for their money instead of one imposed upon them by the Swedish aristocracy, and was, consequently, a movement that had absolutely nothing in common with revolution. At the same time, the dissolution of the union between Sweden and Norway showed once more to what extent, in this case also, the federation which had existed until then was only an expression of purely dynastic interests and, therefore, merely a form of monarchism and reaction." (*Przegad.*)

That is literally all that Rosa Luxemburg has to say on this score! Admittedly, it would have been difficult for her to have revealed the hopelessness of her position more saliently than she has done in this particular instance.

The question was, and is: do the Social-Democrats in a mixed national state need a programme that recognises the right to self-determination or secession?

What does the example of Norway, cited by Rosa Luxemburg, tell us on this point?

Our author twists and turns, exercises her wit and rails at Naprzód, but she does not answer the question! Rosa Luxemburg speaks about everything under the sun so as to *avoid saying a single word* about the actual point at issue!

Undoubtedly, in wishing to have a king of their own for their money, and in rejecting, in a national referendum, the proposal to establish a republic, the Norwegian petty bourgeoisie displayed exceedingly bad philistine qualities. Undoubtedly, *Naprzód* displayed equally bad and equally philistine qualities in failing to notice this.

But what has all this to do with the case?

The question under discussion was the right of nations to self-determination and the attitude to be adopted by the socialist proletariat towards this right! Why, then, does not Rosa Luxemburg answer this question instead of beating about the bush?

To a mouse there is no stronger beast than the cat, it is said. To Rosa Luxemburg there is evidently no stronger beast than the "Fracy". "Fracy" is the popular term for the "Polish Socialist Party", its so-called revolutionary section, and the Cracow newspaper *Naprzód* shares the views of that "section". Rosa Luxemburg is so blinded by her fight against the nationalism of that "section" that she loses sight of everything except *Naprzód*.

If *Naprzód* says "yes", Rosa Luxemburg considers it her sacred duty to say an immediate "no", without stopping to think that by so doing she does not reveal independence of *Naprzód*, but, on the contrary, her ludicrous dependence on the "Fracy" and her inability to see things from a viewpoint any deeper and broader than that of the Cracow anthill. *Naprzód*, of course, is a wretched and by no means Marxist organ; but that should not prevent us from properly analysing the example of Norway, once we have chosen it.

To analyse this example in Marxist fashion, we must deal, not with the vices of the awfully terrible "Fracy", but, first, with the concrete historical features of the secession of Norway from Sweden, and secondly, with the tasks which confronted the *proletariat* of both countries in connection with this secession.

The geographic, economic and language ties between Norway and Sweden are as intimate as those between the Great Russians and many other Slav nations. But the union between Norway and Sweden was not a voluntary one, and in dragging in the question of "federation" Rosa Luxemburg was talking at random, simply because she did not know what to say. Norway was *ceded* to Sweden by the monarchs during the Napoleonic wars, against the will of the Norwegians; and the Swedes had to bring troops into Norway to subdue her.

Despite the very extensive autonomy which Norway enjoyed (she had her own parliament, etc.), there was constant friction between Norway and Sweden for many decades after the union, and the Norwegians strove hard to throw off the yoke of the Swedish aristocracy. At last, in August 1905, they succeeded: the Norwegian parliament resolved that the Swedish king was no longer king of Norway, and in the referendum held later among the Norwegian people, the overwhelming majority (about 200,000 as against a few hundred) voted for complete separation from Sweden. After a short period of indecision, the Swedes resigned themselves to the fact of secession.

This example shows us on what grounds cases of the secession of nations are practicable, and actually occur, under modern economic and political relationships, and the *form* secession sometimes assumes under conditions of political freedom and democracy.

No Social-Democrat will deny—unless he would profess indifference to questions of political freedom and democracy (in which case he is naturally no longer a Social-Democrat)—that this example *virtually* proves that it is the *bounden duty* of class-conscious workers to conduct systematic propaganda and prepare the ground for the settlement of conflicts that may arise over the secession of nations, not in the "Russian way", but *only in the way* they were settled in 1905 between Norway and Sweden. This is exactly what is meant by the demand in the programme for the recognition of the right of nations to self-determination. But Rosa Luxemburg tried to get around a fact that was repugnant to her theory by violently attacking the philistinism of the Norwegian philistines and the Cracow *Naprzód*; for she understood perfectly well that this historical fact *completely refutes* her phrases about the right of nations to self-determination being a "utopia", or like the right "to eat off gold plates", etc. Such phrases only express a smug and opportunist belief in the immutability of the present alignment of forces among the nationalities of Eastern Europe.

To proceed. In the question of the self-determination of nations, as in every other question, we are interested, first and foremost, in the self-determination of the proletariat within a given nation. Rosa Luxemburg modestly evaded this question too, for she realised that an analysis of it on the basis of the example of Norway, which she herself had chosen, would be disastrous to her "theory".

What position did the Norwegian and Swedish proletariat take, and indeed had to take, in the conflict over secession? *After* Norway seceded, the class-conscious workers of Norway would naturally have voted for a republic,[2] and if some socialists voted otherwise it only goes to show how much dense, philistine opportunism there sometimes is in the European socialist movement. There can be no two opinions about that, and we mention the point only because Rosa Luxemburg is trying to obscure the issue by speaking *off the mark.* We do not know whether the Norwegian socialist programme made it obligatory for Norwegian Social-Democrats to hold particular views on the question of secession. We will assume that it did not, and that the Norwegian socialists left it an open question as to what extent the autonomy of Norway gave sufficient scope to wage the class struggle freely, or to what extent the eternal friction and conflicts with the Swedish aristocracy hindered freedom of economic life. But it cannot be disputed that the Norwegian proletariat had to oppose this aristocracy and support Norwegian peasant democracy (with all its philistine limitations).

And the Swedish proletariat? It is common knowledge that the Swedish landed proprietors, abetted by the Swedish clergy, advocated war against Norway. Inasmuch as Norway was much weaker than Sweden, had already experienced a Swedish invasion, and the Swedish aristocracy carries enormous weight in its own country, this advocacy of war presented a grave danger. We may be sure that the Swedish Kokoshkins spent much time and energy in trying to corrupt the minds of the Swedish people by appeals to "handle" the "elastic formulas of political self-determination of nations carefully" by painting horrific pictures of the danger of the "disintegration of the state" and by assuring them that "people's freedom" was compatible with the traditions of the Swedish aristocracy. There cannot be the slightest doubt that the Swedish Social-Democrats would have betrayed the cause of socialism and democracy if they had not fought with all their might to combat both the landlord and the "Kokoshkin" ideology and policy, and if they had failed to demand, *not only* equality of nations in general (to which the Kokoshkins also subscribe), but also the right of nations to self-determination, Norway's freedom to secede.

The close alliance between the Norwegian and Swedish workers, their complete fraternal class solidarity, *gained* from the Swedish workers' recognition of the right of the Norwegians to secede. This convinced the Norwegian workers that the Swedish workers were not infected with Swedish nationalism, and that they placed fraternity with the Norwegian proletarians above the privileges of the Swedish bourgeoisie and aristocracy. The dissolution of the ties imposed upon Norway by the monarchs of Europe and the Swedish aristocracy strengthened the ties between the Norwegian and Swedish workers. The Swedish workers have proved that in spite of *all* the vicissitudes of bourgeois policy—bourgeois relations may quite possibly bring about a repetition of the forcible subjection of the Norwegians to the Swedes!—they will be able to preserve and defend the complete equality and class solidarity of the workers of both nations in the struggle against both the Swedish and the Norwegian bourgeoisie.

Incidentally, this reveals how groundless and even frivolous are the attempts sometimes made by the "Fracy" to "use" our disagreements with Rosa Luxemburg against Polish Social-Democracy. The "Fracy" are not a proletarian or a socialist party, but a petty-bourgeois nationalist party, something like Polish Social-Revolutionaries. There never has been, nor could there be, any question of unity between the Russian Social-Democrats and this party. On the other hand no Russian Social-Democrat has ever "repented" of the close relations and unity that have been established with the Polish Social-Democrats. The Polish Social-Democrats have rendered a great historical service by creating the first really Marxist, proletarian party in Poland, a country imbued with nationalist aspirations and passions. Yet the service the Polish Social-Democrats have rendered is a great one, not because Rosa Luxemburg has talked a lot of nonsense ahout §9 of the Russian Marxists' Programme, but despite that sad circumstance.

The question of the "right to self-determination" is of course not so important to the Polish Social-Democrats as it is to the Russian. It is quite understandable that in their zeal (sometimes a little excessive, perhaps) to combat the nationalistically blinded petty bourgeoisie of Poland the Polish Social-Democrats should overdo things. No Russian Marxist has ever thought of blaming the Polish Social-Democrats for being opposed to the secession of Poland. These Social-Democrats err only when, like Rosa Luxemburg, they try to deny the necessity of including the recognition of the right to self-determination in the Programme of the *Russian* Marxists.

Virtually, this is like attempting to apply relationships, understandable by Cracow standards, to all the peoples and nations inhabiting Russia, including the Great Russians. It means being "Polish nationalists the wrong way round", not Russian, not international Social-Democrats.

For international Social-Democracy stands for the recognition of the right of nations to self-determination. This is what we shall now proceed to discuss.

The Resolution Of The London International Congress, 1896

This resolution reads:

"This Congress declares that it stands for the full right of all nations to self-determination [*Selbstbestimmungsrecht*] and expresses its sympathy for the workers of every country now suffering under the yoke of military, national or other absolutism. This Congress calls upon the workers of all these countries to join the ranks of the class-conscious [*Klassenbewusste*—those who understand their class interests] workers of the whole world in order jointly to fight for the defeat of international capitalism and for the achievement of the aims of international

Social-Democracy."[3]

As we have already pointed out, our opportunists—Semkovsky, Liebman and Yurkevich—are simply unaware of this resolution. But Rosa Luxemburg knows it and quotes the full text, which contains the same expression as that contained in our programme, viz., "self-determination".

How does Rosa Luxemburg remove this obstacle from the path of her "original" theory?

Oh, quite simply…the whole emphasis lies in the second part of the resolution…its declarative character…one can refer to it only by mistake!

The feebleness and utter confusion of our author are simply amazing. Usually it is only the opportunists who talk about the consistent democratic and socialist points in the programme being mere declarations, and cravenly avoid an open debate on them. It is apparently not without reason that Rosa Luxemburg has this time found herself in the deplorable company of the Semkovskys, Liebmans and Yurkeviches. Rosa Luxemburg does not venture to state openly whether she regards the above resolution as correct or erroneous. She shifts and shuffles as if counting on the inattentive or ill-informed reader, who forgets the first part of the resolution by the time he has started reading the second, or who has never heard of the discussion that took place in the socialist press *prior* to the London Congress.

Rosa Luxemburg is greatly mistaken, however, if she imagines that, in the sight of the class-conscious workers of Russia, she can get away with trampling upon the resolution of the International on such an important fundamental issue, without even deigning to analyse it critically.

Rosa Luxemburg's point of view was voiced during the discussion which took place prior to the London Congress, mainly in the columns of *Die Neue Zeit*, organ of the German Marxists; *in essence this point of view was defeated in the International* ! That is the crux of the matter, which the Russian reader must particularly bear in mind.

The debate turned on the question of Poland's independence. Three points of view were put forward:

1. That of the "Fracy", in whose name Haecker spoke. They wanted the International to include in *its own* programme a demand for the independence of Poland. The motion was not carried and this point of view was defeated in the International.

2. Rosa Luxemburg's point of view, viz., the Polish socialists should not demand independence for Poland. This point of view entirely precluded the proclamation of the right of nations to self-determination. It was likewise defeated in the International.

3. The point of view which was elaborated at the time by K. Kautsky, who opposed Rosa Luxemburg and proved that her materialism was extremely "one-sided"; according to Kautsky, the International could not at the time make the independence of Poland a point in its programme; but the Polish socialists were fully entitled to put forward such a demand. From the socialists' point of view it was undoubtedly a mistake to ignore the tasks of national liberation in a situation where national oppression existed.

The International's resolution reproduces the most essential and fundamental propositions in this point of view: on the one hand, the absolutely direct, unequivocal recognition of the full right of all nations to self-determination; on the other hand, the equally unambiguous appeal to the workers for *international* unity in their class struggle.

We think that this resolution is absolutely correct, and that, to the countries of Eastern Europe and Asia at the beginning of the twentieth century, it is this resolution, with both its parts being taken as an integral whole, that gives the only correct lead to the proletarian class policy in the national question.

Let us deal with the three above-mentioned viewpoints in somewhat greater detail.

As is known, Karl Marx and Frederick Engels considered it the bound duty of the whole of West-European democracy, and still more of Social-Democracy, to give active support to the demand for Polish independence. For the period of the 1840s and 1860s, the period of the bourgeois revolutions in Austria and Germany, and the period of the "Peasant Reform" in Russia [the abolition of serfdom in 1861], this point of view was quite correct and the only one that was consistently democratic and proletarian. So long as the masses of the people in Russia and in most of the Slav countries were still sunk in torpor, so long as *there were no* independent, mass, democratic movements in those countries, the liberation movement [1863-64] of the *gentry* in Poland assumed an immense and paramount importance from the point of view, not only of Russian, not only of Slav, but of European democracy as a whole.[4]

But while Marx's standpoint was quite correct for the forties, fifties and sixties or for the third quarter of the nineteenth century, it has ceased to be correct by the twentieth century. Independent democratic movements, and even an independent proletarian movement, have arisen in most Slav countries, even in Russia, one of the most backward Slav countries. Aristocratic Poland has disappeared, yielding place to capitalist Poland. Under such circumstances Poland could not but lose her *exceptional* revolutionary importance.

The attempt of the P.S.P. (the Polish Socialist Party, the present-day "Fracy") in 1896 to "establish" for all time the point of view Marx had held in a *different epoch* was an attempt to use the *letter* of Marxism against the *spirit* of Marxism. The Polish Social-Democrats were therefore quite right in attacking the extreme nationalism of the Polish petty bourgeoisie and pointing out that the national question was of secondary importance to Polish workers, in creating for the first time a purely proletarian party in Poland and proclaiming the extremely important principle that the Polish and the Russian workers must maintain the closest alliance in their class struggle.

But did this mean that at the beginning of the twentieth century the International could regard the principle of political self-determination of nations, or the right to secede, as unnecessary to Eastern

Europe and Asia? This would have been the height of absurdity, and (theoretically) tantamount to admitting that the bourgeois-democratic reform of the Turkish, Russian and Chinese states had been consummated; indeed it would have been tantamount (in practice) to opportunism towards absolutism.

No. At a time when bourgeois-democratic revolutions in Eastern Europe and Asia have begun, in this period of the awakening and intensification of national movements and of the formation of independent proletarian parties, the task of these parties with regard to national policy must be twofold: recognition of the right of all nations to self-determination, since bourgeois-democratic reform is not yet completed and since working-class democracy consistently, seriously and sincerely (and not in a liberal, Kokoshkin fashion) fights for equal rights for nations; then, a close, unbreakable alliance in the class struggle of the proletarians of all nations in a given state, throughout all the changes in its history, irrespective of any reshaping of the frontiers of the individual states by the bourgeoisie.

It is this twofold task of the proletariat that the 1896 resolution of the International formulates. That is the substance, the underlying principle, of the resolution adopted by the Conference of Russian Marxists held in the summer of 1913. Some people profess to see a "contradiction" in the fact that while point 4 of this resolution, which recognises the right to self-determination and secession, seems to "concede" the maximum to nationalism (in reality, the recognition of the *right of all* nations to self-determination implies the maximum of *democracy* and the minimum of nationalism), point 5 warns the workers against the nationalist slogans of the bourgeoisie of any nation and demands the unity and amalgamation of the workers of all nations in internationally united proletarian organisations. But this is a "contradiction" only for extremely shallow minds, which, for instance, cannot grasp why the unity and class solidarity of the Swedish and the Norwegian proletariat *gained* when the Swedish workers upheld Norway's freedom to secede and form an independent state.

To sum up.

As far as the theory of Marxism in general is concerned, the question of the right to self-determination presents no difficulty. No one can seriously question the London resolution of 1896, or the fact that self-determination implies only the right to secede, or that the formation of independent national states is the tendency in all bourgeois-democratic revolutions.

A difficulty is to some extent created by the fact that in Russia the proletariat of both the oppressed and oppressor nations are fighting, and must fight, side by side. The task is to preserve the unity of the proletariat's class struggle for socialism, and to resist all bourgeois and Black-Hundred nationalist influences. Where the oppressed nations are concerned, the separate organisation of the proletariat as an independent party sometimes leads to such a bitter struggle against local nationalism that the perspective becomes distorted and the nationalism of the oppressor nation is lost sight of.

But this distortion of perspective cannot last long. The experience of the joint struggle waged by the proletarians of various nations has demonstrated all too clearly that we must formulate political issues from the all-Russia, not the "Cracow" point of view. And in all-Russia politics it is the Purishkeviches and the Kokoshkins who are in the saddle. Their ideas predominate, and their persecution of non-Russians for "separatism", for *thinking* about secession, is being preached and practised in the Duma, in the schools, in the churches, in the barracks, and in hundreds and thousands of newspapers. It is this Great-Russian nationalist poison that is polluting the entire all-Russia political atmosphere. This is the misfortune of one nation, which, by subjugating other nations, is strengthening reaction throughout Russia. The memories of 1849 and 1863 form a living political tradition, which, unless great storms arise, threatens to hamper every democratic and *especially* every Social-Democratic movement for decades to come.

There can be no doubt that however natural the point of view of certain Marxists belonging to the oppressed nations (whose "misfortune" is sometimes that the masses of the population are blinded by the idea of their "own" national liberation) may appear at times, *in reality* the objective alignment of class forces in Russia makes refusal to advocate the right to self-determination tantamount to the worst opportunism, to the infection of the proletariat with the ideas of the Kokoshkins. And these ideas are, essentially the ideas and the policy of the Purishkeviches.

Therefore, although Rosa Luxemburg's point of view could at first have been excused as being specifically Polish, "Cracow" narrow-mindedness,[5] it is inexcusable today, when nationalism and, above all, governmental Great-Russian nationalism, has everywhere gained ground, and when policy is being shaped by this *Great-Russian nationalism*. In actual fact, it is being seized upon by the opportunists of *all* nations, who fight shy of the idea of "storms" and "leaps", believe that the bourgeois-democratic revolution is over, and follow in the wake of the liberalism of the Kokoshkins.

Like any other nationalism, Great-Russian nationalism passes through various phases, according to the classes that are dominant in the bourgeois country at any given time. Up to 1905, we almost exclusively knew national reactionaries. After the revolution, *national-liberals* arose in our country.

In our country this is virtually the stand adopted both by the Octobrists and by the Cadets (Kokoshkin), *i.e.*, by the whole of the present-day bourgeoisie.

Great-Russian national-democrats will *inevitably* appear later on. Mr. Peshekhonov, one of the founders of the "Popular Socialist" Party, already expressed this point of view (in the issue of *Russkoye Bogatstvo* for August 1906) when he called for caution in regard to the peasants' nationalist prejudices. However much others may slander us Bolsheviks and accuse us of "idealising" the peasant, we always have made and always will make a clear distinction between peasant intelligence and peasant prejudice, between peasant strivings for democracy and opposition to Purishkevich, and the peasant desire to make peace with the priest and the landlord.

Even now, and probably for a fairly long time to come, proletarian democracy must reckon with the nationalism of the Great-Russian peasants (not with the object of making concessions to it, but in order to combat it).[6] The awakening of nationalism among the oppressed nations, which became so pronounced after 1905 (let us recall, say, the group of "Federalist-Autonomists" in the First Duma, the growth of the Ukrainian movement, of the Moslem movement, etc.), will inevitably lead to greater nationalism among the Great-Russian petty bourgeoisie in town and countryside. The slower the democratisation of Russia, the more persistent, brutal and bitter will be the national persecution and bickering among the bourgeoisie of the various nations. The particularly reactionary nature of the Russian Purishkeviches will simultaneously give rise to (and strengthen) "separatist" tendencies among the various oppressed nationalities, which sometimes enjoy far greater freedom in neighbouring states.

In this situation, the proletariat of Russia is faced with a twofold or, rather, a two-sided task: to combat nationalism of every kind, above all, Great-Russian nationalism; to recognise, not only fully equal rights for all nations in general, but also equality of rights as regards polity, *i.e.*, the right of nations to self-determination, to secession. And at the same time, it is their task, in the interests of a successful struggle against all and every kind of nationalism among all nations, to preserve the unity of the proletarian struggle and the proletarian organisations, amalgamating these organisations into a close-knit international association, despite bourgeois strivings for national exclusiveness.

Complete equality of rights for all nations; the right of nations to self-determination; the unity of the workers of all nations—such is the national programme that Marxism, the experience of the whole world, and the experience of Russia, teach the workers.

This article had been set up when I received No. 3 of *Nasha Rabochaya Gazeta*, in which Mr. Vl. Kossovsky writes the following about the recognition of the right of all nations to self-determination:

> "Taken mechanically from the resolution of the First Congress of the Party (1898), which in turn had borrowed it from the

decisions of international socialist congresses, it was given, as is evident from the debate, the samf meaning at the 1903 Congress as was ascribed to it by the Socialist International, *i.e.*, political self-determination, the self-determination of nations in the field of political independence. Thus the formula: national self-determination, which implies the right to territorial separation, does not in any way affect the question of how national relations within a given state organism should be regulated for nationalities that cannot or have no desire to leave the existing state."

It is evident from this that Mr. Vl. Kossovsky has seen the Minutes of the Second Congress of 1903 and understands perfectly well the real (and only) meaning of the term self-determination. Compare this with the fact that the editors of the Bund newspaper *Zeit* let Mr. Liebman loose to scoff at the programme and to declare that it is vague! Queer "party" ethics among these Bundists... The Lord alone knows why Kossovsky should declare that the Congress took over the principle of self-determination mechanically. Some people want to "object", but how, why, and for what reason—they do not know.

FOOT NOTES:

1. A certain L. Vl. [L. Vladimirov (pseudonym of M. K. Sheinfinkel)—a Social-Democrat.] in Paris considers this word un-Marxist. This L. Vl. is amusingly "*superklug*" (too clever by half). And "this too-clever-by-half" L. Vl. apparently intends to write an essay on the deletion of the words "population", "nation", etc., from our minimum programme (having in mind the class struggle!).

[A] This refers to the *Second All-Ukraine Students' Congress* held in Lvov on June 19-22 (July 2-5), 1913, to coincide with anniversary celebrations in honour of Ivan Franko, the great Ukrainian writer, scholar, public figure, and revolutionary democrat. A report, "The Ukrainian Youth and the Present Status of the Nations," was made at the Congress by the Ukrainian Social-Democrat Dontsov, who supported the slogan of an "independent" Ukraine

2. Since the majority of the Norwegian nation was in favour of a monarchy while the proletariat wanted a republic, the Norwegian proletariat was, generally speaking, confronted with the alternative: either revolution, if conditions were ripe for it, or submission to the will of the majority and prolonged propaganda and agitation work.
3. See the official German report of the London Congress: *Verhandlungen und Beschlüsse des internationalen sozialistischen Arbeiterund Gewerkschafts-Kongresses zu London, vom 27. Juli bis 1. August 1896*, Berlin, 1897, S. 18. A Russian pamphlet has been published containing the decisions of international congresses in which the word "self-determination" is wrongly translated as "autonomy".
4. It would be a very interesting piece of historical research to compare the position of a noble Polish rebel in 1863 with that of the all-Russia revolutionary democrat, Chernyshevsky, who (like Marx), was able to appreciate the importance of the Polish movement, and with that of the Ukrainian petty bourgeois Dragomanov, who appeared much later and expressed the views of a peasant, so ignorant and sluggish, and so attached to his dung heap, that his legitimate hatred of the Polish gentry blinded him to the significance which their struggle had for all-Russia democracy. (Cf. Dragomanov *Historical Poland and Great-Russian Dcmocracy.*) Dragomanov richly deserved the fervent kisses which were subsequently bestowed on him by Mr. P. B. Struve, who by that time had become a national-liberal.
5. It is not difflcult to understand that the recognition by the Marxists of the *whole of Russia*, and first and foremost by the Great Russians, of the *right* of nations to secede in no way precludes *agitation* against

secession by Marxists of a particular oppressed nation, just as the recognition of the right to divorce does not preclude agitation against divorce in a particular case. We think, therefore, that there will be an inevitable increase in the number of Polish Marxists who laugh at the non-existent "contradiction" now being "encouraged" by Semkovsky and Trotsky.

6. It would be interesting to trace the changes that take place in Polish nationalism, for example, in the process of its transformation from gentry nationalism into bourgeois nationalism, and then into peasant nationalism. In his book *Das polnische Gemeinwesen im preussischen Staat* (*The Polish Community in the Prussian State*; there is a Russian translation), Ludwig Bernhard, who shares the view of a German Kokoshkin, describes a very typical phenomenon: the formation of a sort of "peasant republic" by the Poles in Germany in the form of a close alliance of the various co-operatives and other associations of *Polish* peasants in their struggle for nationality, religion, and "Polish" land. German oppression has welded the Poles together and segregated them, after first awakening the nationalism of the gentry, then of the bourgeoisie, and finally of the peasant masses (especially after the campaign the Germans launched in 1873 against the use of the Polish language in schools). Things are moving in the same direction in Russia, and not only with regard to Poland.

THE SOCIAL REVOLUTION AND ON THE DAY AFTER THE SOCIAL REVOLUTION

Karl Kautsky

Chapter-9

Introduction

The greater part of the first half of this translation was already completed before the numbers of *Justice* containing the translation of J. B. Askew reached us. Hence little use could be made of that work. Some comparisons with the first few pages were made in the proofs, and a few alterations made in accordance with suggestions there received, for which we wish to give due credit. The present translation has also been compared with the French translation of the first part which appeared in Le Mouvemente Socialiste.

Finally we wish to extend our thanks to Comrade Kautsky for his kind permission to bring this translation of what we believe to be one of the most important contributions made to Socialist literature during the last decade before American readers.

The following writings owe their existence to the action of a Socialist Reading Circle in Amsterdam, a society largely comyoscd of Academics, who invited me to speak there and in Delft. Among the themes that I suggested was that of Social Revolution. But as the comrades in both cities selected the same theme, and I did not wish to repeat myself, I divided my subject into tmo essays practically independent from one another, but connected in their general thought, and called it "Reform and Revolution" and "On the Day After the Revolution."

The Society wished to publish these essays and naturally I had no reason to object to this, but in the interest of their circulation I proposed that they be issued br the German Party Publishing House, to which the Holland comrades very gladly agreed.

It is not a stenographic report of the lectures that is here given. I have included many lines of thought, in the writing which would have been too long to have given in the lectures. But in general I have kept within the limits of the lecture and have not sought to make a book of it.

The purpose of the work shows for itself and needs no explanation. It had a special application for Holland in that shortly before my lectures, which took place on the 22d and 24th of April, 1902, the former minister Pierson had made an assertion in a public assemblage, and argued for it, that a proletarian revolution must, for certain necessary reasons, be avoided, my lectures form a direct answer to this. The Minister was, however, so friendly as to attend the second one, where he made industrious notes and did not offer a word against me.

Because of the predominating academic character of the public that attended, aside from local and propagandist reasons, I was led to choose the theme of Social Revolution for the lecture. The Academics are those among us who are least friendly to the idea of revolution, at least in Germany. All things considered, however, the case appeared somewhat different in Holland and the applause of my audience there very pleasantly surprised me. Ms assertions raised scarcely any antagonism, but only approval. I hope that this is not entirely because of international politeness. If not, Marxism has a body of strong representatives among the Academics of Holland.

I can wish nothing better than that my attempt should receive the same approval among German comrades that it has found among those of Holland, and I extend my thanks to the latter for the friendly reception they have given me in a very agreeable duty.

The Social Revolution

The Concept of Social Revolution

There are few conceptions over which there has been so much contention, as over that of revolution. This can partially be ascribed to the fact that nothing is so contrary to existing interests and prejudices as this concept, and partially to the fact that few things are so ambiguous.

As a rule, events can not be so sharply defined as things.

Especially is this true of social events, which are extremely complicated, and grow ever more complicated the further society advances—the more various the forms of co-operation of humanity become. Among the most complicated of these events is the Social Revolution, which is a complete transformation of the wonted forms of associated activity among men.

It is no wonder that this word, which every one uses, but each one in a different sense, is sometimes used by the same persons at different times in very different senses. Some understand by Revolution barricades, conflagrations of castles, guillotines, September massacres and a combination of all sorts of hideous things. Others would seek to take all sting away from the word and use it in the sense of great but imperceptible and peaceful transformations of society, like, for instance, those which took place through the discovery of America or by the invention of the steam engine. Between these two definitions there are many grades of meaning.

Marx, in his introduction to the "Critique of Political Economy," defines social revolution as a more or less rapid transformation of the foundations of the juridical and political superstructure of society arising from a change in its economic foundations. If we hold close to this definition we at once eliminate from the idea of social revolution "changes in the economic foundations," as, for example, those which proceeded from the steam engine or the discovery of America. These alterations are the causes of revolution, not the revolution itself.

But I do not wish to confine myself too strictly to this definition of social revolution. There is a still narrower sense in which we can use it. In this case it does not signify either the transformation of the juridical and political superstructure of society, but only some particular form or particular method of transformation.

Every socialist strives for social revolution in the wider sense, and yet there are socialists who disclaim revolution and would attain social transformation only through reform. They contrast social revolution with social reform. It is this contrast which we are discussing today in our ranks. I wish here to consider social revolution in the narrow sense of a particular method of social transformation.

The contrast between reform and revolution does not consist in the application of force in one case and not in the other. Every juridical and political measure is a force measure which is carried through by the force of the State. Neither do ally particular forms of the application of force, as, for example, street fights, or executions, constitute the essentials of revolution in contrast to reform. These arise from particular circumstances, are not necessarily connected with revolutions, and may easily accompany reform movements. The constitution of the delegates of the third Estate at the National Assembly of France, on June 17, 1789, was an eminently revolutionary act with no apparent use of force. This same France had, on the contrary, in 1774 and 1775, great insurrections for the single and in no way revolutionary purpose of changing the bread tax in order to stop the rise in the price of bread.

The reference to street fights and executions as characteristic of revolutions is, however, a clue to the source from which we can obtain important teachings as to the essentials of revolution. The great transformation which began ill France in 1789 has become the classical type of revolution. It is the one which is ordinarily in mind when revolution is spoken of. From it we can best study the essentials of revolution and the contrast between it and reform. This revolution was preceded by a series of efforts at reform, among which the best known are those of Turgot. These attempts in many cases aimed at the same things which the revolution carried out. What distinguished the reforms of Turgot from the corresponding measures of the revolution? Between the two lay the conquest of political power by a new class, and in this lies the essential difference between revolution and reform. Measures which seek to adjust the juridical and political superstructure of society, to changed economic conditions, are reforms if they proceed from the class which is the political and economic ruler of society. They are reforms whether they are given freely or secured by the pressure of the subject class, or conquered through the power of circumstances. On the contrary, those measures are the results of revolution if they proceed from the class which has been economically and politically oppressed and who have now captured political power and who must in their own interest more or less rapidly transform the political and juridical superstructure and create new forms of social co-operation.

The conquest of the governmental power by an hitherto oppressed class, in other words, a political revolution, is accordingly the essential characteristic of social revolution in this narrow sense, in contrast with social reform. Those who repudiate political revolution as the principal means of social transformation or wish to confine this to such measures as have been granted by the ruling class are social reformers, no matter how much their social ideas may antagonize existing social forms. On the contrary, any one is a revolutionist who seeks to conquer the political power for an hitherto oppressed class, and he does not lose this character if he prepares and hastens this conquest by social reforms wrested from the ruling classes. It is not the striving after social reforms but the explicit confining of one's self to them which distinguishes the social reformer from the social revolutionist. On the other hand, a political revolution can only become a social revolution when it proceeds from an hitherto socially oppressed class. Such a class is compelled to complete its political emancipation by its social emancipation because its previous social position is in irreconcilable antagonism to its political domination. A split in the ranks of the ruling classes, no matter even if it should take on the violent form of civil mar, is not a social revolution. In the following pages we shall only discuss social revolution in the sense here defined.

Evolution and Revolution

A social reform can very well be in accord with the interests of the ruling class. It may for the moment their social domination untouched, or under certain circumstances, can even strengthen it. Social revolution, on the contrary, is from the first incompatible with the interests of the ruling class, since under all circumstances it signifies annihilation of their power. Little wonder that the present ruling class continuously slander and stigmatize revolution because they believe that it threatens their position. They contrast the idea of social revolution with that of social reform, which they praise to the very heavens, very frequently indeed without ever permitting it to become an earthly fact. The arguments against revolution are derived from the present ruling forms of thought. So long as Christianity ruled the minds of men the idea of revolution was rejected as sinful revolt against divinely constituted authority. It was easy to find proof texts for this in the New Testament, since this of the Roman Empire, during an epoch in which every revolt against the ruling powers appeared hopeless, and all independent political life had ceased to exist. The revolutionary classes, to be sure, replied with quotations from the Old Testament, in which there still lived much of the spirit of a primitive pastoral democracy. When once the judicial manner of thought displaced the theological, a revolution was defined as a violent break with the existing legal order. No one, however, could have a right to the destruction of rights, a right of revolution was an absurdity, and revolution in all cases a crime. But the representatives of the aspiring class placed in opposition to the existing, historically descended right, the right for which they strove, representing it as an eternal law of nature and reason, and an inalienable right of humanity. The re-conquest of these latter rights, that plainly could have been lost only through a violation of rights, was itself impossible without a violation of rights, even if they came as a result of revolution.

Today the theological phrases have lost their power to enslave, and, most of all, among the revolutionary classes of the people. Reference to historical right has also lost its force. The revolutionary origin of present rights and present government is still so recent that their legitimacy can be challenged. Not alone the government of France, but the dynasties of Italy, Spain, Bulgaria, England and Holland, are of revolutionary origin. The kings of Bavaria and Wurtemburg, the grand duke of Baden and Hesse, owe, not simply their titles, but a large share of their provinces, to the protection of the revolutionary parvenu Napoleon; the Hohenzollerns attained their present positions over the ruins of thrones, and even the Hapsburgers bowed before the Hungarian revolution. Andrassy, who was hung in effigy for high treason in 1852, was an imperial minister in 1867, without proving untrue to the ideas of the national Hungarian revolution of 1848.

The bourgeoisie was itself actively engaged in all these violations of historical rights. It cannot, now, since it has become the ruling class, well condemn revolution in the name of this right to revolution, even if its legal philosophy does everything possible to reconcile natural and historical rights. It must seek more effective arguments with which to stigmatize the revolution, and these are found in the newly-arising natural science with its accompanying mental attitude. While the bourgeoisie were still revolutionary, the catastrophic theory still ruled in natural science (geology and biology). This theory proceeded from the premise that natural development came through great sudden leaps. Once the capitalist revolution was ended, the place of the catastrophic theory was taken by the hypothesis of a gradual imperceptible development, proceeding by the accumulation of countless little advances and adjustments in a competitive struggle. To the revolutionary bourgeoisie the thought of catastrophes in nature was very acceptable, but to the conservative bourgeoisie these ideas appeared irrational and unnatural.

Of course I do not assert that the scientific investigators had all their theories determined by the political and social needs of the bourgeoisie. It was just the representatives of the catastrophe theories who were at the same time most reactionary and least inclined to revolutionary views. But every one is involuntarily influenced by the mental attitude of the class amid which he lives and carries something from it into his scientific conceptions. In the case of Darwin we know positively that his natural science hypotheses were influenced by Malthus, that decisive opponent of revolution. It was not wholly accidental that the theories of evolution (of Darwin and Lyell) came from England, whose history for 250 years has shown nothing more than revolutionary beginnings, whose point the ruling class have always been able to break at the opportune moment.

The fact that an idea emanates from any particular class, or accords with their interests, of course proves nothing as to its truth or falsity. But its historical influence does depend upon just these things. That the new theories of evolution were quickly accepted by the great popular masses, who had absolutely no possibility of testing them, proves that they, rested upon profound needs of those classes. On the one side these theories—and this gave them their value to the revolutionary classes—abolished in a much more radical manner than the old catastrophic theories, all necessity of a recognition of a supernatural power creating a world by successive acts. On the other side—and this pleased most highly the bourgeoisie—they declared all revolutions and catastrophies to be something abnormal, contrary to the laws of nature, and wholly absurd. Whoever seeks to-day to scientifically attack revolution does it in the name of the theory of evolution, demonstrating that nature makes no leaps, that consequently any sudden change of social relations is impossible; that advance is only possible through the accumulation of little changes and slight improvements, called social reforms. Considered from this point of view revolution is an unscientific conception about which scientifically cultured people only shrug their shoulders.

It might be replied that the analogy between natural and social laws is by no means perfect. To be sure, our conception of the one will unconsciously influence our conception of the other sphere as we have already seen. This is however, no advantage and it is better to restrain rather than favor this transference of laws from one sphere to another. To be sure, all progress in methods of observation and comprehension of any one sphere can and will improve our methods and comprehension in others, but it is equally true that within each one of these spheres there are peculiar laws not applying to the others.

First of all must be noted the fundamental distinction between animate and inanimate nature. No one would claim on the ground of external similarity to transfer without change a law which applied to one of these spheres to the other. One would not seek to solve the problem of sexual reproduction and heredity by the laws of chemical affiliation. But the same error is committed when natural laws are applied directly to society, as for example when competition is justified as a natural necessity because of the law of the struggle for survival, or when the laws of natural evolution are invoked to show the impossibility of social revolution.

But there is still more to be said in reply. If the old catastrophic theory is gone forever from the natural sciences, the new theory which makes of evolution only a series of little, insignificant changes meets with ever stronger objections. Upon one side there is a growing tendency toward quietistic, conservative theories that reduce evolution itself to a minimum, on the other side facts are compelling us to give an ever greater importance to catastrophes in natural development. This applies equally to the geological theöries of Lyell and the organic evolution of Darwin.

This has given rise to a sort of synthesis of the old catastrophic theories and the newer evolutionary theories, similar to the synthesis that is found in Marxism. Just as Marxism distinguishes between the gradual economic development and the sudden transformation of the juridical and political superstructure, so many of the new biological and geological theories recognize alongside of the slow accumulation of slight and even infinitesimal alterations, also sudden profound transformations—catastrophies—that arise from the slower evolution.

A notable example of this is furnished by the observations of de Bries reported at the last Congress of Natural Sciences held at Hamburg. He has discovered that the species of plants and animals remain unchanged through a long period; some of them finally disappear, when they have become too old to longer adapt themselves to the conditions of existence, that have in the meantime been changing. Other species are more fortunate; they suddenly "explode," as he has himself expressed it, in order to give life to countless new forms, some of which continue and multiply, while the others, not being adapted to the conditions of existence, disappear.

I have no intention of drawing a conclusion in favor of revolution from these new observations. That would be to fall into the same error as those who argue to the rejection of revolution from the theory of evolution. But these observations at least show that the scientists are themselves not wholly agreed as to the part played in organic and geologic development by catastrophies, and for this reason it would be an error to attempt to draw from either of these hypotheses any fixed conclusions as to the role played by revolution in social development.

If in spite of these facts such conclusions are still insisted upon, then we can reply to them with a very popular and familiar illustration, which demonstrates in an unmistakable manner that nature does make sudden leaps: I refer to the act of birth. The act of birth is a leap. At one stroke a fetus, which had hitherto constituted a portion of the organism of the mother, sharing in her circulation, receiving nourishment from her, without breathing, becomes an independent human being, with its own circulatory system, that breathes and cries, takes its own nourishment and utilizes its digestive tract.

The analogy between birth and revolution, however, does not rest alone upon the suddenness of the act. If we look closer we shall find that this sudden transformation at birth is confined wholly to functions. The organs develop slowly, and must reach a certain stage of development before that leap is possible, which suddenly gives them their new functions. If the leap takes place before this stage of development is attained, the result is not the beginning of new functions for the organs, but the cessation of all functions—the death of the new creature. On the other hand, the slow development of organs in the body of the mother can only proceed to a certain point, they cannot begin their new functions without the revolutionary act of birth. This becomes inevitable when the development of the organs has attained a certain height.

We find the same thing in society. Here also the revolutions are the result of slow, gradual development (evolution). Here also it is the social organs that develop slowly. That which may be changed suddenly, at a leap, revolutionarily, is their functions. The railroad has been slowly developed. On the other hand, the railroad can suddenly be transformed from its function as the instrument to the enrichment of a number of capitalists, into a socialist enterprise having as its function the serving of the common good. And as at the birth of the child, all the functions are simultaneously revolutionized—circulation, breathing, digestion—so all the functions of the railroad must be simultaneously revolutionized at one stroke, for they are all most closely bound together. They cannot be gradually and successively socialized, one after the other, as if, for example, we would transform to-day the functions of the engineer and fireman, a few years later the ticket agents, and still later the accountants and book-keepers, and so on. This fact is perfectly clear with a railroad, but the successive socialization of the different functions of a railroad is no less absurd than that of the ministry of a centralized state. Such a ministry constitutes a single organism whose organs must cooperate. The functions of one of these organs cannot be modified without equally modifying all the others. The idea of the gradual conquest of the various departments of a ministry by the Socialists is not less absurd than would be an attempt to divide the act of birth into a number of consecutive monthly acts, in each of which one organ only would be transformed from the condition of a fetus to an independent child, and meanwhile leaving the child itself attached to the navel cord until it had learned to walk and talk.

Since neither a railroad nor a ministry can be changed gradually, but only at a single stroke, embracing all the organs simultaneously, from capitalist to socialist functions, from an organ of the capitalist to an organ of the laboring class, and this transformation is possible only to such social organs as retain a certain degree of development, it may be remarked here that with the maternal organism it is possible to scientifically determine the moment when the degree of maturity is attained, which is not true of society.

On the other hand, birth does not mark the conclusion of the development of the human organism, but rather the beginning of a new epoch in development. The child comes now into new relations in which new organs are created, and those that previously existed are developed further in other directions; teeth grow in the mouth, the eyes learn to see; the hands to grasp, the feet to walk, the mouth to speak, etc. In the same way a social revolution is not the conclusion of social development, but the beginning of a new form of development. A socialist revolution can at a single stroke transfer a factory from capitalist to social property. But it is only gradually, through a course of slow evolution, that one may transform a factory from a place of monotonous, repulsive, forced labor into an attractive spot for the joyful activity of happy human beings. A socialist revolution can at a single stroke transform the great bonanza farms into social property. In that portion of agriculture where the little industry still rules, the organs of social and socialist production must be first created, and that can come only as a result of slow development.

It is thus apparent that the analogy between birth and revolution is rather far reaching. But this naturally proves nothing more than that one has no right to appeal to nature for proof that a social revolution is something unnecessary, unreasonable, and unnatural. We have also, as we have already said, no right to apply conclusions drawn from nature directly to social processes. We can go no further upon the ground of such analogies than to conclude: that as each animal creature must at one time go through a catastrophe in order to reach a higher stage of development (the act of birth or of the breaking of a shell), so society can only be raised to a higher stage of development through a catastrophe.

Revolutions in Antiquity and the Middle Age

Any definite conclusion as to whether revolution is a necessity or not can be drawn only from an investigation of the facts of social development, and not through analogies with natural science. It is only necessary to glance at these earlier stages of development in order to see that social revolution, in the narrow sense in which we are here using it, is no necessary accompaniment of social development. There was a social development and a very far-reaching one before the rise of class antagonisms and political power. In these stages the conquest of political power by an oppressed class, and consequently a social revolution, was as a matter of course impossible.

Even after class antagonisms and political power have arisen it is a long time before we find, either in antiquity or the Middle Ages, anything which corresponds to our idea of revolution. We find plenty of examples of bitter class struggles, civil wars and political catastrophies, but none of these brought about a fundamental and permanent renovation of the conditions of property and therewith a new social form.

To my mind the reasons for this are as follows: In antiquity and also in the Middle ages the center of gravity of the economic and also of the political life lay in the community. Each community was sufficient in itself in all essential points and was only attached to the exterior world through loose bands. The great states were only conglomerates of communities which were held together only through either a dynasty or through another ruling and exploiting community. Each community had its own special economic development corresponding to its own peculiar characteristics and corresponding to these also its special class struggles. The political revolutions also at that time were chiefly only communal revolutions. It was as a matter of course impossible to transform the whole social life of a great territory by a political revolution.

The smaller the number of individuals in a social movement the less there is of a real social movement; the less there is of the universal and law creating, and the more the personal and the accidental dominate. This increased the diversity of the class struggles in the different communities. Because in the class struggle no movement of the masses could appear, because the general was concealed in the accidental and the personal, there could be no deep recognition of social causes and the goals of class movements. However great the philosophy created by the Greeks, the idea of a scientific national economy was foreign to them. Aristotle supplies only outlines of such a system. The Greeks and Romans on the economic field produced only practical instructions for domestic economy, or for agricultural industries, such as those composed by Xenophon and Varro.

While the deeper social causes that gave rise to the condition of individual classes remained concealed and were veiled by the acts of individual persons and local peculiarities, it was not to be wondered at that the oppressed classes also, as soon as they had conquered political power, used it first of all to get rid of individuals and local peculiarities and not to establish a new social order.

The most important obstacle in the road to any revolutionary movements at this time was the slowness of economic development. This proceeded imperceptibly. Peasants and artisans worked as their grandfathers and great-grandfathers had been accustomed to work.

The ancient, the customary, was the only good and perfect thing. Even when one sought to create something new, he endeavored to prove to others that it was really a return to some forgotten tradition. Technical progress did not in itself compel new forms of property for it consisted only in increasing social division of labor, in the division of one trade into many. But, in each of the new trades, hand work was still fundamental, the means of production were insignificant, and the decisive element was manual skill. To be sure, in the last years of antiquity, we find beside the peasants and the artisans great businesses (even industrial establishments), but these were operated by slaves who were considered as aliens outside of the community life. These industries produced only luxuries and could develop no special economic strength, except temporarily in times of great wars which weakened agriculture and made slave material cheap. A high economic form and a new social ideal cannot arise upon a slave economy.

The single form of capital which was developed in antiquity and the Middle Ages was usury and commercial capital. Both of these may, at times, bring about rapid economic changes. But commercial capital could only further the division of the old trades into countless new ones and the advance of the great industry dependent on slave labor. Usurious capital operated simply to stunt existing forms of production without creating new ones. The struggle against usurious capital and against the great agricultural industries which were operated by slaves led to occasional political struggles very similar to the social revolutions of our time. But the goal of these was always only the restoration of an earlier condition and not a social renovation. Such was the case in the liquidation of debts brought about for the Greek peasants, by Solon, and in the movements of the Roman peasants and proletarians from which the Gracchi receive their name. To all of these causes—slowness of economic development, lack of recognition of deeper social relations, division of political life into countless differing communities, must be added the fact that in classical antiquity and many times also in the Middle Ages, the means for the suppression of a rising class were relatively insignificant. There were no bureaucracies, or at least never where there was the most active political life, and where the class struggle was most fiercely waged. In the Roman world, for example, bureaucracy was first developed under the empire. The internal relations of communities as well as their commerce with each other were simple, easy to comprehend and pre-supposed no expert knowledge. The governing classes could easily secure the necessary governing officials out of their own number, and this is all the more true in that at that time the governing class was also accustomed to engage in artistic, philosophic and political activity. The ruling class did not simply reign, it also governed.

On the other side the mass of the people were not wholly defenceless. It was in just the golden age of classical antiquity that the militia system was the rule, under which every citizen was armed. Under those conditions a very slight alteration in the balance of power of classes was sufficient to bring a new class into control. Class antagonisnms could not well reach such a height that the idea of a complete transformation of all existing institutions could become firmly rooted in the minds of an oppressed class, and, moreover, in these oppressed classes, stubborn clinging to all privileges was the rule. As has already been noted this operated to confine political revolution almost wholly to the abolition of individual abuses and the removal of individual persons. This condition also assisted in the avoidance through compromise of all forms of revolution.

Among the great nations of modern times England is the one which most resembles the Middle Ages, not economically, but in its political form. Militarism and bureaucracy are there the least developed. It still possesses an aristocracy that not only reigns but governs. Corresponding to this, England is the great modern nation in which the efforts of the oppressed classes are mainly concerned to the removal of particular abuses instead of being directed against the whole social system. It is also the State in which the practice of protection against revolution through compromise is farthest developed.

If the universal armament of the people did not encourage great social revolutions, it did make it much easier for armed conflict between the classes to arise at the slightest opportunity. There is no lack of violent uprisings and civil wars in antiquity and the Middle Ages. The ferocity with which these were fought was often so great as to lead to the expulsion, expropriation and oftentimes to the extermination of the conquered. Those who consider violence as a sign of social revolution will find plenty of such revolutions in earlier ages. But those who conceive social revolution as the conquest of political power by a previously subservient class and the transformation of the juridical and political superstructure of society, particularly in the property relations, will find no social revolution there. Social development proceeded piece-meal, step by step, not through single great catastrophies but in countless little broken-up, apparently disconnected, often interrupted, ever renewing, mostly unconscious movements. The great social transformation of the times we are considering, the disappearance of slavery in Europe, came about so imperceptibly that the contemporaries of this movement took no notice of it, and one is today compelled to reconstruct it through hypotheses.

Social Revolution under Capitalism

Thing took on a wholly different aspect as soon as the capitalist method of production was developed. It would lead us too far and would be only to repeat things well known if I were here to go into the mechanism of capitalism and its consequences. Suffice it to say that the capitalist method of production created the modern State, made an end to the political independence of communities and at the same time their economic independence ceased, each became part of a whole, and lost its special rights and special peculiarities. All were reduced to the same level, all were given the same laws, the same taxes, same courts, and were made subject to the same government. The modern State was thus forced to become a National State and added to the other equalities the equality of language.

The influence of governmental power upon the social life was now something wholly different from what it was through antiquity or the Middle Ages. Every important political change in a great modern State influences at once with a single stroke and in the profoundest manner an enormous social sphere. The conquest of political power by a previously subject class must, on this account, from now on, have wholly different social results than previously.

As a result the power at the disposal of the modern State has grown enormously. The technical revolution of capitalism reaches also to the technique of arms. Ever since the Reformation the weapons of war have become more and more perfect, but also more costly. They thus become a privilege of governmental power. This fact alone separates the army from the people, even in those places where universal conscription prevails, unless this is supplemented by popular armament, which is not the case in any great State. Most important of all, the leaders of the army are professional soldiers separated from the people, to whom they stand opposed as a privileged class.

The economic powers also of the modern centralized State are enormous when compared with those of the earlier States. They comprehend the wealth of a colossal sphere whose technical means of production leave the higher culture of antiquity far behind.

The modern State also possesses a bureaucracy far more centralized than that of any previous State. The problems of the modern State have grown so enormously that it is impossible to solve them without an extensive division of labor and a high grade of professional knowledge. The capitalist manner of production robs the ruling class of all the leisure that they previously had. Even, if they do not produce but are living from the exploitation of the producing classes, still they are not idle exploiters. Thanks to competition, the motive force of present economic life, the exploiters are continuously compelled to carry on an exhausting struggle with each other, which threatens the vanquished with complete annihilation.

The capitalists have therefore neither time nor leisure, nor the previous culture necessary for artistic and scientific activity. They lack even the necessary qualifications for regular participation in governmental activities. Not only in art and science but also in the government of the State the ruling class is forced to take no part. They must leave that to wage-workers and bureaucratic employees. The capitalist, class reigns but does not govern. It is satisfied, however, to rule the government.

In the same way the decaying feudal nobility before it, satisfied itself by taking on the forms of a royal nobility. But while with the feudal nobility the renunciation of its social functions was the product of corruption, with the capitalists this renunciation arises directly from their social functions and is an essential part of their existence.

With the help of such a powerful government a class can long maintain itself, even if it is superfluous. Yes, even if it has become injurious. And the stronger the power of the State, just so much the more does the governing class rest upon it, just so much more stubbornly will it cling to its privileges and all the less will it be inclined to grant concessions. The longer, however it maintains its domination in this manner, the sharper become class antagonisms, the more pronounced must be the political collapse when it finally does come, and the deeper the social transformation that arises out of it, and the more apt the conquest of political power by an oppressed class to lead to revolution.

Simultaneously the warring classes become more and more conscious of the social consequences of their political struggle. The capitalist system of production tends to greatly accelerate the march of economic evolution. The economic transformation for which the century of invention has prepared the way is continued by the introduction of machines into industry. Since their introduction our economic relations are subject to continual change, not only by the rapid dissolution of the old but by the continuous creation of the new. The idea of the old, of the past, ceases to be equivalent to the tested, to the honorable, to the inviolable. It becomes synonymous with the imperfect and the outgrown. This idea is transplanted from the economic life into the field of art and science and politics. Just as in earlier days people clung without reason to the old, so to-day one gladly throws the old aside without reason just because it is old. And the time which is necessary in order to make a machine, an institution, a theory outgrown becomes ever shorter. And if in former days men worked with the intention of building for eternity with all the devotedness that flows from such a consciousness, so to-day one works for the fleeting effect of a moment with all the frivolity of this consciousness. So that the creation of today is within a short time not simply unfashionable but also useless.

The new is, however, just that thing that one observes, criticizes and investigates the most closely. The ordinary and the commonplace pass as a matter of course. Mankind studied the causes of eclipse much earlier than the rising and setting of the sun. In the same way the incentive to investigate the laws of social phenomena was very slight so long as these phenomena were the ordinary, the matter-of-course, the "natural." This incentive must at once be strengthened as soon as new, hitherto unheard of formations appeared in the social life. It was not the old hereditary feudal economics, but rather the newly appearing capitalist economics that first roused scientific observation at the beginning of the seventeenth century.

Economic science was encouraged still more by another motive. Capitalist production is mass production, social production. The typical modern capitalist state is the great state. Modern economics, like modern politics, must deal with mass phenomena. The larger the number of similar appearances that one observes, the greater the tendency to notice the universal—those indicatings a social law—and the more the individual and the accidental disappear, the easier it is to discover the laws of social movements. The mathematical mass-observation of social phenomena, statistics, and the science of society that rises from political economy and reaches its highest point in the materialistic conception of history, has only been possible in the capitalist stage of production. Now for the first time classes could come to the full consciousness of the social significance of their struggles, and for the first time set before themselves great social goals, not as arbitrary dreams and pious wishes destined to be shattered on the hard facts, but as results of scientific insight into economic possibilities and necessities. To be sure this scientific thought can err, many of its conclusions can be shown to be illusions. But however great these errors may be, it cannot be deprived of the characteristic of every true science, the striving after a uniform conception of all phenomena under an indisputable whole. In social science this means the recognition of the social whole as a single organism in which one cannot arbitrarily and for itself alone change any single part. The socially oppressed class no longer directs its theoretical criticism against individual persons and tendencies, but against the total existing society. And just because of this fact every oppressed class which conquers political power is driven to transform the whole social foundations.

The capitalist society which sprang from the revolution of 1789 and its outcome was foreseen in its fundamental outlines by the physiocrats and their English followers.

Upon this distinction between the modern states and society and the organizations of antiquity and the Middle Ages rests the difference in the manner of their development. The former was predominantly unconscious, split up into local and personal strifes and the rebellion of countless little communities at different stages of development; the latter grows more and more self-conscious and strives towards a great recognized social goal which has been determined and is propagated by scientifically critical work. Political revolutions are less frequent, but more comprehensive and their social results more extensive.

The transition from the civil wars of antiquity and the Middle Ages to social revolutions in the previously used sense of the word was made by the Reformation, which belonged half to the Middle Ages and half to modern times. On a still higher stage was the English revolution of the middle of the seventeenth century, and finally the great French revolution becomes the classical type of social revolution, of which the uprisings of 1830 and 1848 mere only faint echoes.

Social revolution in the sense here meant is peculiar to the stage of social development of capitalist society and the capitalist state. It does not exist previous to capitalism, because the political boundaries were too narrow and social consciousness too undeveloped. It will disappear with capitalism because this can only be overthrown by the proletariat, which as the lowest of all social classes can use its domination only to abolish all class domination and classes and therewith also the essential conditions of social revolution.

There now arises a great question, a question that to-day affects us profoundly, because it has the greatest influence upon our political relations to the present: Is the time of social revolution past or not? Have we already the political conditions which can bring about a transition from capitalism to socialism without political revolution, without the conquest of political power by the proletariat, or must we still expect an epoch of decisive struggles for the possession of this power and therewith a revolutionary epoch? Does the idea of social revolution belong with those antiquated ideas which are held only by thoughtless echoers of outgrown conceptions or by demagogical speculators upon the applause of the unthinking masses, and which every honest modern person who dispassionately observes the facts of modern society must put aside?

That is the question. Certainly an important question which a couple of phrases will not serve to dismiss.

We have discovered that social revolution is a product of special historical conditions. They presuppose, not simply a highly developed class antagonism, but also a great national state rising above all provincial and communal peculiarities, built upon a form of production that operates to level all local peculiarities, a powerful military and bureaucratic state, a science of political economy and a rapid rate of economic progress.

None of these factors of social revolution have been decreasing in power during the last decade. Many of them, on the contrary, have been much strengthened. Never was the rate of economic development more rapid. Scientific economics make, at least, a great extensive, if not intensive growth, thanks to the newspapers. Never was economic insight so broadly dispersed; never was the ruling class, as well as the mass of people, so much in a condition to comprehend the far-reaching consequences of its acts and strivings. This alone proves that we shall not make the tremendous transition from capitalism to socialism unconsciously, and that we cannot slowly undermine the dominion of the exploiting class without this class being conscious of this, and consequently arming themselves and using all their powers to suppress the strength and influence of the growing proletariat.

If, however, the insight into social relations was never so extensive as today, it is equally true that the governmental power was never so strong as now, nor the military, bureaucratic and economic forces so powerfully developed. It follows from this that the proletariat, when it shall have conquered the governmental powers, will have thereby attained the power to at once bring about most extensive social changes. It also follows from this that the personal governing class with the help of these powers can continue its existence and its plundering of the laboring class long after its economic necessity has ceased. The more, however, that the ruling classes support themselves with the State machinery and misuse this for the purposes of exploitation and oppression, just so much more must the bitterness of the proletariat against them increase, class hatred grow, and the effort to conquer the machinery of State increase in intensity.

To be sure it has been claimed that this comprehension of the newest socialist phenomena does not take account of the undeniable fact that the development proceeds in other directions also. It is claimed also that the contrast between proletariat and bourgeoisie is not increasing, and in every modern State there are enough democratic arrangements to make it possible for the proletariat, if not to gain *the* power, still to gain *power* gradually, step by step and steadily increasing, so that the necessity of a social revolution ceases. Let us see in how far these exceptions are justified.

The Softening of Class Antagonisms

Let us turn next to the first objection that the social antagonism between bourgeoisie and proletariat is diminishing. I do not here refer to the question of industrial crises whose amelioration was claimed a few years ago. This idea has been so energetically confuted since then by notorious facts that I only need to refer to it here without attempting to enter upon a discussion which would lead us too far away. I do not wish either to make any further contribution to the debate over the already over-discussed, so-called theory of increasing misery, which, with a sort of cleverness, when one desires, can be endlessly spun out and which with us has more and more tended to, turn on the definition of the word "misery" than on the determination of definite facts. Socialists are all agreed that the capitalist manner of production when unhindered has as a result an increase of physical misery. They are also agreed that in present society the organization of the laboring class and the capture of governmental powers has attained a height where it is able to somewhat ameliorate this misery. Finally they are agreed that the emancipation of the laboring class is not to be expected from its increasing demoralization, but from its increasing strength.

The question of the antagonism between the bourgeoisie and proletariat is a wholly different one. It is primarily a question of increasing exploitation.

That this does increase Marx proved a generation ago, and to my mind no one has yet confuted him. Whoever denies the increasing exploitation of the proletariat must, first of all, set about a refutation of Marx's Capital.

To be sure it will be at once replied that this is purely theory and that for us nothing is to be held as true and proven that we cannot grasp with the hands. We are not given economical laws, but only statistical figures. These are not so easily to be discovered for, as yet, no one has been pleased to set forth the amounts, not simply of the wages, but also of the profits in a statistical form, because of the fact that the fire-proof safes are a castle which even the cowardly and benevolent bourgeois will defend like a lion against every administrative attack.

Meanwhile, there are calculations upon the growth of wages and other incomes. One of these, the latest that I know of, is given herewith:

Many observations can be offered against this presentation. It appears to me too optimistic and gives the appearance of a much greater increase in wages than actually exists. In the reckoning of the total wages the compiler took no notice of the unemployed and besides this he omitted to note a whole list of important variations

Year	Total Annual Wage Income		Income Not Arising From Wages			
			Subject to Income Tax		Not Subject to Income Tax	
	Million Pounds Sterling	% Total Social Income	Million Pounds Sterling	% Total Social Income	Million Pounds Sterling	% Total Social Income
1860	392	47	376	45 1/2	64	7 2/3
1866	464	45	485	47	81	8
1870	486	44 1/2	521	48	85	7 ½
1874	609	45 1/2	635	47 1/2	100	7 ½
1877	591	43	652	47 1/2	130	9 ½
1880	567	42	652	48 1/2	126	9 ½
1883	609	42 2/3	696	49	122	8 ½
1886	605	42	715	49 1/2	125	8 ½
1891	699	43 1/2	782	48 1/2	130	8

inside of the laboring class which, if considered, would greatly change the result. As a statistician, to be sure, he undoubtedly has the right to do this, but these are just the factors that change things to the disadvantage of the laboring class. Such are, for example, the relation between male and female labor and between skilled and unskilled labor.

Of still greater consequence is the fact that the calculation

	1860	1866	1870	1874	1877	1880	1883	1886	1891
Agricultural laborers	100	105	107	130	132	122	117	111	118
Building Trades	100	116	116	126	128	125	123	126	128
Cotton workers	100	125	125	148	148	136	145	155	175
Woolen workers	100	106	112	121	130	123	120	115	113
Iron workers	100	127	127	143	112	112	110	100	124
Machinists	100	108	110	124	123	120	127	120	120
Gas workers	100	115	120	125	128	128	130	130	140
Sailors	100	113	103	129	123	102	118	110	148
Miners	100	?	100	150	115	100	115	100	150
Average	100	113	113	138	132	124	130	125	140

confines itself to a few branches of labor, all of which, with the exception of the farm laborers, are extremely well organized economically. The author has then, without further consideration, concluded that the condition of the whole laboring class has risen at the same average rate as that of these organized laborers which, even in England, did not include at the highest calculation more than one-fifth of all laborers. So it is not without interest that we observe the changes in wages in each of these categories of labor is shown in the table.

We see that the increase in wages of 40 per cent from 1860 to 1891 that Bowley calculates for the whole laboring class of England, does not even hold foe the whole aristocracy of labor. With the exception of the cotton workers who have not vainly been the conservatives of England and the model children of all dreamers of "social peace," the average of 1891 was only exceeded by the gas workers, the sailors and the miners. The gas workers owe their increase, in part, at least, to politicians, for in the larger cities municipalization has brought many improvements. With the gas workers also considerations of competition and exploitation by private capital are of least importance. In part, also, the upward leap of 1891 as well as the sudden appearance of the "new Unionism" which gave rise to such far-reaching hopes has now run into the ground. More even than with the gas workers the rise of wages in 1891 for the sailors and miners appears wholly abnormal and temporary. With the miners the wages of 1888 were the same as those of 1860, but by 1891 they were 50 per cent higher. One cannot consider this as a secure advance. With the wood workers, the woolen workers and the laborers in the iron industry, the increase of wages since 1860 is far less. Bowley would also have us believe that the wages of the unorganized laborers of England had risen 40 per cent during the same time in which the well organized iron workers had only increased 25 per cent.

But let us take the table as it is. What does it really prove? Even by this extraordinarily optimistic presentation wages are becoming an ever smaller portion of the social income. From 1860 to 1874 the average rate of increase was 45 per cent; from 1877 to 1891 only 42

2/3 per cent. If we place in opposition to this, in lack of more reliable figures, the total of the income tax that did not arise from wages but from surplus values then in 1860 this would be eighty million dollars less than the sum of the wages. In 1891 the amount of surplus values exceeded the sum of wages by the significant sum of not less than four hundred million dollars.

This certainly signifies a considerable increase in exploitation. The rate of surplus value, that is to say, the rate of exploitation of the laborer, has accordingly risen during this time from 96 per cent to 112 per cent. Actually, even according to Bowley's figures, exploitation has at least grown very fast among the best organized laborers. The exploitation of the masses of unorganized must have reached a much higher degree.

We do not lay any great stress upon these figures. But as far as they show anything, they speak for, not against, the claim of the increasing exploitation of labor power, that Marx has proven in another way, by examination of the laws of movements, the capitalist system of production, and which has not yet been disproved. To be sure, one can say: Granted that exploitation increases, but wages increase also, even if not to the same degree as surplus values. How then shall the laborer discover this increasing exploitation if it is not plainly evident, but is only to be discovered by painstaking investigation? The mass of the laborers do not study statistics or think about theories of value and profit.

This may be granted. But there is a way in which the increase of exploitation can be made perceptible to the laborers. In the same degree that the mass of profit rises, the standard of living of the bourgeoisie rises also. But the classes are not divided from one another by impenetrable walls. The rising standard of life of the upperclass oozes down through to those beneath and wakens in them new needs and demands to the satisfaction of which the slowly growing wage is by no means satisfactory. The bourgeoisie whine about the disappearance of modesty in the lower classes and about their increasing enviousness, and forget that the growing demands from below are only the reflex of the rising standard of life above, which furnishes the example and rouses the envy of the lower class.

That the capitalist standard of living grows faster than that of the proletariat is self-evident. The laborer's dwelling has not been greatly improved in the last fifty years. But the dwelling places of the bourgeoisie are gorgeous in comparison with the average capitalist house of fifty years ago. The third-class railroad carriage of to-day and the one of fifty years ago differ but little in their interior equipments. But when we compare the first-class railroad carriage of the middle of the nineteenth century with the palace car of the modern train! I do not believe that the sailors in the Transatlantic ships are much better cared for to-day than fifty years ago, while the luxuries to be found in the salon of the modern passenger steamer would have been unheard of fifty years ago even in a royal pleasure yacht.

So much for the increasing exploitation of the proletariat. But is not this economic factor counterbalanced by the increasing political approach of the classes? Do not the bourgeoisie more and more recognize the laborer as their political and social equals?

There is no doubt that the proletariat is gaining rapidly in political and social respects.

If its rise in economic relations remains behind that of the bourgeoisie, this gives rise to a continually increasing enviousness and discontent. Perhaps the most striking phenomenon of the last fifty years is the rapid and unbroken rise of the proletariat in moral and intellectual relations.

Not many decades ago the proletariat was so low that there were even socialists that expected the worst results for culture from the conquest of the proletariat. In 1850 Rodbertus wrote: "The most threatening danger at present is that we shall have a new barbarian invasion, this time coming from the interior of society itself to lay waste custom, civilization and wealth."

At the same time Heinrich Heine declared that the future belonged to the communist. "This confession, that the future belongs to the communist, I make in sorrow and greatest anxiety. This is in no way a delusion. In fact; it is only with fear and shuddering that I think of the epoch when these dark iconoclasts come to power; with their callous hands they will destroy all the marble statues of beauty, etc."

Undeniably it has now become wholly different. It is not by the proletariat that modern civilization is threatened. It is those very communists who to-day constitute the safe refuge of art and science, for which they stand in the most decisive manner.

So it is that the fear is rapidly disappearing, which after the Paris Commune dominated the whole capitalist class; the fear that the conquering proletariat would come into our culture like the Vandals in their race migrations and on its ruins found a government of barbaric ascetics.

It is partially owing to the disappearance of this fear that sympathy with the proletariat and with socialism is on the increase among the bourgeois intellectuals.

Like the proletariat, class intelligence is a peculiarity of the capitalist system of production. I have already shown that this system makes such demands upon the ruling class that they have neither the interest nor the leisure to care for the business of government, or to cultivate art and science, as did the aristocracy of Athens or the clergy of the best days of the Catholic Church. The whole sphere of the higher intellectual activity, that was formerly a privilege of the ruling classes, is now left by these to paid laborers, and the number of these professional scholars, artists, engineers and functionaries is increasing rapidly.

Taken as a whole these constitute the so-called "intellectuals," the "new middle class," but they are distinguished from the old middle class above all by the lack of any especial class consciousness. Certain divisions of them have a peculiar caste consciousness, very often a blindness of caste, but the interests of each one of these divisions is too peculiar for any common class consciousness to develop. Its members unite with various classes and parties and furnish the intellectual fighters for each. One portion defends the interests of the ruling class for whom many of the intellectuals serve professionally. Others have championed the cause of the proletariat. The majority, however, have up to the present time remained entangled in the little bourgeois circles of thought. This is not alone because many of them sprung from this class, but also because their social position as "middle class" is like that of the small bourgeois, a midway position between the proletariat and the ruling class.

It is in these divisions of the intellectuals, as remarked above, that a continually increasing sympathy for the proletariat is evident. Because they have no especial class interest, and are most accessible through their professional, scientific point of view, they are easiest won for our party through scientific considerations. The theoretical bankruptcy of bourgeois economics, and the theoretical superiority of Socialism must become clear to them. Through this they must continually discover that the other social classes continuously strive to still further debase art and science. Many others are finally impressed by the fact of the irresistible advance of the Social Democracy, especially when they compare this with the continuous deterioration of Liberalism. So it is that friendship for labor becomes popular among the cultured classes, until there is scarcely a parlor in which one does not stumble over one or more "Socialists."

If these circles of the cultured class were synonymous with the bourgeoisie, then to be sure we would have won the game, and a social revolution would be superfluous. With this class it is easy to discuss things, and from them a quiet gradual development will meet no forcible hindrance.

Unfortunately, however, they are only a portion of the bourgeoisie, though, to be sure, just those who speak and write in the name of the bourgeoisie, but not those who determine their acts. And men as well as classes must be judged, not by their words, but by their deeds.

It must also be remembered that it is the least effective fighters and least combative portion of the bourgeoisie in which sympathy for the proletariat is developing.

Heretofore, while socialism was branded among all cultured classes as criminal or insane, capitalist elements could only be brought into the Socialist movement by a complete break with the whole capitalist world. Whoever came into the Socialist movement at that time from the capitalist elements had need of great energy, revolutionary passion, and strong proletarian convictions. It was just this element which ordinarily constituted the most radical and revolutionary wing of the Socialist movement.

It is wholly different to-day, when Socialism has become a fad. It no longer demands any especial energy, and no break with capitalist society to assume the name of Socialist. It is no wonder then that more and more these new Socialists remain entangled in their previous manner of thought and feeling.

The fighting tactics of the intellectuals are at any rate wholly different from those of the proletariat. To wealth and power of arms the latter opposes its overwhelming numbers and its thorough organization. The intellectuals are an ever diminishing minority with no class organization whatever. Their only weapon is persuasion through speaking and writing; the battle with "intellectual weapons" and "moral superiority," and these "parlor Socialists" would settle the proletarian class struggle also with these weapons. They declare themselves ready to grant the proletariat their moral support, but only on condition that it renounces the idea of the application of force, and this not simply where force is hopeless—there the proletariat has already renounced it—but also in those places where it is still full of possibilities. Accordingly they seek to throw discredit on the idea of revolution, and to represent it as a useless means. They seek to separate off a social reform wing from the revolutionary proletariat, and they thereby divide and weaken the proletariat.

Zip to the present time this is practically the only result of the beginnings of the conversion of the "Intellectuals" to Socialism.

At the side of this "new middle class" the old one, the small capitalist class, still vegetates. This portion of the middle class was at one time the back bone of the revolution; eager for battle and full of fight, they arose on slight provocation whenever the conditions were favorable, against every form of servitude and exploitation from above, against the tyranny of bureaucracy and militarism, against feudal and clerical privileges. They constituted the picked troops of the bourgeois democracy. At one time this class, like a portion of the "new middle class" at present, was very sympathetic towards the proletariat, co-operated with it, gave to it and received from it intellectual support and material strength. But old or new the present middle class is a very unreliable ally, and this just because of its intermediate position between the exploited and the exploiting classes. As Marx has already noted, the little capitalist is neither wholly proletarian, nor wholly bourgeois, and considers himself, according to the occasion, first one and then the other.

Out of this contradictory position there comes a division in the class of small property owners. One portion identifies itself with the proletariat, the other with its enemies.

The small industry is doomed to ruin, its ruin is now proceeding uninterruptedly. This shows itself but slowly in the actual diminution of the number of small industries, but rapidly in their demoralization. A portion of their owners are in absolute dependence upon capital, being nothing more than home and wage-workers, who labor for a master in their houses instead of in a factory. Others, especially small merchants and innkeepers, remain independent, but find their customers only in laboring circles, so that their existence is absolutely dependent upon the prosperity or adversity of the laboring classes. They have despaired of ever rising by their own exertions, they expect everything from above, and look only to the upper classes and the government for assistance. And as all progress threatens them they place themselves in opposition to all advance. Servility and dependence upon reaction make: them not simply the willing supporters, but the fanatical defenders of the monarchy, the church and the nobility. With all this they remain democratic, since it is only through democracy that they can exercise any political influence, and obtain the assistance of the public powers.

It is this division of the little property owners that is mainly responsible for the decadence of the bourgeois democracy. One of these divisions turns toward the proletarian Social Democracy; the other toward the reactionary democracy, where it appears under the most diverse colors as anti-semitism, nationalism, Christian democracy—factions of the conservative and central parties, but always with the same social content. This reactionary democracy has taken many of its ideas and arguments from the socialist thought, and many have therefore come to consider these as but beginnings which indicate an especial transition form from liberalism to socialism. The untenableness of this position is clear to-day. Socialism has no bitterer enemy than the reactionary democracy. If the socialists demand any advance in civilization, whether that advance be a direct benefit to proletarian class interests or not, the reactionary democracy is driven by its whole being to oppose it, even if it does not directly threaten the interests of the small property owner. Just as the Socialist party is the most progressive party, so the reactionary democracy is the most retrograde party, in that to the hatred of progress which they share with other reactionary parties they add the most gross ignorance of everything that takes place outside their narrow circle of thought. Another reason for this fact is that the little capitalists can maintain their position as exploiters only by the most inhuman torture of the weakest and most unresisting of the possessors of labor power—the women and children. As a consequence they are naturally the first opponents of the Socialists, when the latter seek by means of organization and compulsory legislation to abolish this brutal destruction of human life.

So it is that the class of small property owners, so far as it does not become Socialist, becomes, instead of an ally, or a conciliatory element midway between the proletariat and the ruling classes, a bitter enemy of the proletariat. In place of a softening of class antagonisms we see here the most harsh climax of class antagonism, and moreover a rapidly increasing one, for it is only within the last few years that it has become clearly noticeable.

What we have said of the class of small property owners applies with but few changes to the farming class. They are also divided into two camps, one the proletarian, composed of small farmers, and the other of capitalist proprietors. It is our task to accelerate this process of division, in order that we may make clear the overwhelming proletarian interests of the first class, and thereby lead them to socialism. The reactionary democracy in the country is as hostile to our existence as is the one in the cities even if this opposition is not always clearly recognized. Those comrades who look upon the agrarian confusion as only a transition state of the farmers from the old parties to the social democracy are as badly deceived as those who expect the same thing from the anti-semitism in the cities. The medium and large farmers hate the Socialists, just because they struggle to secure a shorter work-day and higher wages for the laborers, and thereby furnish the principal cause for the farm laborers moving to the city and leaving the farmer in the lurch.

In the country also the social antagonism between the possessors and the proletariat grows sharper.

This is even more true of the antagonism between the great land owners and the wage-worker than of that between the farmer and the wage-worker.

In the great agricultural industries the wage-worker plays a more important role than in ordinary farming. For the great farmer also, the high price of provisions is much more important than for the farmer who consumes a large portion of his product. The antagonism between the producer and consumer of provisions is, to be sure, not the same as between the laborer and exploiter, but rather like that between the city and country. But in the city the proletariat is to-day the most numerous and the most combative class and consequently the seller of provisions sees in the proletariat his most energetic enemy.

It is therefore no wonder that the great land owner looks at the industrial laborer today from a wholly different point of view from what he did. Formerly he was indifferent to the struggle between the industrial capitalist and his laborer and indeed he often followed them with malignant rejoicings at the predicament of the capitalists with which indeed there was often a certain sympathy for the proletariat. It was not the latter that then stood in his road, but rather the capitalist who demanded protection while he needed free trade, and who on the other hand saw in ground rents an invasion of his profits and who sought to take away from the land owners the monopoly of the higher places in the army and bureaucracy.

To-day things are wholly different. The day of the labor friends, such as the Tories and Junkers, of Disraeli, Rodbertus, Vogelsang, is long gone by. Like the class of little property owners and the class of medium and large farmers, the class of land owners is becoming more and more antagonistic to the laborers.

But the *capitalist class?* They are to-day the deciding class. Are they not at least like the "intellectuals" becoming more and more friendly to labor?

I regret to say that I can see no sign of this friendship.

Certainly the capitalist class also is changing. It does not remain always the same. But what are the most important changes that it has undergone in the last decade?

Upon the one side we find a diminution, indeed, in some places the complete abolition, by means of agreements, cartels and trusts, of the competition which the capitalists had formerly to meet in the individual branches of industry. On the other side me see the intensification of international competition through the rise of new capitalist powers, particularly Germany and the United States.

The agreements abolish competition among capitalists not only as opposed to the buyers of their products, but also as opposed to their laborers. Instead of numerous buyers of labor power they now stand as a unit opposed to the workers. How greatly this increases their superiority and how much it sharpens their antagonism to the laborers needs no further explanation.

According to the last census of the United States the wages of laborers in American industries have absolutely decreased during the ten years from 1890 to 1900. If this is correct it is not too much to say that it is one of the results of the trust.

The sharpening of international competition works in the same direction. Here also we find the laborers suffering together with the consumers from this development. Alongside of the increase in the price of goods through protective tariff, which also aid the formation of trusts and combines, we find an increased exploitation of the laborers by which the capitalists seek to meet foreign competition. The consequence of this is the intensification of their struggle against the fighting organizations of the laborers, both political and economic which stand in the way of such exploitation.

Here also we find not a softening but a sharpening of class antagonism.

A third force working in the same direction is the increasing amalgamation of industrial capital with money capital, or "high finance." The industrial capitalist is a manager that possesses an industry in the sphere of production, taking this word in its widest sense (including transportation) in which he exploits salaried wage-workers and draws a profit from them. The money capitalist, on the contrary, is the modernized form of the ancient usurer. He draws his income from interest on the money which he loans, not only, as formerly, to indigent private individuals, but also to capitalist managers, institutions, States, etc.

Between the industrial capitalist and the money capitalist a great antagonism exists, similar to that between the first and the land owners. Interest on borrowed capital like ground rent constitutes a reduction from industrial profits. The interests of both forms of capital are here contradictory. Politically also they are in opposition. The great land owner stands to-day for a strong and preferably monarchical form of government because as a part of the nobility he can personally influence the monarch through them and through him the governmental power.

Furthermore he is a military this offers increased opportunities for offers, careers to which the sons of the bourgeois were little inclined. Again, he formerly demanded a forcible policy in both foreign and internal affairs. In this same way, the financier finds militarism and a strong active governmental policy, both external and internal, very agreeable. The kings of finance need not fear a strong governmental power, independent of people and Parliament, because they can rule such a power either directly as bondholders, or else through personal and social influences. In militarism, war and public debts they have a direct interest, not only as creditors, but also as government contractors, since the sphere of their influence, their exploitation, their power and their wealth is thereby increased.

It is wholly different with industrial capital. Militarism, war and public debts signify high taxes which the wealthy must assist in bearing, or else the cost of production is increased. War signifies besides this a stagnation in the production of commodities, a break in trade, economic difficulties and frequently ruin. Where the financier is rash, extravagant and violent the industrial manager is frugal, timid and peace-loving. A strong governmental power arouses anxiety in him and all the more because he cannot directly control it. His interests demand rather a strong parliament than a strong government. In opposition to the great land owner and to the financier, he inclines rather to liberalism, because its half-heartedness accords with his own position. His profits are limited upon the one side by ground rent, interest and taxes, and upon the other side an aspiring proletariat threatens the whole profit system. When the proletariat becomes too threatening, he prefers to adopt the peaceable method of "divide and govern," of corruption, and of compromise by benevolent establishments, etc., rather than the method of forcible suppression. Where the proletariat has not yet entered the field of independent politics the industrial capitalist willingly serves it as bellwether in order to increase his own political power. To the little bourgeois Socialist the opposition between industrial capital and the proletariat appears less than that between profit upon the one side and ground rent and interest upon the other. For him the solution of the social question consists in the abolition of interest and ground rent.

The opposition between finance and industry continually decreases since with the progressive concentration of capital, finance ever more and more dominates industry. A powerful means to this end is the continuous replacement of private employers by stock companies. Well meaning optimists have seen in this a means of "democratizing" capital so that after a while, in the most peaceable manner without any one noticing it, capital would be transformed into social property. In fact, this movement really means the transformation of all the money of the middle and lower classes, which is not used by them for immediate consumption, into money capital and as such placing it at the disposal of the great financiers for the buying out of industrial managers and thereby assisting in the concentration of industry in the hands of a few financiers. Without the system of stocks the great financiers would only control those businesses which they have bought with their own money. Thanks to stocks, they can make countless industries dependent upon them and thereby accelerate the conquest of those which they have not the necessary money to purchase. The whole fabulous power of Pierpont Morgan & Co., that within the last few years has united in one hand countless railroads, mines, and a majority of the iron works, and now has also monopolized the greatest Transatlantic steamship line—this sudden acquisition of dominion over the industry and commerce of the greatest of civilized worlds would have been impossible without stock companies.

According to the London Economist, five men, John D. Rockefeller, C. H. Harriman, Pierpont Morgan, W. M. Vanderbilt and G. D. Could together possess seven hundred and fifty million dollars; while the total capital of the banks, railroads and the industrial companies of the United States is seventeen thousand five hundred million dollars. Thanks to the stock system they control half of this capital, upon which in turn the entire economic wealth of the Union depends.

As has always been the case, so again when the inevitable crisis comes in America, the little stockholders will be expropriated and the positions of the great ones enlarged and strengthened.

The greater the power of the financier in industry, the greater the tendency of industrial capital to adopt the methods of finance. For the private business man who lives by the side of his laborers, these are still men to whose welfare he cannot be wholly indifferent unless lie has become utterly callous. For the stockholder, nothing exists but dividends, and the laborers are simply figures in a mathematical calculation in the result of which he is in the highest degree interested, for it can usually bring him increased well being and increased power, or retrenchment and social degradation. The remnant of consideration for the laborer which was still preserved in the private employer is here wholly lost.

Money capital is that form of capital which mostly inclines toward violence, which easiest leads to monopoly and thereby attains boundless power over the laboring class, which is most estranged from the laborer, which most threatens the capital of the private industrial capitalist, and more and more comes to rule the whole capitalist system of production.

The necessary result of this is a sharpening of social antagonisms. But England! it will be at once responded. Do we not find in England a perceptible softening of class antagonisms, and has not Marx said that England is the classic land of capitalist production, which to-day shows what our future will be? Is not the present condition of England the one toward which we are moving?

It is always to England that the fanatics of social peace refer us and it is significant that it is these same people who taunt us orthodox Marxians the loudest on the obstinate tenacity with which we cling to every Marxian sentence and who most frequently throw the above Marxian sentence at us.

As a matter of fact, however, conditions have greatly changed since the writing of Capital. England has ceased to be the classic land of capitalism. Its development comes more and more to a standstill, it is more and more becoming subordinate to other nations, especially Germany and America, and now the conditions begin to be reversed. England ceases to show us our future. On the contrary, our present state rather shows England's future in capitalist production. The thing which shows that the investigator of actual relations is really an orthodox Marxian is not that he thoughtlessly follows Marx, but that he applies his methods in order to understand facts.

England was the classic ground of capitalism, the one upon which industrial capital first gained the mastery. English capitalism came into power the economic master not only of the upper class of its own land but also of foreign lands. So it was that all of the characteristics that I have above designated as peculiar to it could most freely develop. It gave up violent suppression of the laboring class and depended much more upon peaceful diplomacy, for a while granted political privileges to the powerfully organized, and sought to purchase and corrupt its leaders by friendly advances in which it was too often successful. At the same time it renounced all violence towards the external world. Peace and free tradc were its watchwords. It adopted a peaceful attitude toward the Beers, and finally feigned to be about to right the century-long injustice of England towards Ireland by granting it home rule.

Meanwhile foreign competition grows powerful, indeed sometimes overpowering, and this compelled the capitalists to resist all opposition to exploitation within, while the most violent means are used to secure external markets. Hand and hand with this goes the usurious growth of the domination of high finance in the process of production. Since then England has taken on another appearance. "The spirit of the times," declare the Webbs in "Socialen Praxis" for March 20th, 1902, "has during the last ten years been turned against the 'corporative self-help' in the relations of employer and employee, that was characteristic of a generation ago. Indeed, the public opinion of the wealthy and professional classes is actually hostile to all that concerns trades-unions and strikes, as was not the case a generation ago."

As a result of this sudden change the unions are most seriously hindered in their activity by the courts. In place of free trade we see the cost of living enhanced by taxation; the policy of colonial conquest begins anew, together with coercive legislation against Ireland. All that is needed is the establishment of a standing army on the Prussian model and England will be fully launched upon the road of German policy, with the same Polish, commercial, social, foreign and military policy.

Does this not clearly show that England's future can today be studied in Germany (and also in the United States), and that England's condition has ceased to represent our future? The stage of "softening of class antagonisms" and the building the road to "social peace" is confined to England, and today is even there a thing of the past. Gladstone was the foremost representative of the policy of concessions for the softening of antagonisms, which corresponded to the industrial capitalism of England at the time when it dominated in an overwhelming manner all other classes and countries. The foremost representative of the domination of the violent, conquering, money capital is Chamberlain. It is one of the strangest ironies of history that the Gladstonian stage should have been looked upon in Germany as foretelling our future and most loudly praised as a firmly acquired conquest, at just the moment when the Gladstonian heritage was being scattered to the minds and Chamberlain was becoming the hero of the English populace.

I will freely grant that I, too, formerly had great hopes of England. While I did not expect that the Gladstonian stage would ever be transported to Germany, still I did hope that because of the peculiarity of English conditions the development from capitalism to Socialism might be peaceably accomplished, not through a social revolution, but by means of a series of progressive concessions by the ruling class to the proletariat. The experience of the last few years has destroyed these hopes for England also. The English internal policy now begins to shape itself on the model of its German competitor. May it have a corresponding reaction upon the English proletariat.

We now see in just how far the acceptance of the idea of a softening of class antagonisms and a drawing together of the bourgeoisie and proletariat is justified. To be sure, it is not wholly built on air, it is supported by certain facts, but its defect consists in having accepted as universal, facts that are really confined to a narrow sphere. It considers a few divisions of the Intellectuals as the whole bourgeoisie, and views a peculiar social tendency of England, which now belongs to a past age, as a universal, ever increasing tendency of the whole capitalist system of production.

Democracy

But does not democracy provide the foundation for a gradual, imperceptible transformation of capitalism into Socialism without any violent break with existing things if we but presuppose the conquest of political power by the proletariat?

There are some politicians who assert that only despotic class rule necessitates revolution; that revolution is rendered superfluous by democracy. It is claimed that we have today sufficient democracy in all civilized countries to make possible a peaceable revolutionless development. Above all it is possible to found cooperatives for consumption whose extension will introduce production for use, and so slowly but surely drive capitalist production out of one sphere after another. Most important of all, it is possible to organize unions that shall continually limit the power of the capitalist in his business, until constitutionalism shall supplant absolutism in the factory, and thus the way will be prepared for the slow transition to the republicanized factory. Still further, the socialists can penetrate into the municipal councils, influence public labor in the interest of the laboring class, extend the circle of municipal activities, and by the continuous extension of the circle of municipal production narrow the field of private production. Finally the socialists are pressing into parliament, where they are ever gaining more influence, and push through one reform after the other, restrict the power of the capitalists by labor legislation, and simultaneously extend ever wider the circle of governmental production, while they work for the nationalization of the great monopolies. So by the exercise of democratic rights upon existing grounds the capitalist society is gradually and without any shock growing into Socialism. Consequently the revolutionary conquest of political powers by the proletariat is unnecessary, and the efforts towards it directly hurtful, since they can operate in no other way than to disturb this slowly but surely advancing process.

So much for the opponents of revolutionary development.

It is an attractive picture they have painted for us, and again it cannot be truthfully said that it is wholly built in the air. The facts upon which it is founded actually exist. But the truth that they tell is only a half-truth. A little dialectical reflection would have shown them the whole.

This idyl becomes true only if we grant that but one side of the opposition, the proletariat, is growing and increasing in strength, while the other side, the bourgeoisie, remains immovably fixed to the same spot. Granting this, it naturally follows that the proletariat will gradually, and with no revolution, outstrip the bourgeoisie and imperceptibly expropriate it.

But things take on another aspect when the other side is considered, and it is seen that the bourgeoisie is likewise gaining in strength and is goaded on by every advance of the proletariat to develop new powers, and to discover and apply new methods of resistance and repression. That which from a one-sided observation appears as a gradual peaceable growth into Socialism is then seen as the organization of ever larger fighting bodies, as the development and application of ever more powerful resources for conflict, as a continuous widening of the battle held. Instead of being a gradual winning of the class struggle through the exhaustion of capitalism, it is rather a reproduction of the struggle upon ever wider stages, and a deepening of the consequences of every victory and every defeat.

Most harmless of all are the cooperatives, of which today the cooperatives of consumption are practically the only ones to be considered. Because of their purely peaceable character these are always highly esteemed by all opponents of revolutionary development. There is no doubt but that they can afford numerous important advantages to the laboring class, but it is laughable to expect even a partial expropriation of the capitalist class from them. So far as they are expropriating any class today it is that of little merchants and numerous grades of handworkers, that have been able to maintain their existence until now. Correspondingly it is noticed that nowhere do the great capitalists attack the cooperatives which it is pretended threaten them. On the contrary it is the little property owners whose rage is aroused against the cooperatives, and those who are injured are just the ones who are most dependent upon the laboring class, and who can be most easily won to the proletarian political cause. While the workingmen's cooperatives bring some material advantages to certain divisions of the laboring class, they also drive away from our movement many classes who stand very close to the proletariat. These means to the peaceable absorption of capitalism and the abrogation of the class struggle tend rather to introduce a new bone of contention and to arouse a new class hatred. Meanwhile the power of capital remains wholly untouched. The cooperative for consumption has so far been victorious only in its battle with the little merchant; the struggle with the great stores' is still in the future. This will not be so easy a victory.

The idea that the dividends of the cooperatives, even if not divided, but kept intact, can increase faster than the accumulation of capital so as to overtake it and contract the sphere of capitalism, is absolutely foolish.

The cooperative can play an important part in the emancipation of the proletariat only where the latter is engaged in an active class struggle. The cooperative can then become a means to supply the battling proletarians with resources. Even then they are wholly dependent upon the condition of legislation and the attitude of the state. So long as the proletariat has not yet attained political power, the importance of cooperatives for the class struggle of the proletariat will always be very limited.

Much more important for the proletariat than the cooperatives are the trade unions. This is true, however, only when these are fighting organizations, and not when they are organizations for social peace. Even where they conclude contracts with employers, either as individuals or as organizations, they can only secure and maintain these through their fighting ability.

However important, or indeed indispensable, unions may be for the battling proletariat, they must sooner or later reckon with the union of employers, which when it takes the form of a close agreement, of a cartel, or of a trust, will find it only too easy to become irresistible to the union. But unions of employers are not the only things that threaten the unions—more important is the governmental power. We in Germany could tell a tale on this point. That, however, even in such a democratic country as England, the unions have not yet overcome all their difficulties in this direction, has been shown by the recent well-known decision of the courts which threatens to completely incapacitate the unions.

On this point the already mentioned article of the Webbs in "Socialen Praxis" offers an interesting example which throws a significant light upon the future of the unions. They refer there to the great irregularity of the development of unions in England. Generally speaking the strong have grown stronger, while those that were formerly weak are now weaker than before. The unions of coal miners, cotton workers, and in the building trades and the iron industry have grown. Those of the farm workers, sailors, clothing trades and unskilled laborers have gone backwards. The whole union world, however, is now threatened by the increasing opposition of the possessing classes. The English laws lend themselves remarkably well to the suppression of undesirable organizations, and the danger that they now offer to the unions "has grown, and the fear of them is increasing with the hostility against the unions and strikes which the judges and officials share with the remainder of the upper and middle classes." The existing laws are of a character "to deliver the laborers into the hands of the employers with hands tied." So that the Webbs are forced to reckon with a position "in which the collective bargain with its undeniably favorable conditions, the collective cessation of labor and the opportune interruption of industry, is, through the legal operation of law, made impossible or at least costly and difficult."

This places the unions in a decidedly embarrassing position in opposition to the capitalists, so that one can scarcely expect any effective restriction of exploitation from them. One may well reflect upon what action the governmental power will take in this former El Dorado of the unions, England, if the unions attempt any forcible restraint upon capital.

In the same way the so-called Municipal Socialism is limited to those States and social organizations where universal suffrage in the municipality rules. It must always remain bound to the general economic and political conditions, and can never proceed independently. To be sure, the proletariat may find the municipal government in the individual industrial communities in their hands before they have the strength to conquer the general government, and they can by means of this control, or at least restrain, action hostile to the proletariat and carry through individual betterments which could not be expected from a bourgeois regime. But such municipal governments find themselves limited not alone by the power of the State, but also by their own economic helplessness. They are mostly poor municipalities, almost exclusively made up of proletarians, that are first conquered by the social democracy. Where shall these obtain the means to carry out great reforms? Ordinarily the taxing power of the municipality is restricted by State laws, and even where this is not the case the taxation of the well-to-do and the rich cannot exceed certain bounds without these residents,the only ones from whom anything can be taken, being driven out of the municipality. Every decisive work of reform demands at once new taxes which are unfavorably received not only by the upper classes but also by wider circles of the population. Many a municipal government which has been captured by socialists, or so-called socialistic reformers, has been taken away from them because of the taxation question, in spite of the fact that their actions have been exceedingly efficient. This was true in London and also in Roubaix.

But the political sphere! that knows no bounds! Shall we not find there an unbroken advance for the protection of laborers, and does not every session of Parliament bring us new restrictions on capitalism, and does not every recurring election increase the number of our representatives in Parliament? And is not thereby our power in the State and our influence upon the government slowly and surely but interruptedly growing, and does not this carry with it a corresponding dependence of capital upon the proletariat? Certainly the number of laws for the protection of labor grow from year to year. But when one looks closely at this he will see that in the last ten years they have been only an extension to new spheres of already existing protection Taking children out of the factory, protecting clerks, bookkeepers, house industries, sailors, etc., an extension of a superficial and doubtful character, and not in any way an increasing strengthening of protection where it already existed. When one considers, on the other hand, how remarkably fact the capitalist system of protection extends its sphere, how quickly it leaps from one calling to another, and from one man to another, it will be found that the extension of the protection of labor follows at a much slower pace; that it can never overtake the extension of capitalism, but always comes limping slowly on behind. And while the extension of the latter continually takes on a more rapid pace, the former tends ever more and more to come to a standstill.

If the advance of the protection of labor extensively is so unsatisfactory, intensively we shall find absolutely nothing. In England in 1847, under the pressure of the Chartist movement and the rapid degradation of the textile industry, the ten-hour day was secured for women and children—that is, actually for the whole laboring class of the textile industry. Where have we today an improvement on the ten-hour day?

The Second Republic of France in 1848 fixed the laboring day at ten hours for all the laborers in Paris, and in the remainder of France at eleven hours. When lately Millerand announced in the Chamber the ten-hour day, and that only upon paper and with many restrictions, for those industries in which women and children worked with laborers, and this not for all industries, this was praised as an admirable act of which only a socialist minister was capable. And yet he offered less than the bourgeois lawmakers of a half century ago, for he extended the ten-hour day only to the children for which in England a labor day of six and a half hours had been fixed in 1844.

At the Geneva Congress of 1866 the "International" had already declared the eight-hour day to be the preliminary condition to any fruitful social reform. Thirty-six years later, at the last French Socialist Congress at Tours, a delegate could still arise and declare that the eight-hour day must be placed as our next demand. He only wished to demand "measures preparatory for the eight-hour day," and get this man was not laughed from the room. On the contrary, he was able to be a candidate at, the last election in Paris.

It appears that the only thing in social reform that makes rapid progress is the modesty of the social reformers.

But how is this possible in spite of the increase of socialist representatives in parliamentary bodies? It becomes perfectly clear if one does not look at the matter wholly from one side, but studies the reverse of the medal. There is no doubt that the number of socialist representatives increases, but simultaneously therewith the bourgeois democracy falls to pieces. Very often this is shown openly in the diminution of their vote at election. More frequently it is seen in the falling off of any results. They are ever more cowardly, characterless, and resist reaction only to prepare the way to carry on a reactionary policy themselves as soon as they come to the helm. Indeed, that is the method by which Liberalism seeks nowadays to conquer political power.

As Bismarck saw his power waning he demanded that the terms of the German Reichstag should be extended from three to live years. This was an undoubtedly reactionary measure that raised a storm of indignation. In France, however, the last radical ministry of the republican defense, in which there was a Socialist minister, demanded an extension of the legislative term from four to six years, and the republican majority consented to grant this. Had it not been for the Senate, this reactionary measure would have become a law.

It is not alone that bourgeois liberalism disappears in the same degree that social democracy increases. At the same time that the influence of social democracy grows in Parliament the influence of Parliament decreases. These two phenomena proceed simultaneously without, however, having any direct connection with each other. On the contrary, the parliaments in which there are no Social Democrats, as, for example, the Saxon and Prussian Chambers, lose their influence and their creative power much more rapidly than the others.

The demoralization of Parliaments has various different causes. The most essential causes are not those that belong to Parliamentary tactics which through an alteration in the order of business, or of the sphere of Parliament, abolish its efficiency. The most essential lies in the character of the classes which are able through Parliament to significantly influence government. If Parliamentarism is to prosper, two preliminary conditions are necessary: the first, a single strong majority, and the second, a great social goal toward which this majority energetically strives and toward which they can force the government also. Both of these existed in the Golden Age of Parliamentarism. So long as capitalism represented the future of the nation, all classes of the people that possessed any Parliamentary significance, and especially the mass of the intellectuals, stood for freedom of capitalism. This was true of a majority of the small capitalists, and even the laborers followed the bourgeois leadership.

Liberalism thus stood as a united party with great aims. The struggle of the Liberalists for Parliament and in Parliament gave the latter its significance. Since then, as I have described above, a new development has risen. A special class consciousness has developed in the proletariat, so that a portion of the intellectuals, of the little property owners and of the small farmers are driven into the socialist camp. The rest of the small bourgeoisie and the farmers become wholly reactionary, while the powerful elements of industrial capital unite with the high finance which cares nothing for Parliament except when it can use it for its purposes—vide Panama.

The Liberal Party then dissolves into its elements without another great Parliamentary party with its united character rising from the governing class to take its position. The more reactionary the possessing classes become, the less are they a united body, and the more they split into little individual pieces, the harder it is to bring a united Parliamentary majority together. The more is it true that a majority is possible only through bringing together the different tendencies for a momentary coalition resting upon most uncertain foundations, because no interior bond, but only considerations of external opportuneness, controls them. Such coalitions are from the beginning doomed to unfruitfulness because their elements are so diverse that they are only held together through disclaiming just that decisive action which would give them life. It is a peculiar misunderstanding of the nature of these coalitions which arise from the downfall of Parliamentarism and signify its social and political impotency, that participation in them should be considered the means to a slow, step-by-step introduction of the proletariat to political power.

Social evolution does not, however, lead merely to the dissolution of the great united Parliamentary parties into countless, diverse and indeed often hostile factions. It leads also to the result that very often the Parliamentary majorities are more reactionary and more hostile than the government. Even if the governments are but agents of the ruling classes, still they have more insight into the sum of political and social relations, and, however willing a servant the official bureaucracy is to the government, it nevertheless develops its own life and its own tendencies that react upon the government. Moreover, the bureaucracy is recruited from the intellectuals, in which, as we have already seen, an understanding of the significance of the prolctariat is advancing, even though timidly.

All this operates so that not seldom the government, with all its reactionary attitudes and hostility to labor, still does not proceed with such blind rage as does the ruling class, with its little bourgeois and agrarian tail, which stands behind the government. The Parliament which was formerly the means of pressing the government forward upon the road to progress becomes ever more and more the means to nullify the little progress that conditions compel the government to make. In the degree that the class which rules through Parliamentarism is rendered superfluous and indeed injurious, the Parliamentary machinery loses its significance.

When, on the other hand, consideration of the proletarian body of voters compels the representative body to move towards friendship for labor and democracy and thereby to overreach the government, the latter easily finds means to circumvent Parliament.

In the United States the battle against the unions is carried on much less through the representative bodies than through the courts. In the same way it is the decisions of the House of Lords, and not the legislation of the popularly elected House of Commons, whereby the road to an attack upon the unions has recently been opened in England; and how the spirit of the abolished laws of exception still lives in the German courts, the German laborers can tell many a tale.

So the candle is burning from both ends, and the ruling parties as well as the government more and more doom Parliament to sterility. Parliamentarism is continually more incapable of following a decisive policy in any direction. It becomes ever more senile and helpless, and can only be reawakened to new youth and strength when it, together with the total governmental power, is conquered by the rising proletariat and turned to serve its purposes. Parliamentarism, far from making a revolution useless and superfluous, is itself in need of a revolution in order to vivify it.

I do not wish to be understood as holding democracy superfluous, or to take the position that cooperatives, unions, the entrance of social democracy into municipalities and parliaments, or the attainment of single reforms, is worthless. Nothing would be more incorrect. On the contrary, all these are of incalculable value to the proletariat. They are only insignificant as means to avoid a revolution.

This conquest of political power by the proletariat is of the highest value exactly because it makes possible a higher form of the revolutionary struggle. This struggle is no longer, as in 1789, a battle of unorganized mobs with no political form, with no insight into the relative strength of the contending factors: with no profound comprehension of the purposes of the struggle and the means to its solution; no longer a battle of mobs that can be deceived and bewildered by every rumor or accident. It is a battle of organized, intelligent masses, full of stability and prudence, that do not follow every impulse or explode over every insult, or collapse under every misfortune.

On the other hand, the elections are a means to count ourselves and the enemy and they grant thereby a clear view of the relative strength of the classes and parties, their advance and their retreat. They prevent premature outbreaks and they guard against defeats. They also grant the possibility that the opponents will themselves recognize the untenability of many positions and freely surrender them when their maintenance is no life-and-death question for them. So that the battle demands fewer victims, is less sanguinary and depends less upon blind chance.

Neither are the political acquisitions that are gained through democracy and the application of its freedom and rights to be undervalued. They are much too insignificant to really restrict the dominion of capitalism and to bring about its imperceptible transition into socialism. The slightest reform or organization may be of great significance for the physical or intellectual *re-birth of the proletariat* that, without them, would be surrendered helpless to capitalism and left alone in the misery that continuously threatens it. But it is not alone the relief of the proletariat from its misery that makes the activity of the proletariat in Parliament and the operation of the proletarian organizations indispensable. They are also of value as a means of practically familiarizing the proletariat with the problems and methods of national and municipal government and of great industries, as well as to the attainment of that intellectual maturity which the proletariat needs if it is to supplant the bourgeoisie as ruling class.

Democracy is also indispensable as a means of ripening the proletariat for the social revolution. But it is not capable of preventing this revolution. Democracy is to the proletariat what light and air are to the organism; without them it cannot develop its powers. But we must not be so occupied with observing the growth of one class that we cannot see the simultaneous growth of its opponent. Democracy does not hinder the development of capital, whose organization and political and economic powers increase at the same time as does the power of the proletariat. To be sure, the cooperatives are increasing, but simultaneously and yet faster grows the accumulation of capital; to be sure, the unions are growing, but simultaneously and faster grows the concentration of capital and its organization in gigantic monopolies. To be sure, the socialist press is growing (to only mention here a point which cannot be further discussed), but simultaneously grows the partyless and characterless press that poisons and unnerves ever wider popular circles. To be sure, wages are rising, but still faster rises the mass of profits. Certainly the number of socialist representatives in Parliament is growing, but still more sinks the significance and efficaciousness of this institution, while simultaneously Parliamentary majorities, like the government, fall into ever greater dependence on the powers of the high finance.

So beside the resources of the proletariat develop also those of capital, and the end of this development can be nothing less than a great, decisive battle that cannot end until the proletariat has attained the victory.

The capitalist class is superfluous, and the proletariat, on the other hand, has become an indispensable social class. The capitalist class is not in a condition either to elevate the proletariat nor to root it out. After every defeat the latter rises again, more threatening than before. Accordingly the proletariat, when it shall hare gained the first great victory over capital that shall place the political powers in its hands, can apply them in no other way than to the abolition of the capitalist system. So long as this has not yet happened, the battle between the two classes will not and cannot come to an end. Social peace inside of the capitalist system is a Utopia that has grown out of the real needs of the intellectual classes, but has no foundation in reality for its development. And no less of a Utopia is the imperceptible growth of capitalism into socialism. We have not the slightest ground to admit that things will end differently from what they begun. Neither the economic nor the political development indicates that the era of revolution which characterizes the capitalist system is closed. Social reform and the strengthening of the proletarian organizations cannot hinder it. They can at the most operate to the end that the class struggle in the higher developed grades of the battling proletariat will be transformed from a battle for the first conditions of existence to a battle for the possession of dominion.

Forms and Weapons of Social Revolution

What will be the precise form under which the decisive battles between the ruling class and the proletariat will be fought out? When may we expect them to occur? What weapons will be at the service of the proletariat?

To these questions it is hard to give definite answers. We can to a certain degree suggest the *direction* of the development but not its *form* nor its *velocity*. The investigation of the direction of evolution concerns itself only with relatively simple laws. Here one can only isolate from the whole confused manifold, the phenomena which we recognize as not regular or necessary, or which appear to us as accidental. These latter on the contrary play an important part in the determination of the form and the velocity of the movement. For example, in all modern civilization the direction of capitalist development during the last century has been the same, but in every one of them the form and the velocity was very different. Geographical peculiarities, racial individualities, favor and disfavor of the neighbor, the restraint or assistance of great individualities, all these and many ether things have had their influence. Many of these could not be foreseen, but even the most easily recognizable of these factors operate upon each other in such diverse ways that the result is so extremely complicated as to be impossible of determination from a previous stage. So it came about that even the people who through fundamental and comprehensive knowledge of the social relations of other civilized countries and by methodical and fruitful methods of research far exceeded all their contemporaries, as for example, Marx and Engels, were able to determine the direction of economic development for many decades in a degree that the course of events has magnificently justified. But even these investigators could strikingly err when it came to the question of predicting the velocity and form of the development of the next month.

There is only one thing I think that one can certainly say to-day about the approaching revolution. It will be wholly different from any of its predecessors. It is one of the greatest mistakes that revolutionists as well as their opponents frequently commit to present the coming revolution according to the model of past ones for there is nothing easier than to prove that such revolutions are no longer possible. The conclusion is then at hand that the idea of a social revolution is an entirely outgrown one. It is the first time in the history of the world that we are confronted with a revolutionary struggle to be fought out under the application of democratic forms by organizations created upon the foundation of democratic freedom against resources such as the world has not yet seen, prominent among which are organizations of employers before which even monarchs bow and whose power will be strengthened by the governmental powers of bureaucracy and militarism, which the modern great nations have inherited from absolutism.

One of the peculiarities of the present situation consists in the fact that, as we have already pointed out, it is no longer the governments which offer us the harshest resistance. Under absolutism, against which former revolutions were turned, the government was supreme and class antagonisms could not clearly develop. The government hindered not alone the exploited but also the exploiting classes from freely defending their interests. On the side Of government there stood only a portion of the exploiting class; another and a very considerable part of the exploiters, namely, the industrial capitalists, mere in the camp of the opposition, together with the whole mass of the laboring class—not simply proletarians, but also the small bourgeois and the peasants—except in some backward localities. Government was also isolated from the people. It had no hold on the broad masses of the populace; it represented the most highly favored strength of the oppression and the exploitation of the people. A *coup d'etat* could under certain circumstances suffice to overthrow it.

In a democracy not alone the exploited but the exploiting class can more freely develop their organization, and it is necessary that they do this if they are to be able to resist their opponents. The strength not only of the former but of the latter as well is greater than under absolutism. They use their forces recklessly and more harshly than the government itself, which no longer stands above them, but rather beneath them.

The revolutionary circles have also to deal not only with the government but also with the powerful organizations of the exploiters. And the revolutionary circles no longer represent as in the early revolutions an overwhelming majority of the people opposed to a handful of exploiters. Today they represent in reality only one class, the proletariat, to which not only the whole body of the exploiting class, but also the great mass of the farmers, and a great majority of the intellectuals stand opposed.

Only a fraction of the intellectuals and the very small farmers and the little bourgeois who are actually wage-workers and dependent on their custom unite with the proletariat. But these are decidedly uncertain allies; they are all greatly lacking in just that weapon from which the proletariat draws all its strength—organization.

While the former revolutions were uprisings of the populace against the government, the coming revolution with the exception perhaps of Russia will have more of the character of the struggle of one portion of the people against another, and therein, and *only* therein, resemble more the struggles of the Reformation than the type of the French Revolution. I might almost say that it will be much less of a sudden uprising against the authorities than a long drawn out *civil war,* if one does not necessarily join to these last words the idea of actual slaughter and battles. We have no ground to think that barricade battles and similar warlike accompaniments will play a decisive role to-day. The reasons for this have been given so often that I have no need of dallying longer concerning them. Militarism can only be overthrown by rendering the military itself faithless to the rulers, not through its being conquered by popular uprisings.

We have just as little to expect from a financial crisis as from an armed uprising in producing a collapse of existing conditions. In this respect the situation is also wholly different from that of 1789 and 1848. At that time capitalism was still weak, the accumulation of capital still slight and capital difficult to obtain. In this relation capital was partially hostile to absolutism or at least distrustful of it. The government was dependent upon capital and especially upon industrial capital and its development was impossible without it, or at least against its will. The dying feudalism, however, led to the drying up of all material sources of help so that the government received even less money from its lands and was ever more dependent upon the money lenders. This finally led to financial collapse or to concessions to the struggling class either of which events were able to bring about a political collapse.

It is wholly different to-day. Capitalism does not, like feudalism, lead to under-production, but to over-production, and chokes in its own fat. It is not a lack of capital, but superfluity of capital which to-day demands profitable investment and in pursuit of dividends draws back from no risk. The governments are completely dependent upon the capitalist class and the latter has every reason to protect and support them. The increase of public debts can only become a revolutionary factor in so far as it increases the pressure of taxes and therewith leads to an uprising of the lower classes, but scarcely (Russia perhaps must be excepted) to a direct financial collapse, or even to a serious financial embarrassment of the government. We have just as little cause to expect a revolution from a financial crisis as from an armed insurrection.

One means which is peculiar to the proletariat for battle and the exercise of influence is the organized withholding of labor—the strike. The more the capitalist manner of production develops and capital concentrates, the more gigantic the dimensions of the strike, and the more the capitalist manner of production presses the small industries, the more will the whole of society become dependent upon the undisturbed continuance of capitalist production and the more will every important disturbance of this latter as for instance, a strike of great dimensions, bring with it national calamities and political results. At a certain height of economic development the thought will at once occur to use the strike as a means for political struggle. It has already appeared as such in France and Belgium and has been used with good results. In my opinion it will play a great role in the revolutionary battles of the future.

That has been my view for a long time. In my articles on the new party programme of 1891 (Neue Zeit, 1890-1891, No. 50, page 757) I pointed out the possibility that "under certain conditions, when a great decision is to be made, when great events have moved the labor masses to their depths an extensive cessation of labor may easily have great political results."

Naturally, I am not using the idea of a general strike in the sense that the anarchists and the French trade unionists use the word. To these latter the political and especially the Parliamentary activity of the proletariat is to be Supplemented by the strike and it is to become a means to throw the social order overboard.

That is foolish. A general strike in the sense that all the laborers of the country at a given sign shall lay down their labor presupposes a unanimity and an organizaiion of the laborers which is scarcely possible in present society, and which if it were once attained would be so irresistible that no general strike would be necessary. Such a strike mould, however, at one stroke render impossible the existence not simply of existing society but all existence, and that of the proletarians long before that of the capitalist, and must consequently collapse uselessly at just the moment when its revolutionary virtue began to develop.

The strike as a political weapon will scarcely ever, certainly not in any time now visible, take on the form of a strike of *all* the laborers of a country. It can also not have the purpose of *displacing* the other means of political struggle but only of *supplementing* and *strengthening* them. We are now entering upon a time where opposed to the overwhelming power of organized capital an isolated non-political strike will be just as hopeless as is the isolated parliamentary action of the labor parties opposed to the pressure of the capitalistically dominated governmental powers. It will be ever more necessary that both should grow and draw new strength from co-operation.

As is the case with all new weapons the best manner to use a political strike must first be learned. It is not a cure-all as the anarchists announce it, and it is not an infallible means, under all conditions, as they consider it. It would exceed my purposes to investigate here the conditions under which it is applicable. Considering the latest events in Belgium I might observe that these have shown how very much it demands its own peculiar methods which do not favorably combine with other methods, as for example, with alliances with Liberals. I do not necessarily reject such an alliance under all conditions. It would be foolish for us not to utilize the disagreements and divisions of our opponents. But one should not expect more from the Liberals than they are able to grant. In the field of proletarian activity it may be easily possible under certain conditions that the opposition between them and us in regard to this and that measure may be less than between them and our bourgeois opponents. At such a time an alliance may have a place. But outside of the parliamentary field any effort for a revolutionary demand cannot be fought with Liberal aid. To seek to strengthen proletarian powers in such a struggle by a Liberal alliance is to attempt to use the weapons *for* a purpose that are ordinarily used to *defeat* that purpose. The political strike is a powerful proletarian weapon that is applicable only in a battle which the proletariat fights alone and in which it enters against the total bourgeois society. In this sense it is perhaps the most revolutionary weapon of the proletariat.

Moreover it is probable that still other means and methods of battle will develop of which we do not even dream to-day. There is this difference between the understanding of the *methods* and *organs* and of the *direction* of the social battle that the latter call be theoretically investigated in advance while the former are created in practice and can only be observed by the logicians afterwards, who can then investigate their significance for further evolution. Unions, strikes, corporations, trusts, etc., have sprung from practice and not from theory. In this field many surprises for us may yet appear.

As a means of hastening the political development and of bringing the proletariat into a position of political power war may play a part. War has already often shown itself to be a very revolutionary factor. There are historical situations in which revolution is necessary to the further progress of society but where the revolutionary classes are still, too weak to overthrow the ruling powers. The necessity of revolution does not always imply that the aspiring classes should have just the right strength at just the right moment. Unfortunately the world is not Set so purposefully planned as this. There are situations where revolution is undoubtedly demanded, where one ruling class should be displaced by another, but where the latter is still held in firm subjection by the former. If this situation continues too long the whole society collapses. Very often in such a situation war fulfills the function to which the aspiring class has not yet grown. It fulfills this in two ways. War can be carried on only by the exercise of all the powers of a people. If there is a deep division in the nation war will compel the governing class to grant concessions to the aspiring class which they would not have attained without the war.

If the governing class is not capable of such a sacrifice or yields too late for it to be effective then war can easily lead to defeat from without which carries with it a collapse within. A government resting mainly upon an army is overthrown as soon as the army is defeated.

So it has not unfrequently happened that war has been an extremely efficient means, even if brutal and destructive, to bring about a progress of which other means were incapable.

The German bourgeois, for example, was rendered too weak by the transference of the economic center of Europe to the sea coast of the atlantic Ocean, and by the thirty years' war and its results to overthrow by its own strength the feudal absolutism It was freed from this only through the Napoleonic wars and then later through the wars of the Bismarckian era. The legacy of 1848 was realized upon mainly through the wars of the counter-revolutionary forces as these forces had themselves been formerly established.

Today we are in a period of external and internal political antagonisms analogous to that which existed in the 50's and 60's. Once more a mass of social tinder has accumulated. The problems of external and internal politics demanding solution become ever more tremendous. But none of the rulings classes or parties dare earnestly to attempt their solution because this is not possible without great upheavals and they shrink back from these because they have learned to know the gigantic power of the proletariat which every such great upheaval threatens to set free.

I have referred above to the decay of the internal political life which finds its most striking expression in the increasing decadence of Parliaments. But hand in hand with this is the decay of external politics. One fears every energetic policy that may lead to an international conflict, not from an ethical dislike of war, but for fear of the revolution, whose forerunner it may be. Accordingly the statesmanship of our rulers consists simply, not alone internally, but also externally, in placing every question upon the shelf and thereby increasing the number of unsolved problems. Thanks to this policy there now exists a row of shadow States such as Turkey and Austria, which an energetic revolutionary race of a half century ago placed on the list of extinct States. On the other side, and for the same reason, the interest of the bourgeoisie has completely ceased to stand for an independent Polish national state.

But these social craters are not put out, they may burst out again any day in devastating war, like Mt. Pelee at Martinique. Economic evolution itself continually creates new craters, new causes of crises, new points of friction and new occasions for warlike developments, in that it awakens in the ruling classes a greed for the monopolization of the markets and the conquest of foreign colonies and in that it substitutes for the peaceful attitude of the industrial capitalist, the violent one of the financier.

The single security for freedom is found to-day in the fear of the revolutionary proletariat. We have yet to see how long this will restrain the ever increasing causes of conflict. And there are also a number of powers who have no independent revolutionary proletariat to fear and many of these are completely dominated by an unscrupulous, brutal clique of men of the "high finance." These powers, hitherto insignificant or peace-loving in international politics, are continuously becoming more prominent as international disturbers of peace. This is true most of all of the United States, but also of England and Japan. Russia has figured previously in the first place in the list of international disturbers; her heroic proletariat has momentarily restrained her. But just as over-confidence of a government in unrestricted interior power with no revolutionary class at its back, so also can the despair of a tottering government kindle a war. This was the case with Napoleon III. in 1870 and perhaps may yet be the case with Nicholas II. The great danger to the peace of the world to-day is from these powers and their antagonisms and not from such as exist between Germany and France, or between Austria and Italy. We must reckon on the possibility of a war within a perceptible time and therewith also the possibility of political convulsions that will end directly in proletarian uprisings or at least in opening the way to them.

Let no one misunderstand me. I am investigating here, not prophesying and still less am I expressing wishes. I investigate what may happen; I do not declare what will happen, least of all do I demand what should happen. When I speak, here of war as a means of revolution, that does not say that I desire war. Its horrors are so terrible that to-day it is only military fanatics whose ghastly courage could lead them to demand a war in cold blood. But even when a revolution is not a means to an end but an end in itself, which even at the most bloody price could not be too dearly purchased, still one cannot desire war as a means to release revolution for it is the most irrational means to this end. It brings such terrible destruction and creates such gigantic demands upon the State that any revolution springing from it is heavily loaded with tasks that are not essential to it but which momentarily absorb all its means and energy. Consequently a revolution which rises from war is a sign of the weakness of the revolutionary class, and often the cause of further weakness, just because of the sacrifice that it brings with it, as well as by the moral and intellectual degradation to which war gives rise. It also increases enormously the tasks of the revolutionary regime and simultaneously weakens its powers. Accordingly a revolution springing from a war is easier wrecked or sooner loses its motive force. How wholly different were the results of the bourgeois revolution in France where it sprung from an uprising of the people, from those in Germany, where it was imported through a number of wars. And the proletarian cause would have received much greater justice from the uprising of the Parisian proletariat if it had not been prematurely brought about by the war of '70 and '71, but had waited until a later period in which the Parisians mould have had sufficient strength to have driven out Louis Napoleon and his band without a war.

We also have not the slightest ground to wish for an artificial acceleration of our advance by a war.

But things do not move according to our wishes. To be sure men make their own history, but they do not choose according to their desires the problems which they have to solve nor the conditions under which they live, nor the means through which these problems are to be solved. If it came according to our wishes who of us would not prefer the peaceable to the violent road for which our present strength has perhaps not sufficiently grown and which perhaps would swallow us up. But it is not our task to express pious wishes and to demand of the world that it move in accordance with them, but to recognize the tasks, conditions and means which arise and to use the latter purposefully to a solution of the former.

Investigation of existing facts is the foundation of any rational policy. If I have arrived at the conviction that we are entering upon a revolutionary epoch, concerning whose conclusions everything is not yet clear, I am driven thereto by the investigation of actual conditions and not by my desires. I desire nothing more than that I may be wrong and that those may be right who maintain that the greatest difficulties of the transition period from capitalism to socialism lie behind us, and that we have all the essential foundations for a peaceful advance to socialism. Unfortunately I see no possibility of accepting this view. The greatest and the most difficult of the battles for political power still lies before us. It will be decided only after a long and hard struggle that will test all our powers to the utmost.

One can do nothing worse to the proletariat than to advise him to rest upon his arms in order to encourage a favorable attitude of the bourgeoisie. Under present conditions this means nothing less than to deliver the proletariat over to the bourgeoisie and bring it into intellectual and political dependence upon the latter, to enervate and degrade it and make it incapable of fulfilling its great historical purposes.

The proof that this is not exaggerated is furnished by the English laborers. Nowhere is the proletariat more numerous, nowhere is its economic organization better developed, nowhere is its freedom greater than in England, here is the proletariat politically more helpless. It has not simply lost all independence in the higher politics. It no longer knows how to even preserve its immediate interests. Herte also we may again refer to the previously cited article of Webb, which certainly cannot be suspected of being consciously revolutionary. "During the upward movement of the last ten years," he says, in the previously mentioned article,"the participation of the English laborers in labor politics has gradually decreased. The eight-hour law and the constructive Socialism of the Fabians to which the unions turned so eagerly in the period of '90 and '93 ceases more and more to occupy their thoughts. The number of labor representatives in the Lower House does not increase."

Even the latest scourgings of their opponents have not served to rouse the proletariat of England. They remain dumb, even when their hands are rendered powerless, dumb when their bread is made more costly. The English labourers to-day stand lower as a political factor than the laborers of the most economically backward country in Europe—Russia. It is the real revolutionary consciousness in these latter that gives them their great political power. It is the renunciation of revolution, the narrowing of interest to the interests of the moment, to the so-called practical politics, that have made the latter a cipher in actual politics.

But in this practical politics the loss of political power goes hand in hand with moral and political degradation.

I have referred above to the moral re-birth of the proletariat which has transformed them from the barbarians of modern society into the most significant factor in the maintenance and furtherance of our culture. But they have only so risen when they have remained in sharpest antagonism to the bourgeoisie; where the strife for political power has kept alive in them the consciousness that they are called to raise themselves together with the whole of society. Here, again, England offers us an illustration of a laboring class who renounce revolution and care only for practical politics, laughing scornfully at their ideals hung on a peg at one side and casting from them every goal of battle that they cannot express in pounds and shillings. From the mouths of the bourgeois themselves come complaints of that moral and intellectual decay of the elite of the English laborers which they share with the bourgeoisie itself and to-day indeed they are scarcely more than little bourgeois and are distinguished from them only by a somewhat greater lack of culture. Their highest ideal consists in aping their masters and in maintaining their hypocritical respectability, their admiration for wealth, however it may be obtained, and their spiritless manner of killing their leisure time. The emancipation of their class appears to them as a foolish dream. Consequently, it is foot-ball, boxing, horse racing and opportunities for gambling which move them the deepest and to which their entire leisure time, their individual powers, and their material means are devoted.

One seeks hopelessly to rouse by political preaching the English laborers to a higher way of life, to a mind capable of nobler considerations. The ethic of the proletariat flows from its revolutionary efforts and it is these which have strengthened and ennobled it. It is the idea of the revolution which has brought about that wonderful elevation of the proletariat from its deepest degradation, which elevation stands as the greatest result of the second half of the nineteenth century.

To this revolutionary idealism we must above all cling fast, then come what will, we can bear the heaviest, attain the highest, and remain worthy of the great historical purpose that awaits us.

On the Day after the Social Revolution

I must first of all clear away a suspicion which will be roused in many people by the title of this work. "On the Day after the Revolution!" Does not that mean that we "orthodox" Marxists are only disguised Blanquists who expect by a *coup d' etat* to make ourselves dictators, and is not it a return to Utopianism when I attempt to describe a movement of which we can know nothing as to the circumstances under which it will take place?

I hasten then to remark that I consider the revolution an historical process that may easily draw itself out into a decade of hard battles. On the other side I am thoroughly convinced that it is not our task to invent recipes for the kitchens of the future, and when more than ten years ago the German Social democracy proposed to include in its program demands for such measures as would accelerate the transformation from a capitalist to a socialist manner of production, I opposed this because I maintained that the party could not lay out a definite road for conditions of which we can have only a dim presentiment and which may easily surprise us with much that is wholly unexpected.

But I maintain that it is a help to political clearness to examine the problems that will grow out of the conquest of political power by us. This is also valuable for propaganda since our opponents frequently assert that our victory will give us unsoluble problems, and we have in our own ranks also people who are unable to paint the results of our victory black enough. According to these people the day of our victory is also the day of our downfall. Therefore it is important to investigate and know how far this is the case.

But if one wishes to attain definite results in this direction and not get lost in endless windings, then we must investigate these problems in a simple form such as never exists in reality and abstracted from all complications. This is a customary process in science whereby one remains entirely conscious that in reality things are never so simple, or develop so smoothly as is the case in the abstraction. I have already said that the social revolution is a process of many years. But to reduce things to their simplest forms we must proceed from the idea that on some fine day the proletariat captures entire political power without restrictions at one stroke and is enabled to exercise it in strict accord with its class interests. The first certainly could not occur and the latter can never be completely the case. The proletariat itself is not sufficiently united nor enough of a uniform mass to permit such a condition. The proletariat divides into perceptibly different grades, different in their rate of development, different also in their intellectual and economic stage of evolution. It is also very probable that simultaneous with the rise of the proletariat other social grades close to them will be raised, such for example as a portion of the small bourgeoisie, or the small farmers, whose intellectual attitude is not yet fully proletarian. Friction and mistakes of manifold forms will rise from this, so that we shall never come to just what we wish and shall never have exactly that which we should have. We must however at this time leave these disturbing factors out of consideration.

On the other hand we must proceed throughout this investigation from certain assumptions. We cannot accept as our foundation a picture of the conditions as they may develop in the future for this would lead us into fantasies. And yet it is certain that we shall not gain our victory under present conditions. Revolution itself presupposes a long and profound struggle that will in itself greatly change our present social and political structure. After the conquest of political power by the proletariat, problems will arise of which we know nothing and many with which we are occupied to-day will by that time be solved. New means to the solution of these different problems will also arise of which we today have no suspicion.

Just as in natural philosophy the laws of falling bodies are investigated in a vacuum and not in moving air so here we investigate the situation of the conquering proletariat under presumptions which cannot occur in their complete purity; that is under the postulate that some morning we shall at a single blow come into complete domination while the means which Will be at hand for the solution of our task will be those that exist to-day. We can by this means attain results that will be differentiated from the actual course of coming events in exactly the same way as the laws of falling bodies differ from the actual fall of various substances. But in spite of these variations the laws of falling bodies actually exist and govern the fall of every single substance and the rate of fall of these can only be determined when we have first understood these laws.

So it is that the outlooks and obstacles for the conquering proletariat actually will be discovered in the road we shall take (taking it for granted that we apply our method correctly) and they will undoubtedly play an important role in the social revolution and its resultants, even if the actuality is something wholly different from that we here consider it. And it is only in this way that one can come to scientifically definite judgments concerning the outcome of the revolution. Those to whom this road appears too uncertain to form a basis for prognostication must remain silent whenever this subject is under discussion and simply declare: "Whoever lives will know how it will come out and what is undeniably the proper road."

Only such problems of the social revolution are capable of discussion as can be determined in this manner. Concerning all others no judgment can be made either in this or in any other direction.

The Expropriation of the Expropriators

Let us imagine then that this fine day has already come, in which at one stroke all power is thrown into the lap of the proletariat. How would it begin? Not how *would* it begin upon the grounds of this or that theory, or opinion, but *must* begin, driven thereto by its class interests and the compulsion of economic necessity.

In the first place it is self-evident that it would recover what the bourgeoisie has lost. It would sweep all remnants of feudalism away and realize that democratic programme for which the bourgeoisie once stood. As the lowest of all classes it is also the most democratic of all classes. It would extend universal suffrage to every individual and establish complete freedom of press and assemblage. It would make the State completely independent of the church and abolish all rights of inheritance. It would establish complete autonomy in all individual communities and abolish militarism. This last could be brought about in two ways; through the introduction of universal armament and the dissolution of the army. Universal armament is a political measure and dissolution of the army a financial one. The former can under certain conditions cost as much as a standing army. But it is essential to the security of democracy, in order to take away from the government its most powerful means of opposing the people. Dissolution again aims mainly at a diminution of the military budget.

It can, however, be carried through in such a manner as to strengthen still further the power of the government, if in place of an army built on universal compulsory military service an army of characterless slum proletariat is substituted which Will lend itself to anything for money. A proletarian regime would necessarily find a way to unite both methods so as to arm the people and to simultaneously make an end of the disturbance brought about by the installation of new weapons, cannons, warships and fortresses.

Undoubtedly the victorious proletariat would also make fundamental reforms in taxation. It would endeavor to abolish all the taxes that today rest upon the laboring population—first of all the indirect ones that increase the cost of living, and would draw the sums necessary to the covering of governmental expenses from the great properties by means of a progressive income tax supplemented by a property tax. I shall return to this point later. This must suffice for the present suggestion.

A particularly important field for us is that of education. Popular schools have always occupied the attention of proletarian parties and they even played a great role in the old communistic sects of the Middle Ages. It must always be one of the aims of the thinking proletariat to deprive the possessing classes of the monopoly of culture. It is self-evident that the new regime would increase and improve the schools and pay their teachers better. But we would go still further. To be sure the victorious proletariat, no matter how radically minded it may be, cannot at a single stroke abolish class differences, for these have risen from many centuries of development and these causes and their results are not swept away as easily as a chalk mark is wiped from a slate with a sponge. But the school can prepare the road in this direction and contribute very essentially to the abolition of class differences in that all children will be equally well nourished and clothed, and instructed in the same manner while at the same time the possibility of a diverse development of their intellectual and bodily activities is retained.

We must not over value the influence of the school. Life is mightier than it and where it comes in opposition to actuality it will certainly be forced to give way. When, for example, the effort is made to-day to abolish class difference through the schools not much progress can be made. But the school can, when it works in the direction of the existing social development, powerfully assist this movement. Where these social conditions are also operating in the direction of class interests the school can co-operate and, at least within a limited sphere, realize for the generation which is growing up in this period what the whole society of this generation is simultaneously growing toward.

All these are means that bourgeois radicalism has already placed before itself, but a certain power, and a disregard of capital of which no bourgeois class is capable are essential to such an attainment. Such a school as is here outlined would, in Germany, for example, according to the reckoning which I have made in my *Agrarfrage* demand one and a half or two million marks yearly. Almost double the present military budget! Such a sum for school purposes can only be obtained by a proletarian ruled community that does not maintain a respectful attitude towards great incomes.

But the revolution would naturally not stop at these transformations. It would not be simply a bourgeois democratic, but a proletarian revolution. We shall not, as we have already stated, investigatc what the proletariat would do upon the basis of this or that theory, for we do not know what theories may appear or under what circumstances the next revolution will be carried through. We will only investigate what a victorious proletariat, if it is to advance purposefully, will be compelled to do by the pressure of economic conditions.

There is one problem above all others with which the proletarian regime must primarily occupy itself. It will in all cases be compelled to solve the question of the *relief of the unemployed.* Enforced idleness is the greatest curse of the laborer. For him it signifies misery, humiliation, crime. The laborer lives only from the sale of his labor power and when he can find no purchaser for this he is delivered up to hunger. And even when the laborer has found his labor the unemployed still torture him, for he is never secure from the loss of his labor and consequent misery. A proletarian regime would in every case make an end to this condition even if the proletarians were not Socialists but simply Liberals as in England. In just what manner the problem of the unemployed would be solved we shall not here attempt to investigate. There are many different methods, and many plans to this end have been made by sociologists. For example it has been sought from the bourgeois point of view to insure against the necessity of unemployment by taxation, and in part this has been done. But a bourgeois society can only create the most insufficient patchwork in this field because it is itself the bough from which unemployment hangs. Only the proletariat and the victorious proletariat can and will enact the measures which are capable of completely abolishing the necessity of the unemployed whether this be through sickness or otherwise. An actually effective maintenance of all the unemployed must completely alter the relative strength of the proletariat and capitalist. It will make the proletariat master in the factory. That the laborer of to-day is compelled to sell himself to the employer and that the latter can exploit and enslave him is because of the ghost of the unemployed and the hunger whip that swings above his head. If the laborer can once be secure of existence even when he is not working, nothing would be easier than for him to overthrow capital. He no longer needs capitalists, while the latter cannot continue his business without him. Once things have gone thus far the employer would be beaten in every conflict with his employees and be quickly compelled to give in to them. The capitalists could then perhaps continue to be the directors of the factories, but they would cease to be their masters and exploiters. Once the capitalists recognized, however, that they had the right to bear only the risk and burdens of capitalist business, these men would be the very first ones to renounce the further extension of capitalist production and to demand that their undertakings be purchased because they could no longer carry them on with any advantage. We have already had similar results. This was the case, for example, in Ireland at the time the anti-rent movement reached its highest point and the land owners were not in a position to forcibly collect their rents. Accordingly it was the landlords themselves who demanded that the State purchase all their landed possessions. We could expect the same from the capitalist undertakers under a proletarian regime, even if this regime was not dominated by socialist theories and did not proceed directly from the point of view of bringing the capitalist means of production into social possession. Capitalists would themselves demand that their means of production be purchased. The political domination of the proletariat and the continuation of the capitalist system of production are irreconcilable. Whoever concedes the possibility of the first must also grant the possibility of the disappearance of the latter.

The question then arises as to what purchasers are at the command of capitalists when they wish to sell their undertakings. A portion of the factories, mines, etc., could be sold directly to the laborers who are working them, and could be henceforth operated co-operatively; another portion could be sold to cooperatives of distribution, and still another to the communities or to the states. It is clear, however, that capital would find its most extensive and generous purchaser in the States or municipalities, and for this very reason the majority of the industries would pass into the possession of the States and municipalities. That the Social Democrats when they came into control would strive consciously for this solution is well recognized. On the other side, even a proletariat which was not governed by socialist ideas would proceed from the point of view of transforming into State or municipal property those industries which for natural reasons—for example, mines—or through the form of their organization—as, for example, trusts—have become monopolies.

These private monopolies have become unbearable, not simply for the wage-workers, but for all classes of society who do not share in their ownership. It is only the weakness of the bourgeois world, as opposed to capital, which hinders it from taking effective action against these monopolies. A proletarian revolution must from its very necessity lead to the abolition of private property in these monopolies. They are to-day very extensive and dominate in a high grade the whole economic life and develop with great rapidity. Their nationalization and communalization signifies simply the domination of the whole productive process by society and its organs,—the State and municipalities.

The industries which are most prepared for nationalization are the national means of transportation, railroads and steamships, together with those which produce raw material and partially produced goods; for example, mines, forests, iron foundries, machine manufactures etc. These are also the very spheres where the great industries and trustification are highest developed. The manufacture of raw material and partially produced articles for personal consumption as well as small trading have many local characteristics, and are still largely decentralized. In these spheres the municipality and co-operatives will come more to the front, leaving the national industries to play a secondary role. But with the increasing division of labor, production for direct personal consumption becomes of less and less importance compared with the production of means of production, and therewith also the sphere of governmental production increases. On the other side this field is extended by the development of commerce and of the great industries, which bursts the local bonds of the market for each branch of production one after another, and transforms one after another from a local into a national industry. For example, gas lighting is clearly a municipal business. The development of electric lighting and the transformation of power in mountainous regions makes the nationalization of water power necessary. This operates also to transform illumination from a municipal to a national business. Again, the business of the shoemaker was formerly confined to the local market. The shoe factory does not supply simply the community, but the whole nation, with its production, and is ripe not for communalization, but for nationalization. The same is true of sugar factories, breweries, etc.

The trend of evolution under a proletarian regime would be towards making the national form of industry predominant.

So much then concerning the property in the *means of production* of the great industries, including those in agriculture. What then is to happen to *money capital* and *landed property?* Money capital is that portion of capital taking the form of interest-bearing loans. The money capitalist fulfills no personal function in the social life, and can without difficulty be at once expropriated. This will be all the more readily done as it is this portion of the capitalist class, the financier, who is most superfluous, and who is continually usurping domination over the whole economic life. He is also the master of the great private monopolies, the trusts, etc., and it is therefore impossible to expropriate industrial capital without including money capital. They are too completely bound up in each other. The socialization of capitalist industry (as one may designate for short the transference to national, municipal and co-operative possession) will carry with it the socialization of the greater part of the money capital. When a factory or a piece of landed property is nationalized, its debts will be also nationalized, and private debts will become public debts. In the case of a corporation the stockholders will become holders of government bonds.

In this connection comes the consideration of landed property. I refer here to property in land, and not agricultural industry. The great capitalistic socially operated agricultural industries will be subject to the same evolution as the other great industries. They will lose their wage-slaves and be compelled to offer their possessions to the State or municipality for purchase, and will thereby become socialized. The little farming industries may well remain private property, But I shall return to this subject later.

But we are not here discussing agricultural industry, but the ownership of land, independent of industry, the private property in the ground that yields to its possessor ground rent, through leasing or renting or interest on a mortgage, whether the property be urban or rural.

What we said of the money capitalist holds true also of the land owner. He likewise has no longer any personal function to fulfill in the economic life, and can easily be shoved to one side. As noted above in the instance of private monopoly, so with regard to private property in land, we find much opposition even in bourgeois circles, which expresses itself in a demand for socialization, since this private land monopoly is constantly growing more oppressive and injurious, especially in the cities. Here also nothing is lacking but the necessary power to bring about socialization. The victorious proletariat will furnish this power.

The expropriation of the exploiting classes presents itself purely as a question of power. It proceeds essentially from the economic necessities of the proletariat, and will be the inevitable result of their victory.

Confiscation or Compensation

The question of the possibility and necessity of the expropriation of the exploiters can be answered with much greater degree of certainty than the question which naturally arises therefrom: Will the expropriation proceed as a process of confiscation or compensation; will the previous possessors be indemnified or not? This is a question which it is impossible to answer to-day. We are not the ones who will have to complete this development. It is now impossible to determine any force inherent in conditions which will make either one answer or the other necessary. In spite of this, there are, however, a number of reasons which indicate that a proletarian regime will seek the road of compensation, and payment of the capitalists and landowners. I will here mention but two of these reasons which appear the most important to me. Money capital, as already stated, has become an impersonal power, and every sum of money can to-day be transformed into money capital without the owner actively functioning as a capitalist. We know that when a man has saved a mark to-day he can put it out at interest without thereby becoming a capitalist. As is well known, this phenomenon has been widely utilized by the optimistic representatives of the existing order. They conclude that this gives an easy way for the expropriation of the capitalist by the laborers depositing their total of saved pennies in the saving banks or purchasing shares in the corporations with them, and thereby becoming partners in capital. At other times these optimists say that if we were to confiscate capital to-day we must confiscate not alone the capital of the rich, but that of the laborers also, in which case we would be taking away the scanty savings of the poor, the widows and the orphans. In this manner we would arouse great discontent among the laborers themselves, another reason which would tend to provoke them to the overthrow of their own domination, a result which these glorifiers of the existing order await with greatest certainty.

The first assumption I do not need to discuss further. It is too foolish. The people who expect to see capital expropriated by the increase of savings are blind to a much more rapid increase of large private capitals. On the other hand, it is not wholly unjustifiable to say that a proletarian regime pledged to universal confiscation would also confiscate the savings of small traders. That would not be a reason why the laborers should find their own rule unnecessary. (One must be hard up for plausible arguments against a social revolution when he makes use of such anticipations.) But it might become a reason for the conquering proletariat to stop in the confiscation of the means of production.

If, however, that should happen, one could ask, What justice has the laboring class received from expropriation? It works simply to make all capital become simple money capital; and all the capital being transformed into national, state and co-operative bonds, any surplus value which the capitalists have drawn directly from the laborers will flow to them from the nations, states and co-operatives. Is this in any way to change the condition of the laborer? This question is wholly justifiable. But even if a proletarian regime should permit the same amount of profit to flow to capital that it had formerly received, the expropriation through a continuance of proletarian rule would have brought great advantages with it, in that a further increase of exploitation from then on would be impossible. Any new application of capital as well as every increase would be excluded together with all increase in ground rent. This alone would be a significant result of proletarian transformation. Every further increase of social wealth would from then on inhere to the good of all society. But together with this there would come still another advantage. As soon as all the capitalist wealth had taken the form of bonds of states, municipalities and. co-operatives, it would be possible to raise a progressive income, property and inheritance tax to a height which until then was impossible. It is one of our demands at the present time that such a tax shall be substituted for all others especially for an indirect tax. But even if we had to-day the power to carry through such a measure with the support of other parties, which is plainly impossible because no bourgeois party would go so far, we would at once find ourselves in the presence of great difficulties. It is a well known fact that the higher the tax the greater the efforts at tax dodging. But when a condition exists where any concealment of income and property is impossible even then me could not be in a position to force the income and property tax as high as we wish because the capitalists, if the tax on their income or property pressed them too closely, would simply leave the State. There have already been instances of this. The State then has the income and property tax without either income or property. Above a certain measure such taxes cannot rise today even if we had the political power. The situation however is completely changed when all capitalist property takes the form of public debts. The property that to-day is so hard to find then lies in broad daylight. It would then only be necessary to declare that all bonds must be public and it would be known exactly what was the value of every property and every capitalist income. The tax could then be raised as high as desired without the possibility of tax frauds. It would then also be impossible to avoid taxation by emigration for it is then a public institution of the country and above all of the nation itself from which all interest must how and the tax could simply be taken from the interest before it was paid out. Under such conditions it would be possible to increase the progressive income and property tax as high as desired. If necessary it might be put so high as to be equivalent, or nearly so, to a confiscation of the great properties.

It might well be asked what advantage is offered by this round-about way of confiscation of great property instead of taking the direct road. Is it not mere jugglery simply for the purpose of avoiding the *appearance* of confiscation if capital is first compensated for at its full value and then confiscated through tax legislation? The difference between this mode and that of direct confiscation appears to be but formal.

But the difference is not so trifling. Direct confiscation of all capitalists would strike all, the small and the great, those utterly useless to labor and those the most essential to labor in the same manner. It is difficult, often impossible, in this method to separate the large possessions from the small when these are united in the form of money capital in the same undertaking. Direct confiscation would complete this quickly, often at one stroke, while confiscation through taxation permits the disappearance of capitalist property through a long drawn out process proceeding in the exact degree in which the new order is established and its benevolent influence made perceptible. It makes it possible to extend the process of confiscation over a decade so that it will only be fully operative in the new generation that will have grown up under the new conditions and is therefore not accustomed to reckon with capital and interest. Confiscation in this way loses its harshness, it becomes more acceptable and less painful. The more peaceably the conquest of the political power by the proletariat is attained and the more firmly organized and enlightened it is, the more we can expect that the primitive forms of confiscation will be softened.

I have lingered somewhat longer with this question because it constitutes one of the main objections of our opponents and not because its carrying out is the greatest difficulty that we will meet. The greatest difficulties begin rather after all of the above events. The expropriation of the means of production is relatively the simplest incident among the great transformations of the social revolution. It requires only the necessary power and it is one of the inevitable presumptions of our whole investigation. The difficulties for the proletarian regime lie not so much in the sphere of property as in that of production.

The Incentive of the Laborer to Lobor

We have seen that the social revolution makes the continuation of the capitalist manner of production impossible, and that the political domination of the proletariat is necessarily bound up with the economic uprising against the capitalist manner of production by which its progress is hindered. Production however must continue. It cannot pause even for a few weeks without the whole of society going down. So it is that the victorious proletariat has the imperative task of ensuring the continuance of production in spite of all disturbances, and to lead the laborer back to the factories, or other places of labor upon which they have turned their backs and to keep them there in order that production may go on undisturbed.

What are the means at the disposal of the new regime for the solution of this problem? Certainly not the whip of hunger and still less that of physical compulsion. If there are people who think that the victory of the proletariat is to establish a prison regimentation where each one will be assigned his labor by his superior then they know the proletariat very poorly. The proletariat which will then make its own laws has a much stronger instinct for freedom than any of the servile and pedantic professors who are crying about the prisonlike character of the future state.

The victorious proletariat will never be satisfied with any prison or barrack-like regulations. Moreover it has no need of anything of the kind since it has other means at its command to hold the laborer to his labor.

In this connection the great power of custom must not be

forgotten. Capital has accustomed the modern laborer to work day in and day out and he will not long remain wholly without labor. There are people who are so much accustomed to their work that they do not know what to do with their free time and that feel themselves unhappy when they are not working, and there will be few people who will feel themselves happy for any length of time without any work. I am convinced that when once labor loses the repulsive character of over-work and when the hours of labor are reduced in a reasonable degree, custom alone will suffice to hold the great majority of workers in regular work in factories and mines.

But it is self-evident that we cannot trust to this motive alone as it is the weakest. Another much stronger motive force is the *discipline* of the proletariat. We know that when the union declares a strike the discipline of organized labor is sufficiently strong to make the laborers freely take upon themselves all the dangers and horrors of unemployment and to remain hungry for months in order to secure a victorious conclusion for the common cause. Now I believe that when it is possible by the strength of discipline to keep the laborers *out* of the factories it will also be possible to hold them *in* by the same force. If the union once recognizes the necessity of the unbroken regular progress of labor we may be sure that the interest of the whole will be so great that scarcely a single member will leave his post. The same force that the proletariat uses to-day as a weapon to destroy production will then become an effective means to secure the regular continuance of social labor. The higher the economic organization develops to-day the better the outlook for the undisturbed progress of production after the conquest of political power by the proletariat.

But the discipline which lives in the proletariat is not military discipline. It does not mean blind obedience to an authority imposed from above. It is democratic discipline, a free will submission to a self-chosen leadership, and to the decisions of the majority of their own comrades. If this democratic discipline operates, in the factory, it presupposes a democratic organization of labor, and that a democratic factory will take the place of the present aristocratic one. It is self evident that a socialist regime would from the beginning seek to organize production democratically. But even if the victorious proletariat did not have this point in view from the beginning they would be driven to it by the necessity of ensuring the progress of production. The maintenance of social discipline in labor could only be secured by the introduction of union discipline into the processes of production.

This would, however, not be everywhere carried out in the same manner, for each industry has its own peculiarities according to which the organization of the laborers must conform. There are, for example, industries which cannot be operated without a bureaucratic organization, as for example railroads. The democratic organization can be so formed that the laborers choose delegates, who will constitute a sort of parliament, which will fix the conditions of labor and control the government of the bureaucratic machinery. Other industries can be given over to the direction of the unions, and others again can be operated co-operatively. There are also many forms of democratic organizations of industry which are possible, and we need not expect that the organization of all industry would be according to one and the same pattern.

We have seen how the various forms of property would vary and that there would be national, municipal and co-operative property. At the same time, as we saw, private property can still exist in many means of production. Now we see also that the organization of industry takes on manifold forms.

But however powerful motives democratic discipline and the custom of labor may be, they are perhaps not sufficient to ensure that the entire labor class would continuously take part in production. We need not expect that at any time in present society the economic organization and discipline will include more than the majority of the laboring class. When these shall come into control only a minority of the members will probably be organized. It will be necessary to look for other motives to labor. There is one especially strong motive that is peculiar to a proletarian regime, that is, the attractive power of labor. It will be necessary to make labor, which to-day is a burden, a joy, so that it will be a pleasure to work, so that the laborer will go to his work with pleasure. To be sure that is not so simple a thing, but at least a beginning to it can be made by the proletariat at the beginning of its rule in that it will shorten the hours of labor. At the same time it will endeavor to make the place of labor more hygienic and friendly and to take from the labor process as much as possible its disagreeable repulsive side.

All of this is simply a continuation of efforts that to-day are somewhat developed in all labor legislation. But great advances in this direction demand building and technical changes which cannot be brought about between one day and the next. It will be neither an easy or rapid task to make the work in factories and mines very attractive. Beside the attractiveness of labor another power of attraction will come into operation through the wages of labor.

I speak here of the wages of labor. What, it will be said, will there be wages in the new society? Shall we not have abolished wage labor and money? How then can one speak of the wages of labor? These objections would be sound if the social revolution proposed to immediately abolish money. I maintain that this would be impossible. Money is the simplest means known up to the present time which makes it possible in as complicated a mechanism as that of the modern productive process, with its tremendous far-reaching division of labor, to secure the circulation of products and their distribution to the individual members of society. It is the means which makes it possible for each one to satisfy his necessities according to his individual inclination (to be sure within the bounds of his economic power). As a means to such circulation money will be found indispensable until something better is discovered. To be sure many of its functions, especially that of the measure of value, will disappear, at least in internal commerce. A few remarks concerning value will not be out of place here since they relate to what will be of much importance in our future discussion.

There could be no greater error than to consider that one of the tasks of a socialist society is to see that the law of value is brought into perfect operation and that only equivalent values are exchanged. The law of values is rather a law peculiar to a society for production for exchange.

Production for exchange is that manner of production in which with a developed division of labor independent producers produce for one another. But no manner of production can exist without a definite proportionality in production. The number of labor powers at the disposal of society is limited, and production can only be continued when a corresponding number of productive forces are active in each branch of existing production. In a communistic society labor will be systematically regulated and the labor power be assigned to the individual branches of production according to a definite plan. In the production for exchange this regulation is obtained through the law of value. The value of each product is determined not by the labor time actually applied to it but by the socially necessary time for its production. With the modification that this law receives in capitalist production by profits rye are not concerned because this would only unnecessarily complicate the analysis without bringing any new knowledge to the question. The socially necessary labor time in each branch of labor is determined on the one side by the height of its technique in any society and the customary exertion of labor, etc., in short through the average productive power of the individual laborers; on the other side, however, by the number of products demanded by the social necessity of a particular branch of labor, and finally by the total number of labor powers at the disposal of society. Free competition sees to it to-day that the price of products, that is to say the amount of money that one can exchange for them, is continually tending towards the value determined. by the socially necessary labor time. In this manner the result is attained that the production in each department of labor, in spite of the fact that it is not regulated from any central point, never goes very far, or continues long away from the proper level. Without the law of value the anarchy that rules in the production for exchange would soon end in an inextricable chaos.

An example will make this plain. We will make it as simple as possible. As the sum of social production only two different forms of goods are necessary, so far as I am concerned—trousers and suspenders.

Considering then that a society demands as the socially necessary labor within a definite time for the production of trousers 10,000 labor days and for suspenders 1,000, that is to say, this amount of labor is necessary in order to satisfy the social need for trousers and suspenders at the present stage of the productivity of labor. If the product of the labor day is worth one dollar, the value of the trousers will be $10,000 and of the suspenders $1,000.

If the individual laborer deviates from the social form in his production and produces for example one-half as many products in a labor day as his colleagues, then, the price of his product for a day's labor would be only the half of that inhering to what was produced by the others in a day of labor. This is well known. This happens also if the proportionality of labor is abnormal, for example, if the manufacturers of trousers attract more labor power today than is socially necessary this labor power must be taken away from other places so that the number of labor powers at the disposal of society in this line would be diminished. Take it in the simplest possible form, that they are all drawn away from the tailors. In place of the socially necessary time of 10,000 labor days here and the 1,000 there, we find only 5,000 actual labor days here and 3,000 there. The world is swamped with suspenders and we do not have enough trousers. What will be the result? The price of suspenders sinks and that of trousers rise. The 3,000 actual salable labor days in the manufacture of suspenders will then represent only the value of the 1,000 socially necessary and the value of the individual suspenders will sink to one-third of their former value. The prices will correspondingly sink below these one-third. The value of the trousers will, however, be determined as before by the socially necessary 10,000 and not by the actually supplied 8,000 labor days and as a result the individual producers will be worth five-fourths of their previous price. As a result of this the manufacture of suspenders will be unprofitable and the number of labor powers devoted to it will decrease and flow again to the manufacture of trousers which has become so extraordinarily profitable.

It is in this manner that the law of value under free competition regulates production. It is not the best conceivable way to regulate production but it is the only one possible with private property in the means of production. With social property in the means of production we shall have instead social regulation of production and the necessity of regulating production by the exchange of equal values will cease. Therewith also will disappear the necessity of money as a measure of value. In place of metallic money we can easily have token money. The price of products themselves can now be determined independent of their value. Meanwhile the amount of labor time embodied will always have an important bearing in determining its value and it is probable that the inherited price would be approximated.

While labor gives value and price to the product and labor must be paid with money there will be wages. In spite of this it would be false if one were to speak of a continuation of the present wage system as is done by many Fabians who say that the object of socialism is not to abolish the wage system but rather to make it universal. That is only superficially correct. As a matter of fact wages under the proletarian regime would be something wholly different from under capitalism. To-day it is the price of the commodity—labor power. This is determined in the last analysis by the cost of subsistence of the laborer, while its minor variations depend upon the operation of supply and demand. In a society ruled by the proletariat this would stop, as the laborer mould no longer be compelled to sell his labor power. This labor power would cease to be a commodity whose price is determined by its cost of re-production, and its price would become independent of the relation between supply and demand. That which to-day determines in the last analysis the height of wages is the number of products to be divided among the laboring class, the larger this number the higher can and will the general level of wages rise. All things considered the proportioning of the wages of labor among the different branches of industry is largely influenced by supply and demand, and since the laborers cannot be assigned by military discipline and against their wishes to the various branches of industry, so it may happen that too many laborers rush into certain branches of industry while a lack of laborers is the rule in others. The necessary balance can then only be brought about by the reduction of wages where there are too many laborers and the raising of them in those branches of industry where there is a lack of laborers until the point is reached where every branch has as many laborers as it can use. But the relation between supply and demand has really no influence upon a universal levelling of the wages of the entire laboring class which is determined only by the amount of existing product. A universal decline in wages as the result of over-production is impossible. The more there is produced the higher in general are the wages.

Now the following question arises. If the continuous progress of production is to be secured it will then be necessary to hold the laborers to production by a universal raising of wages. Whence then shall this increase of wages be paid and whence shall come the necessary amount of product? If we accept the most favorable conditions for the new regime, which we have not done, with all property confiscated, and with the total income of the capitalists flowing to the laborers, this in itself would give a very handsome rise in wages. I have pointed out in my writings on "Reform and Revolution" the statistics of England in the year 1891 where the amount of the income of the laborers was seven hundred million pounds sterling and where the amount of the income of the capitalists was in the neighborhood of eight hundred million pounds sterling. I have further shown that these statistics in my opinion were painted too rosily. I have reason to believe that they calculate the wages too high and the capitalist income too low. If we take, however, these figures of 1891 they will show that if the income of the capitalist was directed to the laborers wages would be doubled. But unfortunately things are not to be done so simply. When we expropriate capital we must at the same time take over its social functions. The most important of these is the accumulation of capital. Capitalists do not consume their entire income. A portion they lay aside for the extension of production. A proletarian regime would be obliged to do the same since it too must extend production. Accordingly for this reason even the most radical confiscation of capital could not turn its entire previous income to the laboring class. Even from the surplus value that the capitalists pocket they must again give up a portion in the form of taxes to the State. This share would increase enormously when the progressive income and property tax are the only forms of state and municipal taxation. And the burden of taxation would not diminish. I have pointed out above at what cost the re-arrangement of the school system alone could be brought about and besides this an old age insurance for all incapable of labor, etc., would be instituted.

We shall see that there is none too much remaining over from the present income of the capitalist to be applied to the raising of wages even if we confiscate capital at one stroke. There is even less if we wish to compensate the capitalist. It would then be absolutely necessary if we were to raise the wages of labor to raise production above its present amount.

It will be one of the imperative tasks of the social revolution not simply to continue but to increase production. The victorious proletariat must extend production rapidly if it is to be able to satisfy the enormous demands that will be made upon the new regime.

Increase in Production

There are various means by which production can be increased. Two of the most important of these have already attained great significance. Both have been applied with great results by the trusts of america from which very much can be learned concerning the methods of the social revolution. They show us how at a single stroke the productivity of labor can be increased simply by concentrating the total production in the most perfect industrial plants and throwing all those out of operation which do not attain a definite standard. The Sugar Trust, for example, a few years ago consigned all but about one-fourth of the industrial plants which it possessed to idleness and in this one-fourth it has produced as much as previously in the whole number. The whiskey trust also obtained eighty large distilleries and, at once put out of operation sixty-eight out of the eighty. It is only operating twelve distilleries but in these twelve it produces even more than hitherto in the eighty. A proletarian regime could proceed in the same manner. It could do this even easier because it would not be hindered by private property. Where individual industries are private property, the culling out of the inefficient by way of free competition is a very slow process. The trusts can only displace the less productive industries through the fact that they have destroyed private property in them by uniting all under one head. The method which the trusts can only apply to a relatively small sphere of production may be extended by a proletarian regime to the whole sphere of social production, since it will have totally abolished capitalistic private property. This method of increasing productivity by the culling out of inefficient industries will not be distinguished from the similar operation by the trusts of to-day simply by the extent of the operation but also in that it will include other methods and other purposes. The new regime will carry out this change principally in order to increase wages. The Trust on the other hand goes its way without regard to the laborers. Those laborers who are rendered superfluous by reduction of surplus industries it simply discharges. It utilizes them mainly as a means of pressing down the wages of the laborers who are at work and in increasing their dependence. Very naturally a victorious laboring class would proceed differently. It would transfer the laborers rendered superfluous by the closing of industries to other industries where their activity would continue. The trusts rather make the laborers superfluous because it is not their intention to perceptibly increase production. The greater the increase in the amount of products the greater the supply and the lower, under otherwise equal conditions, is the price. The trusts fight against all decline in prices. They would much rather limit production than extend it. When they produce only in the most efficient plants, this is done simply to reduce the cost of production and to increase profits, with the same or even an increased price, and not for the purpose of extending production. A proletarian regime, however, would act for the purpose of extending production, for it does not desire to raise profits but rather wages. It also would increase the number of laborers in the best industrial plants and it would thereby increase production, because in each plant more classes of laborers would work together. How possible this is and how much production will be influenced thereby I can explain by an example whose figures are taken wholly from the imagination and have no equivalent in reality but that nevertheless are not simply fantastic pictures but a real representation of things which find their counterpart in the trusts. Take, for example, the German textile industry which includes to-day a round million laborers (in 1895 993,257). Of these the great majority (in 1895 587,579) were occupied in plants which employed not more than 50 laborers. We take it for granted that the larger and the more comprehensive plant is always technically the more perfect. To be sure this is not true in all cases. It is possible that a factory with 20 laborers may be technically better organized than one in the same branch of industry with 80 laborers. But on an average the former statement would hold true and we can accept it all the more readily as we use it only as an example for the purpose of illustration and not as a proposition. Let us take it for granted that the most imperfect factories are those employing less than 50 laborers. All these would be closed and the work in them transferred to those factories in which more than 50 laborers were employed. These could then be divided into two shifts working one after the other. If the hours of labor are ten to eleven a day now each shift could then have its hours reduced to eight. From that time on the industry would run daily six hours more and its machinery would be so much the better used, while at the same time the hours of labor for each laborer would be shortened by two hours. We can take it for granted that the production of each individual would not be decreased thereby as we have had countless examples showing that the advantages of the shortened labor time generally, at least, outweigh the disadvantages. Considering that a laborer in the most imperfect industry to-day produces an amount of product which represents the value of 2,000 marks and that labor in the great industries is 100 per cent, more productive (Sinzheimer makes a similar estimate of the productivity of the large and small industries) so that each laborer in a great industry would produce the value of 4,000 marks. The half million laborers in the small factories of the textile industries produce an amount of products having a value of a billion marks. The other half million laborers in the great industries produce in the same time an amount of products valued at two billion marks. The million of laborers can produce a product of the value of three million marks.

Under the new regime when the laborers were all concentrated in the great factories with more than fifty laborers, each laborer would produce to the value of 4,000 marks a year and the total production of the textile laborers would amount to four billion marks or one billion more than they formerly produced. For the purpose of comparison we consider that values would still be produced.

We can go still further and close not simply the small but the medium sized factories and concentrate the total textile production in the great factories employing more than 200 laborers. The total number of laborers employed in such factories in 1895 amounted to 350,306, or almost one-third of the total textile workers. Under these conditions it would be necessary to work the laborers in three shifts in order to employ all the laborers in the great factories alone and in order to avoid the night work while shortening the labor time of a day to five hours or half of the present time. To-day the laborer in the great industry produces perhaps four times as much as the one in the small industry, or according to our previous wholly arbitrary illustration about 8,000 marks a year. By the shortening of the labor time his product would not be reduced in equal degree because the better rested laborer will produce more than the over-worked one. We may accept the hypothesis that he could produce as much in eight hours as he to-day produces in ten. We would not be reckoning things too optimistically if we went further and considered that by shortening the labor time from eight to five hours the production of the laborer would not be lowered more than 25 per cent, certainly not as much as 37 per cent. Accordingly each laborer would produce at least 5,000 perhaps 6,000 marks in each year, and all together would produce five to six billion. The total production would therefore, as compared with the present, be doubled and the wages could be correspondingly doubled and this absolutely without any reference to confiscation of capital while at the same time the labor time would be reduced one-half. Indeed under certain conditions the increase of wages on the basis of the figures here given could be still greater. Let us assume that of the present yearly product of the textile industry, which we have called three billion, one billion is applied to wages and the second to the purchase of raw materials, machines, etc., and the third to the profit of capital. Now under the new regime six billion would be produced. Of this two would be applied to raw materials, machines and such like. One would serve for compensation to the expropriated capitalists and the completion of the previously mentioned social activity. This would leave three billion for wages. This mould permit a tripling of wages. And all this without any new plans or new machinery, but simply through the closing of the little industries and transference of their laborers to the large ones. We simply need to do on a large scale what the trusts are doing on a small. It is only the private ownership of the means of production that hinders the development of modern production.

This method develops still another side. Our critics are very ready to tell us that for a long time it will be impossible to socialize production because the number of existing productive establishments is much too great and it will take too long a time for competition to crush out all the little industries and therewith create a possibility of socialist production. If the number of all the industrial plants in the German empire amounts to 2 1/2 million and those of the textile alone to over 200,000, how could one possibly manage such a number of industries nationally?

Certainly the task appears alarming but it is very much reduced when we consider that the proletarian regime will apply the methods of the trust, and while it will expropriate all the industries at once, only the best equipped large industries will be further operated. Of the 200,000 textile industries there are only 3,000 which employ more than 50 workingmen. It is clear that the concentration of industry in these latter plants mould very much simplify the task of the social regulation of production. It will be still simpler when we consider that the new regime will have closed up all plants employing less than 200 laborers. Of the 200, 000 there would then only remain 800. To control and supervise this number of industries is certainly no longer an impossibility.

Here again there is another significant point of view. Our opponents and the pessimists in our own ranks measure the ripeness of our present society for social production by the number of ruins which are still strewn round it and of which it is still incapable of ridding itself. Over and over again the great number of little industries that still exist is triumphantly pointed out. But the ripeness for Socialism does not depend on the number of little industries that yet remain but upon the number of great industries which *already* exist. Without a developed great industry socialism is impossible. Where, however, a great industry exists to a considerable degree it is easy for a socialist society to concentrate production and to quickly rid itself of the little industry. The socialist birds of ill omen, that simply know enough to announce the coming of ill luck by their warning croaks, continuously raise an obstinate clamor about the fact that the number of little industries in the German empire has increased 1 1/8 per cent from 1882 to 1895. But they are blind to the fact that in the same period the number of large industries with more than fifty employees increased about 90 per cent, while the gigantic industries employing over 1,000 persons increased in the neighborhood of 100 per cent. It is this increase that is the preliminary condition of socialism and this is richly fulfilled. Even if the small industry does not absolutely decrease, that simply shows that the number of ruins which the proletarian regime will have to sweep away is still considerable. Meanwhile the trusts promise to greatly assist us in this respect.

In other directions also they offer us a forecast. The present trusts increase their profits not merely through increasing the productivity of their employees but also by economies of different forms. Socialist production must make use of these same methods in still higher degree. Among these economies are those relating to machinery, by products and cost of transportation. Taking an example from the textile industry, which demands a wholly different expenditure to transport the raw material and accessories to production for 200,000 than for 800,000 industrial plants. The same is the case with the cost of the supervision of industries. Of the 200,000 industries, the smallest to be sure demands practically no supervision. In this class are those with less than five laborers. Here the manager is also a worker. Over 12,000 exceed this limit. But their supervision also demands considerably more directive power than those of 800. Other savings are attained in that the trusts abolish the struggle of competing industries for markets. Since their appearance in the United States the number of commercial travelers employed has decreased. One of the most striking of these cases is instanced by J. W. Jenks in his treatise concerning the trust. The extension of production has so increased that the number of unskilled laborers employed in these plants have increased 51 per cent and of the skilled 14 per cent. At the same time the number of commercial travelers has decreased 75 per cent. Jenks also states that many trusts have, according to their own statements, saved from 40 to 85 per cent of their advertising expenses.

Finally the raising of wages in industry would set free a large number of labor powers whose existence to-day is merely parasitic. They maintain a wretched existence to-day in their little shops, not because these shops are a necessity but because their possessors are in despair of finding their bread in any other place or because they cannot earn enough by wage labor and seek a supplementary occupation.

Of the almost two million people who are occupied to-day in the German Empire in trade and commerce (exclusive of the post office and railroads) and hotel keeping perhaps a million would, with a sufficiently high wage in industry and sufficient demand for labor powers, be transferred from parasitic to productive activity.

These are the two methods for increasing the productive powers of the laboring class: The abolition of parasitic industry and the concentration of industries in the most perfect plants. By the application of these two means a proletarian regime can raise production at once to so high a level that it mould be possible to considerably increase wages and simultaneously reduce the hours of labor. Every increase in wages and reduction of hours must again increase the attractiveness of labor and draw new laborers to production who were formerly parasitic, such for example as servants, small merchants, etc. The higher the wages the more laborers. But in a socialist society one can transform this saying into "the more workers the fewer the ill doers in society, the more produced and the greater the wages." This law would be absurd in a society of free competition where the greater the supply of laborers, under otherwise equal conditions, the lower the descent of wages. It is a law of wages for the socialist system of production.

The Organization of the Productive Process

The application of the two above mentioned methods of the trust to production have not exhausted the resources of the proletarian regime in relation to the increase of production. The productive process considered as a continuous transaction, as a reproductive process demands an undisturbed continuation, not simply of production, but also of circulation. If production is to go on without interruption it is necessary not simply that there be laborers for the creation of products, but it is also necessary that there be no break in the securing of raw materials and essentials of production, the necessary tools and machines, and the means of sustenance for the laborers, and that no interruption occur and that the finished product find a sale.

A stoppage in circulation signifies an economic crisis. It stops in some cases because too much is produced of some wares. In this case the industrial plants from which these products came cannot further function in their full capacity because of the lack of sale for their products. They receive no money for their products and the result of this is they lack the means to buy raw materials, to pay wages and so forth.

But crises can also occur because too little of many of certain wares have been produced, as for instance was the case in the crisis of the English cotton industry at the time of the war of the Rebellion in the United States, which for some time greatly disturbed the production of cotton.

The crises are the worst scourges of the modern productive system. To abolish them is one of the most important tasks of a proletarian regime. This can be done only through the systematic regulation of production and circulation as well as of re-production.

It has already been admitted that the object of socialism is the organization of production. But a portion of this problem is already solved by capital in that it substitutes for a number of little independent industries the organization of production into one great industry in which thousands of laborers are employed. The trusts have already accomplished the organization of whole branches of industry.

What, however, only a proletarian regime can accomplish is the systematic regulation and circulation of products, the exchange between industry and industry, between producers and consumers, in which the idea of consumption is taken in its highest sense, so as to include not simply personal but productive consumption. The weaver for example consumes yarn in productive consumption while the piece of bread that he eats is included in personal consumption.

The proletarian can only accomplish this regulation of the circulation of products by the abolition of private property in industry, and it not only can do this but it must do it if the process of production is to proceed under its direction and its regime is to be permanent. It must fix the height of production of each individual social productive plant according to the basis calculated upon the existing productive power (laborers and means of production) and of the existing needs, and see to it that each productive plant has not only the necessary laborers but also the necessary means of production and that the necessary products are delivered to the consumers.

Is not this task however insoluble in the great modern States? It would presuppose that in Germany the State is to become the director of production of two million productive plants and to act as medium for the circulation of this product, which will come to it partially in the form of means of production and partially as means of consumption to be distributed to sixty million consumers, of which each one has a special and changing need. The task appears overwhelming if one does not proceed from the point of view of regulating the necessities of humanity from above according to a very simple pattern and assigning to each one, barrack fashion, his portion, which would mean the lowering of modern civilization to a much lower stage. Are we destined then to come to a barrack or prison-like State? Certainly the problem is not simple. It is the most difficult which will come to the proletarian regime and will furnish it with many hard nuts to crack. But its difficulties must not be exaggerated.

In the first place it must be remembered that we are not compelled to create out of nothing over night a complete organization of production and circulation. There is one existing at present of a certain character, or otherwise the existence of the present society would be impossible. The question is simply to transform this organization, which has hitherto been an unconscious one going on behind the shoulders of those engaged in it with friction, sorrow and woe, bankruptcies and crises, under the operation of the law of value, ever being readjusted, into a conscious system in which a previous calculation of all modifying factors will take the place of the retroactive corrections through the play of supply and demand. There is a proportionality between the different branches of labor today even though it is wholly incomplete and incompetent; it is necessary, not to introduce, but rather to make complete and permanent. As with money and with prices it is necessary to connect with that which is historically descended and not to build everything from the ground anew; but only to broaden out at some points or to restrict others and to formulate more clearly the loose relations.

This problem is considerably restricted by the fact already discussed that the concentration of production in the most perfect productive plants has already perceptibly decreased the number of industries. Of the 2,146,972 businesses which constituted the industry of the German Empire in 1895 there were only 17,941 great businesses having more than 50 laborers (and these contained three million laborers out of the total number of eight million industrial workers). To be sure I do not assert that only these great industries will be retained in activity. To attempt to give absolutely exact figures of a future condition would be absurd. All the numbers herewith printed have simply the purpose of illustrating the problems which arise and not of narrowly setting forth how things will be formulated in reality. The relation of two million industrial plants to 18,000 great industries shows that the number of industrial plants would be perceptibly decreased under a proletarian regime.

But the difficulties of the organization of production and circulation can be diminished in other directions as well as by a decrease in the number of plants. Production can be divided into two great fields; those in which the production is for consumption and those in which production is for production. The production of means of production, thanks to the extensive division of labor, has become to-day the most important portion of production and it continues to increase steadily. Scarcely a single article of consumption comes from the hand of a single producer, but all run through a number of productive processes so that those who finally fit it for our use are only the last in a long row of producers. The production of articles for consumption and for the means of production have a wholly different character. The production for further production belongs to the domain of gigantic industries such as the iron industry, mining, etc. These are all highly organized in owner's agreements, cartels, etc. But even among the users of these means of production, operator's agreements are already very extensive. In most cases in this held to-day the individual operator does not deal with individual operators, but union of operators with union of operators, industrial branch deals with industrial branch, and those places where the union of operators is least developed are just the regions in which there are relatively few producers and few consumers dealing with each other. For consumption is here not by an individual but by a whole industry. In the manufacture of spinning and weaving machines, for example, there were in 1895 1,152 businesses with 17,047 laborers. Of these, however, there were 774 industries which had only 1,474 laborers and were scarcely to be considered. Among the great industries there were only 73 with 10,755 laborers. Opposed to these were 200,000 textile industries (not simply spinners and weavers) whose numbers, as we have seen, may be reduced to a thousand or perhaps to a hundred. On the one side there remained after the completion of the concentration of production in the most perfect industries perhaps 50 manufacturers of machinery and on the other side 2,000 spinning and weaving establishments. Is it then so impossible that the former should agree with the latter in regard to the demand for machines, and that their production should be systematically regulated? With this relatively small number of purchasers and consumers it is easily conceivable that in the sphere of the production of the means of production to-day, production for the open market has already disappeared and production for orders, that is to say, regulated, thoughtful production and circulation has taken its place.

The production of articles for consumption has another character. To be sure we have here the gigantic industries (sugar factories and breweries), but as a general thing the little industry is still generally dominant. Here it is necessary to satisfy the individual needs of the market, and the small industry can do this better than the large. The number of productive plants is here large and would not ordinarily be capable of reduction as in the production of means of production. Here also production for the open market still rules. But because of the greater number of consumers this is much more difficult to supervise than is production for production. The number of operators' agreements is fewer here. The organization of the production and circulation of all articles of consumption accordingly offers much greater difficulties than that of the means of production.

Here also we must again distinguish the two forms, namely: the production of necessary articles of consumption, and of luxuries. The demand for necessary articles of consumption ordinarily shows rather small fluctuations. It is quite definite. Day in and day out one needs the same amount of flour, bread, meat and vegetables. Year in and year out there is little change in the demand for boots and linen. On the other hand, the demand for means of consumption changes the more readily the more these take on the character of unnecessary luxuries, whose possession or use is agreeable but not indispensable. Here consumption is much more whimsical, but when we look closer we see that this really proceeds much less from the purchasing individual than from the industry itself. Changes in fashion, for example, springs not so much from the changes in taste of the public as from the necessity of the producer to render impossible of further use the old wares which have already been sold, in order to thereby appeal to consumers to purchase new wares. The new and modern goods must accordingly be very strikingly distinguished from the old. Next to the restlessness which lies in the very nature of the modern manner of production, this strife of the producer is the main cause of the rapid changes of fashion. It is this which first produces the new fashions and then makes them necessary to the public.

The variations in demand for articles of consumption, especially of luxuries, are influenced much more by the variations in the income of the consumers than by variations in taste. These last variations again, so far as they do not remain isolated but really have a wide extension through society, so as to perceptibly influence consumption, arise from the contrast between prosperity and crises, from the contrast between the strong demand for labor and the increase of enforced idleness. When, however, we investigate the source of these variations we find that they spring from the held of the production of the means of production. It is universally known and recognized that to-day it is the iron industry especially which gives rise to crises.

The alternation between prosperity and crises and therewith the great variations in the demand for articles of consumption also arises out of the sphere of the production of the means of production. In the other sphere, as we have already seen, the concentration of industry and the organization of production is already so far developed that it has made possible a really complete organization of production and circulation. Stability in the production of means of production carries with it stability in demand for means of consumption, and this can be easily established by the State without direct regulation of consumption.

Only one phase of the disturbances in circulation which spring from production is of importance to the proletarian regime,—only under-production, never over-production. Today the latter is the principal cause of crises, for the greatest difficulty at present is the sale, or getting rid of the product. The purchase of goods, the procuring of the products that one needs, ordinarily causes very little complaint from those lucky ones who have the necessary small change in their pockets. Under proletarian regime this relation mould be reversed. There will be no need of anxiety regarding the disposal of the products when completed. Private individuals will not be purchasing for sale to other private individuals, but society will be purchasing for its own necessities. A crisis can then only arise when a sufficient amount of a number of products has not been produced to supply the need either for production or personal consumption. If accordingly there are here and there, or even anywhere, too much produced this will signify only a wasting of labor power and a loss for society, but will not hinder the progress of production and consumption. It will be the principal anxiety of the new regime to see to it that there is not insufficient production in any sphere. Accordingly it will, to be sure, also take care that no labor power is wasted in superfluous production, for every such waste signifies an abstraction from all the others and an unnecessary extension of the labor time.

The Remnants of Provate Property in the Means of Production

We havé seen that the proletarian regime would make short work of the smaller businesses where they represent the little, undeveloped plants, not only in industry but also in exchange.

The efforts referred to above for the organization of circulation would also lead to the greatest possible abolition of the little middlemen by crushing them out, partially through co-operatives for consumption, partly through extension of municipal activity. Superintendence and organisation of the productive processes will be much easier when it is not necessary to deal with countless operators, but rather with only a few organizations.

Besides the work of the middle-men the direct producers of articles of consumption for local necessity would fall to the cooperatives and municipalities—for example, bakeries, milk and vegetable production and erection of buildings.

But it is not to be expected that all small private industries will disappear in this manner. This will be specially true in agriculture. To be sure those agricultural plants which have already become capitalist industries would fall with the wage system and be transformed into national, municipal or co-operative businesses. Therewith a large number of the little competing farmers of to-day would cease to exist and go as laborers into the industrial or agricultural great industry, because they could there secure a respectable existence. But we may be sure that some farmers would always remain with their own family, or at the most with one assistant, or maid that will be reckoned as part of the family, and would continue their little industry. With the present conservative nature of our farmers it is highly probable that a number of them would continue to work in the present manner. The proletarian governmental power would have absolutely no inclination to take over such little businesses. As yet no socialist who is to be taken seriously has ever demanded that the farmers should be exappropriated, or that their goods should be confiscated. It is much more probable that each little farmer would be permitted to work on as he has previously done. The farmer has nothing to fear from a socialist regime.

Indeed it is highly probable that these agricultural industries would receive considerable strengthening through the new regime. It would bring an abolition of militarism, of burdens of taxation, bring self-government and nationalism of schools and road taxes, an abolition of poor relief and perhaps also a lowering of mortgage burdens, and many other advantages. We have also seen that the victorious proletariat has every reason to increase the amount of products, and among those products for which the demand would be increased, the most important are agricultural products. In spite of all the refutation of the theory of increasing misery there is still much hunger to satisfy, and this fact alone justifies us in the opinion that the raising of wages mould show itself above all in an increase of the demand for agricultural products. The proletarian regime would also have the greatest interest in increasing the production of the farmers and it would have powerful forces at its disposal for this purpose. Its own interests demand that the agricultural industry should be brought to a higher stage through the care of animals, machines and fertilizers, through improvement of the soil, etc. It mould in this manner assist in Increasing agricultural products, including those in the industries not yet socialized.

But here, as well as in every sphere, conditions would make it necessary to simplify the circulation process by substituting for a large number of private individuals trading their products with one another a few organizations united for economic purposes. The State would much prefer instead of selling breeding animals, machines and fertilizers to the individual farmers to deal with the farmers' societies and co-operatives. These societies and co-operatives would find as the purchasers of their products no longer private middle-men, but either co-operatives, unions for consumption, municipalities or national industries (mills, sugar factories, breweries and such like). So here also the private industry would continually recede before the social, and the latter would finally transform the agricultural industry itself and permit the development of many such industries through the co-operative or municipal co-operative into one great social industry. The farmers will combine their possessions and operate them in common, especially when they see how the social operation of the expropriated great industry proves that with the same expenditure of labor perceptibly more can be produced, or that with the same number of products the laborers can be granted considerably more leisure than is possible in the small industry. If the small industry is still able to assert itself in agriculture this is due not a little to the fact that it can pump more labor out of its laborers than the great industry. It is undeniable that farmers work harder than the wage workers of the great land owners. The farmer has scarcely any free time, and even during the little free time that he has he must be continually studying how he can improve his business. There is nothing else in his life but his business, and that is also one of the reasons why he is so hard for us to gain.

But this holds true only for the older generation; the younger generation is conscious of other things. They feel a strong impulse towards enjoyments and pleasures, towards joy, and also towards a higher culture, and because they cannot satisfy these impulses in the country they stream into the cities and populate the level plains. When once the farmer sees, however, that he can remain in agriculture without being compelled to renounce leisure and culture he will no longer flee from agriculture, but will simply move from the little industry to the great and therewith the last fortress of private property will disappear.

But the victorious proletariat will not consider a violent hastening of this development, and this for the very good reason that it does not feel itself called upon to get its head cracked without any necessity. And this has been the result of every attempt to force the farmers to a new stage of production. However high may be my

	Number of Factories with:		
	1 to 5 workers	6 to 50 workers	Number of motors
Makers of whetstones	77	2	52
Makers of violins	1037	24	5
Preparation of anatomical material	126	3	
Scavengers	971	2	11
Spinners (materials not given)	275	3	2
Weavers (materials not given)	608	6	5
Rubber toys	4	-	
Barbers, hairdressers wigmakers	60,035	470	6
Cleaners of clothes and bootblacks	744	4	7
Chimneysweeps	3,860	26	
Sculptors and painters	5,630	84	2

estimate of the belligerency and fearlessness of the proletariat, its struggle is not directed against the little people that are themselves exploited, but against the great exploiters.

Along with agriculture the small industry in business comes into consideration. This also need not completely disappear at once. To be sure the new regime, as we have already seen, would, whenever poorly organized industry came in competition with the more perfect, strive to concentrate production in the well directed great industries. This could be easily attained, however, without the application of force by the simple raising of wages. But there will always be branches of industry in which the machine cannot compete successfully with hand labor, or, cannot accomplish what the latter can accomplish. It is highly significant that an investigation of the factory statistics of the German empire did not yield a single form of production in which the small industry still exclusively rules, with one insignificant exception (four plants each with one laborer). A few figures that, so far as I know, have never yet been published are here given. In the following branches of industry the small business rules almost exclusively, more than 97 per cent of all industries, while the great business with more than fifty laborers does not exist at allin the table.

If we exclude painters, barbers, chimneysweeps, violin makers and, according to my opinion, also scavengers and bootblacks, this reduces the held of existing small businesses, in industries which are outside the field of competition of great industries, to practically nil.

Nevertheless it may be granted that the small industry will have a definite position in the future in many branches of industry that produce directly for human consumption, for the machines manufacture essentially only products in bulk, while many purchasers desire that their personal taste shall be considered. It is easily possible that even under a proletarian regime the number of small businesses may increase as the well being of the masses increases. The demand for products of hand labor as a result of this may become active. Artistic hand work may accordingly receive a new impulse. However, we need not expect the realization of the picture of the future that William Morris has painted for us in his beautiful Utopia, in which the machine plays no role whatever. The machine will remain the ruler of the productive process. It will never give up this position again to hand labor. This, however, does not exclude the possibility that hand work in many artistic branches will again flourish and that it will even conquer many new fields. Meanwhile it to-day too often maintains its existence only as the product of extreme misery. As a house industry hand work in a socialist society call only exist as an expensive luxury which may in a universal well being find an extensive distribution. The foundation of the productive process will still remain the machine-driven great industry. The problematical small industries will at the most be maintained as islands in the ocean of the great social businesses.

These little industries, again, can take on the most various forms in regard to the ownership of their means of production and the disposal of their products. They may be dependent upon a great national or municipal industry, from which they receive their raw material and tools and to which they dispose of their products. They can produce for private customers, or for the open market, etc. as to-day, so then, a laborer can occupy himself in the most diverse occupations one after another. A seamstress, for example, can occupy herself for a time in a national factory and at another time make dresses for private customers at home, then again can sew for another customer in her own house, and finally she may, with a few comrades, unite in a co-operative for the manufacture of clothing for sale.

In this, as in every other relation, the greatest diversity and possibility of change will rule. Nothing is more false than to represent the socialist society as a simple, rigid mechanism whose wheels when once set in motion run on continuously in the same manner.

The most manifold forms of property in the means of production—national, municipal, cooperatives of consumption and production, and private can exist beside each other in a socialist society—the most diverse forms of industrial organization, bureaucratic, trades union, cooperative and individual; the most diverse forms of remuneration of labor, fixed wages, time wages, piece wages, participation in the economics in raw material, machinery, etc., participation in the results of intensive labor the most diverse forms of circulation of products, like contract by purchase from the warehouses of the State, from municipalities, from co-operatives of production, from producers themselves, etc., etc. The same manifold character of economic mechanism that exists to-day is possible in a socialistic society. Only the hunting and the hunted, the struggling and resisting, the annihilated and being annihilated of the present competitive struggle are excluded and therewith the contrast between exploiter and exploited.

Intellectual Production

So much for the most important economic problems that arise from the political victory of the proletariat and the means to their solution. It would be very alluring in this connection to follow these conditions further, to investigate the problems which housing and international commerce, the relations of city and country, etc., carry with them, all of which will be deeply touched by the domination of the proletariat and cannot continue in their present manner. But I must turn from the discussion of these themes at this point because I have said elsewhere the most essential things that I have to say upon them (the position of a socialist community in relation to colonies and world's commerce I have discussed in my preface to "Atlanticus, A View of the Future State," p. XIX, and "The Future of the Individual Home," in my Agrarfrage, p. 447, etc.). I wish to discuss only one point in this connection about which much indefiniteness exists—the future of intellectual production.

We have here hitherto only investigated the problem of material production which is most fundamental. But upon this basis there arises a production of artistic works, scientific investigation and literary activities of various forms. The continuation of this production is no less necessary for modern civilization than the undisturbed continuance of the production of bread and meat, coal and iron. A proletarian revolution, however renders its continuance in the former manner impossible. What has it to substitute therefor? That no reasonable man to-day fears that the victorious proletariat will cause a return to the old condition of barbarism or that it will fling art and science and superfluous rubbish into the lumber room but that on the contrary it is just among those broad popular sections of the proletariat that the most interest and the highest regard for art and science is to be found, I have already shown in my essay concerning "Reform and Revolution." But my whole inquiry is not so much in the nature of an investigation into what the victorious proletariat might do as to what by virtue of the power of logic and facts it can and must do.

There will be no lack of the necessary material objects for art and science. We have already seen that it is one of the strong points of the proletarian regime that through the abolition of private property in the means of production the possibility will be created of wiping out in the quickest possible manner the ruins of the outgrown means and methods of production which to-day prevent the unfolding of the modern productive powers and which beneath the present dominion of private property can only be slowly and incompletely swept out of the road by competition. The wealth of society must thereby at once attain a level far above that inherited from capitalist society.

But material objects alone are not sufficient to secure this elevation. Wealth alone does not give rise to a great ideal life. The question is whether the conditions of production of material goods in socialist society are consistent with the necessary conditions of a highly developed intellectual production. This is strongly denied by our opponents.

Let us nest examine some forms of existing intellectual production. It takes on three forms: production through organs of society for direct satisfaction of social needs; then, the production of goods in individual industries, and finally the production of goods under capitalist industry.

To the first form of intellectual production belongs the whole system of education from kindergartens to universities. If we disregard the insignificant private schools, this is to-day almost wholly in the hands of society and is conducted by the State not for the purpose of making profits or on account of gain. This holds above all of the modern national and municipal schools, but also of those which are mainly ruins descended from the Middle Ages, but which still exist under clerical organization and community support, and which are especially prominent in the land of Anglo-Saxon culture.

This social educational system is of the highest significance for the intellectual life, especially for the scientific, and this is not simply through its influence upon the growing youth. It controls ever more and more scientific investigation in that its teachers, especially in the high schools, have more and more a monopoly of scientific apparatus without which scientific investigation is to-day almost impossible. This is especially true in the field of the natural sciences whose technique has become so highly developed that, aside from a few million sires, the State alone is able to supply the means demanded for the establishment and maintenance of the necessary scientific apparatus. But in many branches of social science, ethnology and archaeology and others, the scientific apparatus of investigation has become ever more comprehensive and expensive. Because of this, science becomes ever more and more an unremunerative occupation, by which a man cannot live and to which only those people can devote themselves who are paid by the State unless they have been very fortunate in the choice of their parents—or of their wives. Attainment of the necessary preliminary knowledge for productive scientific activity demands again a great and ever increasing amount of money. So it is that science is more and more monopolized by the governmental powers and the possessing classes.

At the very least a proletarian regime can abolish the conditions which hamper scientific activity at present. It must formulate its educational system, as was previously pointed out, so that each genius will have within his reach all the knowledge that the social educational system has at its disposal. It will increase enormously the demand for educated people, and therewith also for the power of scientific investigation. Finally it will operate through the abolition of class antagonisms to make the investigators in the sphere of social science, where employed by the State, internally and externally free. So long as there are class antagonisms there will be very different standpoints from which society will be observed. There is no greater hypocrisy or self-deception than the talk about an existing science which is above class antagonisms. Science exists only in the heads of investigators and these are the products of society and cannot get out of it or reach above it. Even in a socialist society science will be dependent upon social conditions but these will then at least be uniform and not antagonistic.

Even worse than the internal dependence upon social conditions, from which no investigator can free himself, is the external dependence of many of those from governmental or other dominating institutions, for example, clerical. These compel the intellectual workers to direct their views according to those of the governing classes and will not permit them to investigate freely and independently, and it compels them to seek in a scientific manner for arguments that will justify the existing order and repel the aspiring classes. So the class dominion operates directly to demoralize science. The intellectual workers will have every reason to breathe freer when the proletarian regime sweeps away the direct and indirect dominion of the class of capitalists and land owners. The intellectual life so far as it is connected with education has nothing to fear and everything to hope from the victory of the proletariat.

How is it, then, with the production of intellectual commodities? In this connection we will first study individual production. Here painting and sculpture come most prominently into consideration, together with a portion of literary writing.

A proletarian regime will no more make this form of commodity production impossible, than it will abolish the little private industry in material production. Just as little as the needle and thimble, will brush and palette, or ink and pen belong to those means of production which must under all conditions be socialized. But one thing is well possible and that is that with the cessation of capitalist exploitation the number of purchasers that heretofore constituted the market for the commodities produced by the little artistic industry will be reduced. This will certainly not be without influence on the articles of artistic production. It will not abolish such production but only alter its character. The easel painting and statuettes which can most easily change their places and possessors, that can be placed wherever we wish, are the special form of commodity production in art. They include those forms of artistic work that can easiest take the form of commodities, which, like jewelry, can be accumulated and stored either for the purpose of re-selling at a profit or to hoard as treasures. It is possible that their production for the purposes of sale will find many obstacles in a socialist society. But in place of these, other forms of artistic production will appear.

A proletarian regime will immensely increase the number of public buildings. It will endeavor to make attractive every place occupied by the people, whether for labor, for consultation, or for pleasure. Instead of accumulating statuettes and pictures that will be thrown into a great impersonal market from whence they finally and a place utterly unknown to the artist and are used for wholly unthought of purposes, the artist will work together with the architect as was the case in the Golden Age of art in Athens under Pericles and in the Italian Renaissance. One art will support and raise the other and artistic labor will have a definite social aim so that its products, its surroundings and its public will not be dependent on chance.

On the other side the necessity to producc artistic works for sale as commodities will cease. Above all there will no longer be need to offer individual labor for profit or as wage labor, or for the production of commodities.

I have already pointed out that a proletarian regime would endeavor, as is perfectly evident from the standpoint of the wage-worker, to shorten the labor time and raise the wages. I have also shown to how high a degree this can be done, particularly in the line of highly developed capitalist production, simply through the concentration of industry in the most perfect centers of production and through the most perfect utilization of these most perfect industries. It is by no means fantastic to conclude that a doubling of the wages and a reduction of labor time to half of the present one is possible at once, and technical science is already sufficiently advanced to expect rapid progress in this field. The further one goes in this direction the more the possibility increases for those who are engaged in material production to give themselves up also to intellectual activity and especially to those forms that bring no material gain, but rather find their reward in themselves and which are the highest forms of intellectual activity. The greater increased leisure may in part, indeed in overwhelming part, lead to pure intellectual *enjoyment.* With the talented the creative genius will be free and the union of material with artistic literary and scientific production will be made possible.

This union, however, will not be simply possible. It will be an *economic necessity.* We have seen that a proletarian regime must aim to make culture a universal good. If we should seek to extend culture in the present sense of the word it would end in making the growing generation useless for material production and hence would undermine the foundations of society. To-day the social division of labor is developed in such a manner that material and intellectual labor are well-nigh mutually exclusive. Material production exists under such conditions that only the few who have been favored by nature or by special conditions are able to engage in the higher intellectual labor. On the other side intellectual labor as it is carried on to-day makes those who follow it incapable of and disinclined toward physical labor. To give culture to all mankind under such conditions would simply make all material production impossible because then no one would be found who could or would carry it on. If we are to make the higher intellectual culture a common good without endangering the existence of society, then not simply pedagogical but economic necessity demands that this be done in such a manner that the growing generation will be made familiar in schools not simply with intellectual but also with physical labor and the habit of uniting intellectual and material production will be firmly rooted.

The proletarian regime must proceed from two directions to secure the union of material and intellectual production and to free the latter in the mass of the population from its present material fetters. On the one side this must be done through the continuous shortening of the labor time of the so-called hand laborers. This will come as a result of the increasing productivity of labor whereby more time will be continuously granted for intellectual labor to those engaged in material production. On the other side this will be accomplished by an increase of the physical labor of the cultured, an unavoidable result of the continual increase in numbers of the latter.

It is, however, plain that with this union, physical labor for gain and for the necessary labor in the interest of society, and intellectual labor for the free exercise of personality would be freed from every social compulsion. For intellectual labor is much more incompatible with such compulsion than physical. This liberation of intellectual labor by the proletariat is not the pious wish of the Utopian but the economically necessary consequence of its victory.

Finally we must observe the third form of intellectual production—that which is capitalistically exploited. Since the first of these three forms of intellectual production includes mainly science and the second the fine arts, so what we have to say now applies to the utilization of all spheres of intellectual activity, but particularly, however, to the heroes of the pen and the stage, to whom now stand opposed as capitalist directors of industry, the publishers, periodical owners and theater directors.

Capitalist exploitation in such a form is impossible of continuance under a proletarian regime. It rests, however, upon the fact that to get even a questionable intellectual production to the public requires an expensive technical apparatus and extensive co-operative powers. The individual cannot here act for himself. Does that, however, not mean that here again the alternative to capitalist industry is national industry? If this is so, must not the centering of so great and important a part of the intellectual life in the State threaten in the highest degree that intellectual life with uniformity and stagnation? It is true that the governmental power will cease to be a class organ, but will it not still be the organ of a majority? Can the intellectual life be made dependent upon the decisions of the majority? Would not every new truth, every new conception and discovery be comprehended and thought out by the insignificant minority? Does not this new order threaten to bring at once the best and keenest of the intellectual thinkers in the various spheres into continuous conflict with the proletarian regime? And even if this creates increased freedom for the artistic and scientific development would not this be more than offset by the fetters that it will lay upon the intellectual activity when this can only be pursued by social means? Here is certainly an important but not an insoluble problem.

We must first notice that as for all production so also for the social necessities of intellectual production the *State* will from the beginning not be the only leading and means granting organ which will come into consideration, but there will also be *municipalities*. Through these alone all uniformity and every domination of the intellectual life by central power is excluded. As another substitute for the capitalist industry in individual production, still other organizations must be considered; those of *free unions* which will serve art and science and the public life and advance production in these spheres in the most diverse ways, or undertake them directly as even today we have countless unions which bring out plays, publish newspapers, purchase artistic works, publish writings, fit out scientific expeditions, etc. The shorter the hours of labor in material production and the higher the wages the more will these free unions be favored. They must increase in numbers, in enthusiasm and in the intelligence of their members as well as in the resources which the intellectuals can contribute to support the common cause. I expect that these free unions will play an even more important role in the intellectual life. It is their destiny to enter into the place now occupied by capital and individual production and to organize and to lead the social nature.

Here also the proletarian regime leads not to greater bondage but to greater freedom.

Freedom of education and of scientific investigation from the fetters of capitalist dominion; freedom of the individual from the oppression of exclusive, exhaustive physical labor; displacement of the capitalist industry in the intellectual production of society by the free unions,—along this road proceeds the tendency of the proletarian regime in the sphere of intellectual production.

We see that the problems in the field of production are of a contradictory nature. The capitalist system of production has created the task of formulating the social process of production in a simple and systematic manner. This task consists in placing the individual in a fixed order to whose rules he must conform. On the other side this same manner of production has more than ever brought the individual to a self-consciousness, placed him on his own feet and freed him from society. More than ever mankind demands to-day the possibility of developing a personality and its relation to other men in order to determine in the freest manner the more sensitive and individual of these relations, especially the marriage relation, but also their relation as artists and thinkers to the external world.

Regulation of social chaos and liberation of the individual—these are the two historical tasks that capitalism has placed before society. They appear to be contradictory, but they are simultaneously soluble because each of them belongs to a different sphere of social life. Undoubtedly whoever should seek to rule both spheres in the same manner would find himself involved in insoluble contradictions. It is on this point that anarchism is wrecked. Anarchism arises out of the reaction of the little bourgeois against the repressive and oppressive capitalism. The little handworker who was accustomed to direct his labor according to his own pleasure rebels against the discipline and the monotony of the factory. His ideal remains the free labor of the individual and when this is no longer possible he seeks to replace it by common working together in free unions wholly independent of each other.

The "new middle class," the intellectuals, is, as we have already seen many times, in its social position only a refined and more sensitive expression of the earlier little bourgeois. Its manner of working develops in them the same need for free labor, the same repugnance to discipline and uniformity. So it is that their social ideal becomes the same as that of the small bourgeois, that is the anarchist. But that which is a progressive ideal in their sphere of production shows itself to be reactionary in the field of material production where it corresponds to the conditions of production of the now extinct hand work.

In the present stage of production there are only two possible forms of *material production* so far as production in quantities is concerned, aside from a few remnants which are mainly curiosities:

on the one side *communistic* with social property in the means of production, and the systematic direction of production from a central point, or the *capitalistic.* The anarchistic system of production can, under the best conditions, be only a transitory episode. Material production through free unions without central production leads to chaos unless the commodities produced exchange on the basis of the law of value determined by free competition. We have seen above what the consequence is for individual industry under free competition. It determines the correct proportionality of individual means of production to one another and prevents any one from swamping society with buttons or leaving it without bread. Production of commodities under the present conditions of social production must continuously take on some form of capitalist production, as countless productive co-operatives have shown. To strive for an anarchist ideal in material production is at best a Sisyphus task.

It is wholly different with intellectual production. This is built upon material production, on the surplus of products and labor powers which proceed from material production. It is possible only when material life is secured. If the latter falls into confusion then our whole existence is threatened. Consequently it is absolutely unimportant for society in what relations the existing surplus of products and labor powers are applied to the individual fields of free intellectual creation. The exception to this is the educational system which has its special laws, and has not yet been turned over to free competition in any society, but has been socially regulated. Society would fall into bad condition if all the world should set to work at the manufacture of one kind of commodities such, for example, as buttons, and thereby direct too much labor power to this, so that not enough was left for the production of others, such for example, as bread. On the other hand the relation between lyric poems and tragedies, works on Assyriology and botany which are to be produced is no essential one; it has neither maximum nor minimum point. If to-day there should be twice as many dramas as yesterday, and at the same time one-half as many lyrics, or if to-day twenty works on Assryiology should appear and only ten Botanical, while yesterday the relations were reversed, still the existence of society would not be touched in the slightest thereby. These facts and their economic expression in that the law of value, in spite of all psychological theories of value, only holds good for material production and not for intellectual. In this held a central direction of production is not only unnecessary, but absolutely foolish. Here free production can rule without the necessity of production of commodities of value or of capitalist production.

Communism in material production, anarchism in the intellectual. This is the type of the socialist productive system which will arise from the dominion of the proletariat or, in other words, out of the social revolution by the logic of economic facts whatever may be the wishes, ideas and theories of the proletariat.

The Preliminary Psychical Conditions to the Dominion of the Proletariat

It will have occurred to very many readers that in this investigation I have spoken only of economic conditions. I have not investigated what are to be the ethical foundations of the new society, whether they shall rest upon Kantian or Spencerian, upon the categorical imperative, or whether the greatest good to the greatest number shall be the principal motive. I have not investigated which of the above theories shall constitute the juridical foundation, whether the right to the complete product of labor, or the right to existence, or some other one of the fundamental economic rights which the judicial socialists have discovered. No doubt laws and ethics will play a part in the social revolution, but the determining factor will always be the demands of economics.

But beside law and ethics psychology also comes into consideration. Will not problems arise therefrom for the proletarian regime and those of great significance? Does not the socialist society presuppose extraordinary people, actual angels in unselfishness, joy in labor, and intelligence? Will not the social revolution with the present race full of egoism and brutality be the signal for a raging battle for spoils or lead to a universal idleness? All transformations of economic foundations amount to nothing so long as mankind is not ennobled.

The treatment and the text are not new. They were sung a hundred years ago as the song arose of the crushed oppressed classes. The gentle landlords of the Holy Alliance would gladly have given their beloved children all possible freedom, but these children must first attain the necessary ripeness.

I do not intend to deny that every system of production demands certain definite technical and also psychological preliminary conditions in order to enable it to be realized. What shall be the necessary forms of these psychological conditions of a given manner of production depends upon the character of the economic tasks which it sets forth.

No one will claim that in my investigation I have presupposed mankind of an angelic character. The problem that we have to solve presupposes *intelligence, discipline and talent for organization.* These are the psychological foundations of a socialist society. Those are just the ones that the capitalist society has created. It is the historical task of capital to discipline and organize the laborers, and to widen their intellectual horizon beyond the boundaries of the workshop and the church door.

For socialism to rise on the basis of hand work or agricultural industry is impossible, not simply on economic grounds because of the low productivity of industry, but also for psychological reasons. I have already shown how small bourgeois psychology inclines towards anarchy and opposes the discipline of the social industry. It is one of the greatest difficulties that capital meets in the beginnings of capitalist production, in that it must take its first laborers directly from hand work or from agriculture. It had to fight with this in the eighteenth century in England and to-day in the Southern States of America which renders very difficult the rapid advance of the great industry not-withstanding the nearness to raw materials greatly favors such industry.

Not discipline alone but also the talent for organization is difficult of development in little bourgeois and agricultural positions. There are no great bodies of men to be united in systematic co-operation. On this economic stage it is only the soldiers who offer the opportunity to organize in great bodies. The great generals are also great organizers. Capitalist production transplants the task of organization of great masses of the community to industry. The capitalists constitute naturally the head people, the field generals of those who are under them and become prominent factors in organization. Correspondingly the organizing talent in its appointees is very highly valued and rewarded by capital. Under these conditions the organizing talent grows rapidly. It can be applied equally well to the uses of a proletarian regime that will also need numerous directors of factories and organizers of trusts.

Capital also demands intelligent labor power, so we see that the competitive struggle above all enforces the betterment of the industrial school. On the other side the development of industry and the existence of newspapers contributes to extend the intellectual horizon of the laborer.

But not alone the pressure of capital in the exploitation of great bodies of labor, but the struggle of the proletarian against this exploitation develops the psychological conditions for socialist production; it develops discipline in every way, as we have already seen, of a wholly different character and from that given capital, and this struggle develops also a talent for organization, for it is only through the unanimous co-operation of the great body of mankind that the proletariat can assert itself against capital and the capitalist state. Organization is the most important weapon of the proletariat and nearly all its great leaders are also great organizers. To the money of capital, and the weapon of the military States, the proletariat has nothing to oppose save its economic indispensability and its organization. That its intelligence grows with these and through these needs no proof.

The social revolution requires high intelligence, strict discipline and complete organization of this great mass and these must exist simultaneously with and be indispensable to economic life if it is to attain strength to overcome so extremely powerful an opponent. We may expect that it will only succeed when these peculiarities are developed in the highest degree and also that the victory of the proletariat and therewith the social revolution will not come before not only the economic but also the psychological conditions to a socialist society are present in a high degree. This does not mean that mankind should be angels nor that we shall need to wait so very long for its psychological ripeness.

While the modern proletariat has need of no great change in order to make it ripe for socialist society, nevertheless we may expect that this society will greatly alter the character of mankind. That which is demanded as a *preliminary condition* to a socialist society, and which the capitalist society makes impossible, and which would be therefore the most impossible preliminary condition, that is, the creation of a higher type of mankind than the modern one, that will be the natural *result* of socialism. It will bring security, rest and leisure to mankind; it will raise their minds above the commonplace because they will no longer need to continuously think of where the bread for the morrow is to come from. It will make personalities independent of other personalities, so that the feeling of slavery as well as of human adoration will disappear. It will at the same time create a balance between country and city, make the treasures of the cultured rich attainable to all mankind and give back to them the nature which arises from the strength and joy of living.

Simultaneously with the abolition of the physiological roots of pessimism it will do away with the social ones also, together with the misery and degradation of the one who makes a virtue of necessity, and the satiety of the other who in idle luxury has drained the cup of enjoyment even to the dregs.

Socialism will abolish poverty and satiety and unnaturalness, make mankind joyful, appreciative of beauty, capable of happiness, and thereby it will bring freedom in scientific and artistic creation for all.

May we not expect that under such conditions a new type of mankind will arise which will be far superior to the highest type which culture has hitherto created? An over-man (*Uebermensch*), if you will, not as an exception but as a rule, an over-man compared with his predecessors, but not as opposed to his comrades, a noble man who seeks his satisfaction not by being great among crippled dwarfs, but great among the great, happy among the happy—who does not draw his feeling of strength from the fact that he raises himself upon the bodies of the down-trodden, but because a union with his fellow-workers gives him courage to dare the attainment of the highest tasks.

So we may expect that a realm of strength and of beauty will arise that will be worthy the ideal of our best and noblest thinkers.